Native American Freemasonry

Native American Freemasonry

Associationalism and Performance in America

JOY PORTER

University of Nebraska Press
Lincoln & London

Library of Congress Cataloging-in-Publication Data

Porter, Joy, 1967–
Native American freemasonry: associationalism and
performance in America / Joy Porter.
p. cm.
Includes bibliographical references and index.
ISBN 978-0-8032-2547-3 (cloth: alk. paper)
1. Indians of North America—Societies, etc. 2. Freemasons—
United States—History. I. Title.
E75.P67 2011
366'.1—dc22
2011017087

Set in Adobe Garamond.

For my husband, Jan Simons

History: An account mostly false, of events mostly unimportant, which are brought about by rulers mostly knaves, and soldiers mostly fools.

—AMBROSE BIERCE, *The Cynic's Word Book*

In general, life is better than it has ever been, and if you think that, in the past, there was some golden age of pleasure and plenty to which you would, if you were able, transport yourself, let me say one single word: "Dentistry."

—P. J. O'ROURKE, *All the Trouble in the World*

The religion of beauty, imagination, and philosophy, without constraint moral or intellectual, a religion speculative and self-indulgent. Pantheism, indeed, is the great deceit which awaits the Age to come.

—JOHN HENRY NEWMAN, *Difficulties of Anglicans*

Contents

Illustrations

Acknowledgments

This book owes much to institutional support, including a Research Award from the Leverhulme Trust, which allowed me a one-year break from teaching to conduct primary research, and support from Anglia Ruskin University in Cambridge, UK, which provided research funds to permit travel to a wide range of U.S. research institutions and personal visits to a number of key Masonic figures in the United States and elsewhere. This book also owes much to a large number of Native and non-Native thinkers, academics, Masons, and friends, none of whom is in any way responsible for any omissions, slippages, misdirection, or errors should they be unearthed. A number of academic colleagues gave vital intellectual guidance as this long project developed. Professor Phil Deloria of the University of Michigan provided deeply appreciated advice and directional input at a key stage. His pathbreaking work on some of the themes considered here remains the touchstone for all research of this sort. Professor Bernt Peyer of Goethe Universität in Frankfurt was kind enough to boost the level of analysis herein and to give this book new dimension. Thank you also to Joe Roach, Sterling Professor of Theater and English in the Department of English at Yale University; to David Stevenson, the distinguished authority on Masonic origins and emeritus professor of Scottish history of St. Andrews University; to Professor Andrew Prescott of the Centre for Research into Freemasonry at the University of Sheffield, UK; and to Professor Jessica Harland-Jacobs of the University of Florida. Professor David Murray of the School of American and Canadian Studies at the University of Nottingham, UK, supported the project from the outset, and Professor Judy Newman, also of the School, provided vital critical intervention in the book's later stages. Sincere thanks are due to friends and colleagues, including Professor Emeritus LaVonne Brown Ruoff of the University of Chicago, Professor Lee Schweninger of the University of North Carolina, Wilmington, and the participants in the Montpellier Indian Literature symposia run under the auspices of Professor Simone Pellerin of the University of Montpellier, France.

Heartfelt thanks are due to Professor Michel Prum and those in the research groups Groupe de recherché sur L'Eugenisme et la Racisme / Research Group on Eugenics and Racism and Identités, Cultures, Territoires at the Université de Paris VII, who were kind enough to host me as a visiting professor in March 2008. Thank you to Bruce Johansen, the Isaacson University Research Professor at the University of Nebraska at Omaha, whose guidance, friendship, and good humor are an inspiration to all who attempt scholarship in Native American studies. Special thanks are due to my colleagues in the College of Arts and Humanities at the University of Wales, Swansea, and to visiting scholar Dr. Don Davis of the Office of the Governor of the State of Oklahoma. Thank you to Associate Professor of English Susan Gardner of the University of North Carolina at Charlotte, who was kind enough to allow me to quote from her manuscript on Ella Deloria; to Professor Tony Badger, Master of Clare College, Cambridge; to Professor Jim Smyth of Notre Dame University; to Mark C. Carnes, the Ann Whitney Olin Professor of History at Barnard College; to the distinguished scholar of things Iroquois Art Einhorn of New York; to Patrick Minges of Davidson Early College, North Carolina; to David Hackett of the Department of Religion at the University of Florida; and to Donald Smith, professor emeritus of history at the University of Calgary. Sincere thanks also to scholar, author, and editor Matthew Bokovoy of the University of Nebraska Press and to Judith Hoover.

A number of senior Masons were kind enough to give pivotal research direction and advice as this book developed, and their input is deeply appreciated. Special thanks are due to Jim Tresner, director of the Masonic Leadership Institute of one of the finest temples in the world, that of the Ancient Free and Accepted Masons of the State of Oklahoma at Guthrie. Mr. Tresner was exceptionally helpful with the research for this book, making his vast knowledge and the state lodge's library available as well as supplying many of the photographs and illustrations to be found in the succeeding pages. Thank you to Arturo de Hoyos, Grand Architect and Grand Historian of the Supreme Council, 33°, of the Ancient and Accepted Scottish Rite of Freemasonry; to Tully Choate, director of the Oklahoma Masonic Degree Team; to Charles F. Scott of the Scottish Rite Temple in Guthrie; to Kenneth G. Hope, Grand Secretary Recorder of the Grand York Rite Bodies of California (Grand Chapter, Royal Arch Masons of California, Grand Council, Cryptic Masons of California, Grand Commandery, Knights Templar of California); to José De Luna, general secretary of the San Diego Scottish Rite Masonic Library; and to John McKenzie, research librarian, Long Beach Scottish Rite, California, and all those who work with him. Thanks are also due to writer Michael Baigent of London and to Susan Snell, archivist at the Library and Museum of Freemasonry, Freemason's Hall, Great Queen Street, London. Thank you to Geraint Griffiths of Swansea University.

This book draws directly and indirectly on contemporary manuscripts, newspapers, and pamphlets, on Masonic sermons, orations, and lodge records, and on writings by Masonic historians and antiquarians held in archives in more than twenty sites in New

York, Philadelphia, Oklahoma, California, and London. My sincere thanks are extended to the following individuals and institutions who helped to provide this material: Dr. Glenys Waldman and Kenneth McCarthy of the Grand Lodge Library of the Masonic Temple, Philadelphia; Thomas Savini, director of the Chancellor Robert R. Livingston Library and Museum of the Grand Lodge, New York; David Francis Philps, Los Angeles Scottish Rite; Kristina L. Southwell, manuscripts librarian, Western History Collections, University of Oklahoma; Joel Springer, Assistant Grand Secretary, Grand Lodge Free and Accepted Masons of California, San Francisco; Michael L. Bruce of the Oklahoma Historical Society, Oklahoma City; Laura R. Jolley, senior manuscript specialist, State Historical Society of Missouri, Western Historical Manuscript Collection, University of Missouri; Cherokee National Historical Society, Tahlequah, Oklahoma; Shawnee Masonic Lodge, Shawnee, Oklahoma; Thomas Gilcrease Institute of American History and Art; American Philosophical Society Library, Philadelphia; Rochester Museum and Science Center, Rochester, New York; Special Collections, Reed Library, State University of New York; Buffalo and Erie Historical Society, Buffalo, New York; New York State Library, Albany; New York Public Library, New York City; Manuscripts, Western History Collections and Government Documents Collection, University of Oklahoma; Bureau of Indian Affairs, Muskogee Agency, Muskogee, Oklahoma; Huntington Research Library, San Marino, California; State Historical Society of Wisconsin; Logan County Genealogical Society, Inc., Guthrie, Oklahoma; Scottish Rite Cathedral, Long Beach, California; Supreme Council, 33°, Southern Jurisdiction, Washington DC; Braun Research Library of the Southwest Museum of the American Indian on Mt. Washington, Los Angeles; San Diego Scottish Rite Masonic Library; Institute for Masonic Studies, California Grand Lodge, San Francisco; Oklahoma Grand Lodge, Guthrie; National Cowboy Hall of Fame and Western Heritage Center, Oklahoma; Most Worshipful Prince Hall Grand Lodge Free and Accepted Masons of Pennsylvania Masonic Temple, Philadelphia; Great Council of Pennsylvania Improved Order of Red Men, Philadelphia; Grand Masonic Lodge of Texas, Houston; San Francisco Scottish Rite Masonic Center; Museum of the Civilized Tribes, Creek Nation, Oklahoma; Tahlequah Museum, Cherokee Nation, Oklahoma.

Thanks are also due to Naples Library in New York, which lent me a number of very old and valuable books; to John Kahionhes Fadden of the Six Nations Indian Museum, Onchiota, New York; to Chief Tom Porter of the Kanatsioharekee Mohawk Community; and to Bob Wicks, director of the Miami Art Museum. Thank you to Mrs. Pat Webster of Albany, New York; Martha Anne Parker of Naples, New York; and Russell Hammond of the London fashion house Alice Temperley, who remarkably and enjoyably took a brief interlude from his work in high-end couture to help with the American stage of the archival work. Thank you to Sue and Alan Bevan, Sue and Dave Harvey, Elaine Porter, and the inestimable M. R. Porter, who remained at my side through every step of the writing process. Finally, thank you to young Artur Porter-Simons, who arrived in the middle of that writing process but who makes all things that bit more wonderful.

Introduction

Many of us working in Native American studies have always been aware that a significant proportion of male Native American political and literary figures over time have been directly involved with the Masonic fraternity in one form or another. However, what this involvement entailed and just what it meant to both Indian and non-Indian Masonic brothers have remained tantalizingly obscure. Part of the reason is that the sources necessary to explain the phenomenon are widely spread and, when it comes to American Masonic libraries in particular, difficult to access. This last difficulty is not in the least because Masonic institutions are unfriendly or unapproachable to either gender, or because Masonic librarians are in any sense unwilling to help. To the contrary, I have found Masons themselves and the staff who look after their archives unfailingly helpful, friendly, and enabling. Rather it is because such a wealth of valuable, unexamined, and often uncatalogued material lies within Masonic libraries that the task of accessing it meaningfully is dauntingly formidable for library staff and scholars alike. Although Masonic library holdings are voluminous, aside from records attesting to their membership status the amount of available written data on specific Indian Masons, even famous ones, is comparatively small. Indian Masons were, after all, part of a secret society or, to use the nuance many Masons prefer, part of a society with secrets. An individual Indian's Masonic involvement may well have been politically and socially very important and have lasted from that man's early manhood until his death, but the records that survive to chart its meaning are often few, perfunctory, unreliable, or buried from even the most diligent historian's view. The fraternity's operations have always been primarily social and ritualistic, focused on conviviality and the practice of carrying out successive rites among like-minded friends—none of which lends itself naturally to the production of detailed written material examining Indians' roles. Yet as I hope to make clear, Indian involvement in Freemasonry has always been significant, and the amount of nonspecific material about Indians within Masonic archives is substantial. Masonic archives do not offer up Indian lives on a plate, but we must be thankful that for most of its history a central part of Masonic life has been the keeping of records, the receipt and retention of dues, the operation of committees, the recording of names matched to roles, and the production of aide-mémoires to the performance of ritual that has stayed relatively consistent though it has dramatically evolved over time. Although many of the records on Indian Masonry that survive were not produced by Indians, where Indian life and Freemasonry intersect and when we can find sources we find a raw chord of cultural interaction and an opportunity to comprehend an important part of social history that would otherwise be lost.

I ask the reader to approach this first book-length study of an unusual topic in an underresearched area with specific expectations. Because this work deals with a fraternity that placed a premium on secrecy it will not surprise readers to find few direct, causative links between the actions of individual Indians and Freemasonry; indeed it would be rather dubious if many links were presented. Instead Freemasonry and its amorphous Indian links and valencies are what lie at the core of this volume, connections and relationships as complex and powerfully rooted as fraternal links between individuals often were in themselves. It is important to recognize that this is a book about Masons who happened to be Native Americans and not a book about Native American Freemasonry as a discrete practice, since there is no such thing. There have simply been Masons across time who were Indian and who found something of value and a distinct kind of fellowship in specific lodges. This is also a book about Freemasonry more generally, its relationships with actual and imagined Native Americans, and about the use non-Indian Freemasons at points made of Indian motifs, costumes, and role-playing in their rituals.

With these provisos established, I nonetheless attempt to go some way toward rectifying the absence of knowledge about Indian Masons. I seek to develop understanding of American Masonry in particular and of Masonry in a wider sense as a social and political phenomenon. I add what I can to the small chorus of contemporary voices who strive to displace some of the prevalent, salacious suggestions made about the fraternity, in particular the dramatic and, for many, attractive idea that for most of its history it operated malevolently in the shadows as a sinister secret society. Instead I suggest something more rewarding and closer to the truth: that in the American context at least Freemasonry was and remains a fraternity of men, developmental in terms of its activities and makeup, united by a set of social and moral values, and committed to fostering the spiritual development of its members through the practice of ritual and group solidarity. Although the concept of Native Americans as Freemasons might initially strike the reader as unlikely in light of Freemasonry's reputation for exclusivity and the constellation of "primitive" imagery that surrounds Native American identity, I will show that Masonry was in fact a significant avenue for Indian and non-Indian people to come together. As the strength of the Oklahoma Masonic Indian Degree Team and the Akdar Shrine Indian Dance Unit of Tulsa, Oklahoma, attest, this is a process with a unique history that continues successfully today. Organized in 1948 after the death of the famous part-Cherokee Freemason Will Rogers, the Oklahoma Masonic Indian Degree Team, like the Akdar Shrine Indian Dance Unit, is intertribal. The work of each group—raising Masons to the third degree and performing traditional dances, respectively—promotes, as Indian Masonic involvement has always tended to, both Indian interests and those of the fraternity.

I argue that Indian involvement in Freemasonry was significant to American Indian leadership over time; that Freemasonry's ritualistic dramas deserve careful consideration; and that Indians' involvement should be seen in terms of their repeated but varied performance. Native American links to Freemasonry were subtle and deep-seated, but Freemasonry should now be recognized as an important forum where Indian and non-Indians exchanged, and at points co-created, cultural forms.

In the first two chapters I consider how Native American Freemasonry might be approached intellectually given that it is a new area of study. In chapter 1 I look at the recent turn toward analysis of performance and its potential usefulness for understanding Masonry. I also look at why Freemasonry may have provided an attractive spiritual sanctuary for so many Indian individuals over time and at how Masonic membership permitted Indian peoples unique access to the discourse of history. In chapter 2 I extol the benefits of performance as a lens through which to understand Indian Masonry but also ask readers to consider its potential pitfalls. I conclude the chapter by suggesting that we see recovery of Indian Masonry primarily as part of a wider imperative spearheaded by Phil Deloria, of continuing to locate Indians historically where hitherto they have not been expected.

Chapters 3 and 4 provide a definition and an analytical genealogy of American Freemasonry, tracking its journey in form and philosophy from Europe to the United States. In chapter 3 I explore debates over the fraternity's earliest origins, look at the role of pantheism and republicanism in its development, and urge readers to recognize it as transatlantic and transoceanic. In chapter 4 I consider Freemasonry as ornamentalism and as a powerful reflector of class, race, and social hierarchy. I plot the new egalitarianism that accompanied the rise within Freemasonry of American "Antients" before considering the growth of black, or Prince Hall, Freemasonry; the Indian role in the 1826 Morgan affair and its anti-Masonic political aftermath; and the revealing sets of relationship among Mormons, Masons, and Indians.

In chapters 5 and 6 I consider in depth what it is about Freemasonry that might explain why it has been it so attractive over time to Indians and others. Thus in chapter 5 I look at the role of magic, irrationality, and enchantment. I go behind Masonic ritual to analyze the specifics of the Masonic journey and understand the significance of death and resurrection within the all-important Masonic third degree. I explore Masonic ritual's relationship to capitalism and some of its complexities as a specific type of performance. Where correspondences can be said to exist between aspects of Indian tradition and those of Freemasonry, I question just what they might mean. Then in chapter 6 I discuss the established strain in Masonic writing that ties Indians and Masons together, looking in particular at the Masonic rescue stories in William R. Denslow's 1956 publication, *Freemasonry and the American Indian*. This leads to a discussion of two exemplary Masonic Indians who played with and variously promoted this idea in the American context, the early twentieth-century Seneca Iroquois writer, museum man, and anthropologist Arthur Caswell Parker and his great-uncle, the nineteenth-century Seneca Iroquois politician and leader Ely S. Parker. I discuss the multivalencies of memory and the power of the Masonic invention of tradition. This leads to an exploration of what I call the "Pocahontas syndrome," the conqueror's desire to perceive some form of universal solvent (such as Masonry or, in Pocahontas's case, romantic love) capable of washing away both difference and the specifics of colonial inequality. I conclude the chapter by analyzing these themes with reference to their greatest proselytizer, Rudyard Kipling, examining the ways his work put forward the fantasy that Masonry established (or reestablished) a timeless global brotherhood.

In chapters 7, 8, and 9 I discuss specific Native American Freemasons during the revolutionary era, the Civil War era, and the nineteenth and twentieth centuries, respectively. In chapter 7 I consider "Indianness" as it was performed at the Boston Tea Party and its Masonic links. I also consider the first Indian Freemason, Joseph Brant, and the performative relationships of the Irish Mason and sometime Iroquois sachem Sir William Johnson. In chapter 8 I explore the role Indian Masonry played in the "settlement" of the West, the pivotal Masonic figure and Civil War defender of Indian Territory Alfred Pike, and the Masonic underpinnings to the Cherokee Keetoowah Society, the fourth wave of Cherokee revitalization generated in the nineteenth century. In chapter 9 I discuss the variants of Freemasonry that are likely to be most familiar to today's readers. I chart nineteenth- and twentieth-century Masonry, exploring how fraternal Indianness related to ideas about how to be a man. I also explore the theatrical nature of modern Freemasonry, the "righteous satisfaction" Masonic performance provided, and the relationship between nostalgia and Freemasonry's rise and decline as the twentieth century progressed.

I conclude in chapter 10 with a full explanation of the twentieth-century decline of Native American Freemasonry in the context of a wider documented decline in American Freemasonry and associationalism more generally. I argue that Freemasonry's organizational diminution is linked to a curtailment of social mobility and to a decrease in the extent to which Americans now mix across generational, social, and ethnic boundaries. However, I point out that the future direction of the fraternity, like the future of how Americans may choose to associate, is by no means set in stone.

A Note on Terms

Although I recognize that Freemasonry has significantly changed over time and that it has been interpreted and practiced differently in different places, I posit that Masonry has a core consistency. Aside from its "Blue Lodge" initiatory framework, Masonry has its own sense of "Masonic time" that is transcendent of time as we commonly think of it;[1] its own sense of history, with a central figure (Hiram Abiff) not found in the Bible but held to be central to biblical events; and its own stated and unstated approaches to religious and ethnic identity. Yet like most truly interesting things, Masonry is a mass of seeming contradictions. To give just three examples, a core organizational concept is that of unity of practice and form (an impulse formalized in the nineteenth century), but deviation from centralized practice and a particular responsiveness in terms of ritual to specific societies and environments have always existed. Masonry is also constitutionally committed to democratic principles, but this is heavily qualified such that for most of its history it has remained the preserve of a middle-class elite. Furthermore although the fraternity creates its own hierarchy, it has always advised members to respect externally bestowed high status. Thus although Freemasonry could be said to be a fraternity obsessed by history and committed to its ritualistic preservation, it is also an association *within* history always operating in relationship to the larger communities it serves.

In this book I refer to one or more *Indian traditions*, a term fraught with complexity and often justifiably contested as being too broad to be meaningful. Where possible it has been replaced with information specific to the people or indigenous communities concerned within defined time periods. Even though Indian communities are at least as diverse as Euro-American ones and any all-encompassing term or generalized set of perceived characteristics is inadequate, it is important to be able to speak of tradition in the sense that Raymond Williams wrote of it, as an active process within communities where ideas and beliefs (which may require only two generations to become "traditional") are nonetheless valuable, dynamic, enabling, and historically significant.[2] It is important to get beyond the Western intellectual tradition of thinking about tradition (here I exclude a number of anthropologists), where the term is seen as stultifying and liable to enforce cultural homogeneity, and as analogous, if juxtaposed to progress, to other nineteenth-century dichotomies like nature/nurture, primitive/civilized, and mind/body. This negative Western intellectual tradition includes Durkheim, Weber, Tönnies, and Marx, the last of whom went so far as to write of the tradition of all the dead generations weighing "like a nightmare on the brain of the living." Indeed even for more recent scholars such as Jürgen Habermas, who recognize that traditions are not static, the continuity of tradition is still seen as coercive and change deemed to be solely the outcome of rationality and reflectivity.[3] In contrast a more productive way to think about tradition when it comes to Freemasonry as well as a number of other Native practices is to recognize what Arnold Krupat has dubbed a *both/and* modality of thought at work. Thus a Native American can be a practitioner of both indigenous ritual *and* Masonic ritual, both a staunch resister of acculturation politically *and* a Mason in good standing, both a Christian, a Mason, *and* a Native patriot, keenly defending his people's interests as he perceives them. This indigenous, complementary way of thinking, of comprehending difference in terms of balance as opposed to the Aristotelian, analytic, *either/or* mode of thought more familiar in the West, is what makes Indian tradition so flexible, inclusive, and, arguably, ultimately indestructible.[4] It is this awareness, rather than any homogenizing, synoptic gloss, that surrounds use of the term *tradition* in the chapters that follow.

A point needs to be made about this book's selective use of yet another problematic term, *spirituality*. The reader might ask, What terms *are* available to a writer foolish enough to attempt to discuss issues surrounding Native American ritual and practice and Masonic ritual and practice? Certainly to speak of Native American religions is problematic. The Western word *religion* sits uneasily with indigenous spiritual practices and traditions, which number in the hundreds and have their own associated ritual systems and applications to everyday life. A number of indigenous communities actively discourage use of the term in conjunction with their beliefs because their spirituality constitutes a seamless part of their being in a way the term *religion* cannot encompass. *Religion* also seems unable to encompass the fundamental significance of place and of cultural community within indigenous spiritual traditions, and it suggests things indigenous spiritual traditions tend not to have, such as central didactic texts, prescribed theology and rituals, and the urge to proselytize. There is also a strong argument that only Native language can express any form of Native transcendent experience, and that in any case such experience can be understood only through embeddedness and personal commitment to a specific Native community. Even so anthropologists have listed themes they deem common to indigenous American spiritualities: certain cosmological approaches; the idea of a pervasive supernatural force; respect for dreams and visions and for song and dance; varying understandings of the afterlife; respect for ancestors; a sense of kinship with all things, including the animate and inanimate; and specific reverence for certain symbols and items such as tobacco and medicine bundles. In contrast to the word *religion* the word *spirituality* is at least a broader, more inclusive term to use when discussing Native American belief systems since it has more to do with a person's beliefs, values, and behavior than with a person's involvement in a religious tradition and institution. Added to this the term *religion* has suffered in relation to the larger term *spirituality* in the past fifteen years or so in popular usage, even though a number of theorists have derided *spirituality* as being "fuzzy" and described it as "a word that encompasses obscurity with a passion."[5] Yet the term is still useful and is defended because it is fluid, allowing for a wide range of experiences rejected by many conservative religious traditions. Thus it is used here.[6]

Approaching Native American Freemasonry, Part One

I

On Ritual, Rhetoric, and the Performative Turn in Contemporary Scholarship

Although it does not confine itself to one period, in approach this book draws on the performative turn discernible in recent studies of early American culture and literature. This is appropriate given how central ritual performance has always been to Masonic identity. As one now largely forgotten source explained back in 1940, dramatic pageantry is something that has been at the very heart of the organizational functioning of many secret orders, and of Freemasonry in particular, for a long time. "The dramatic roles, the titles of the 'actors,' the symbolic themes, the fraternal uniforms, the badges and tokens, the music, the lighting," Noel P. Gist pointed out, "all transform the ceremony into a form of pageant which in certain occasions assumes the proportions of an awe-inspiring spectacle."[1] Such an emphasis on Masonic performance does not deny that mutual aid and brotherhood were and remain the primary concerns of the fraternity, nor is Steven Bullock necessarily wrong in his claim that in the colonial period Masonry's spiritual and mysterious side was "virtually ignored by colonial brothers." Yet the significance of drama and of what might be called the Masonic imagination has until now been underemphasized and bears fresh consideration. Bullock has argued that before 1800 rituals were "mainly the means of establishing the order," but after 1800 they became "ends in themselves." Around this time Masonry adopted a new sanctity and its ritual a new significance, but performance was always, and remains still, at the heart of Masonic practice.[2]

The types of performative analyses with which this book connects repeatedly call for a rethinking of the recognized parameters of the historical discipline and for a broadening of the sphere of information normally permitted to constitute our understanding of the past. To better understand performance as a possible framework for understanding Native American Freemasonry it is worth considering in some detail the key texts that have applied the idea to American history. In doing so we begin to understand the ideas surrounding performance of things Indian in general, and we get a firmer sense of the porous, interlinked nature and disjointed processes whereby culture gets exchanged.

The new approach could be said to have begun in 1993 with Jay Fliegelman's *Declaring Independence: Jefferson, Natural Language, and the Culture of Performance.* Fliegelman is concerned with "rethinking and expanding the kinds of 'facts' that are traditionally judged to be relevant to understanding a major historical document" and sets about analyzing what he dubs the "social dramaturgy" of Jefferson and his times. He argues that Jefferson's draft of the Declaration of Independence was written to be read aloud; it was a "performative utterance," and Jefferson inserted pause marks to divide it in the same way poetry is delineated. The public readings demanded by various audiences, including Congress, "made the Declaration an event rather than a document." Fliegelman asks us to view Jefferson's Declaration as part of a larger "elocutionary revolution" in political discourse and public speech in England and America in the mid-eighteenth century, a shift away from classical argumentation and style toward delivery and a concern to generate emotional force and sympathy with the audience via sounds, tones, and facial expressions.[3] His approach flies in the face of previous studies of the period, such as Michael Warner's *The Letters of the Republic: Publication and the Public Sphere in Eighteenth Century America*, where, rather than the affective power of voice, the impersonal printed word is deemed primary. Warner's depiction of a "civic and emancipatory" American print culture is analogous to the bourgeois public sphere theorized by Jürgen Habermas in *The Structural Transformation of the Public Sphere*, whereas Fliegelman's *Declaring Independence*, with its performative emphasis, has much more in common with Garry Wills's *Inventing America: Jefferson's Declaration of Independence* and Stephen E. Lucas's "Justifying America: The Declaration of Independence as a Rhetorical Document."

One of the most interesting things about *Declaring Independence* is the way Fliegelman puts the bond of sentiment and common feeling at the heart of the revolutionary ideal. The "new rhetoric" of the era, he suggests, was rooted in contemporary, especially Scottish, aesthetic theory, in which the objective was to produce an involuntary response in the listener through speech. This ability to work directly on the passions of the listener was a rhetorical skill associated at the time with Native Americans, and in the Masonic lodge specifically rhetoric and the meaningful recitation of learned speech were absolutely central. Fliegelman thus provides one of the key ways to understand why Masons might permit Indians into the very heart of their exclusive, white, Protestant, and predominantly middle-class organization.[4] He quotes the contemporary thinker James Burgh on the ideal passionate, elocutionary act, "which, by influencing the will, makes one proceed to action. . . . Like irresistible beauty, it transports, it ravishes, it commands the admiration of all. . . . The hearer finds himself as unable to resist it as to stop the flow of a river with his hand. . . . His passions are no longer his own. The orator has taken possession of them: and with superior power, works them to whatever he pleases."[5] In fact it was witnessing Indian oratory that allowed the young Jefferson to first feel such feelings and be moved emotionally by speech.[6] A rather pathetic orator himself, he recalled being in awe of the Overhills Cherokee chief Outacite when Outacite delivered a parting oratory to his people the night before embarking on a trip to London after a peace settlement had been struck following the Cherokee War in North Carolina and present-day Tennessee in about 1758–60. Jefferson remembered Outacite speaking under a full moon: "His sounding voice, distinct articulation, animated action, and the solemn silence of his people at their several fires, filled me with awe and veneration, altho' I did not understand a single word he uttered."[7] One could add to Fliegelman's record of Jefferson's reverence for Indian oratory by referencing Jefferson's *Notes on the State of Virginia*, where he repeats a favorite theme, the supposed similarities between Indian and classical cultures: "I may challenge the whole orations of Demosthenes and Cicero, and of many more prominent orators, if Europe has furnished any more eminent, to produce a single passage, superior to the speech of Logan, a Mingo chief, to Lord Dunmore when Governor of this State."[8]

In stark contrast to this positive stereotype of Indians that tied them to the republican virtue he saw as foundational to American identity, Jefferson saw blacks as being an emotional void, empty of and insensible to the sensibility that defined the nation. Black Americans, it is worth noting, were excluded from mainstream Freemasonry even though certain Indians were allowed access to its inner echelons. I suggest that, in the revolutionary period at least, in part this was because Indians were deemed to be exemplary exponents of the new oratory, possessors of qualities that marked them as being capable potentially of inclusion in American political life. Fliegelman makes explicit this link between aesthetic virtue during the "elocutionary revolution" and political inclusion by referencing his fellow scholar John Barrell: "If the dominant object of both eighteenth-century oratory and fine arts was, as John Barrell puts it, 'to promote the public performance of acts of public virtue,' then oratory and the arts were necessarily addressed to and produced by 'those imagined to be capable of performing such acts'—to citizens, those 'capable not only of being ruled but also of ruling.' . . . Full membership in the republic of letters, the republic of taste, or the republic of virtue—either as producer or consumer—required prior political enfranchisement."[9]

This idea, that the ability to speak eloquently on Euro-American terms was linked with the capacity of different racial groups for inclusion in the nation—the idea that certain groups possessed a set of sympathies shared by Euro-Americans—has also been explored by Stephen Conn in his study *History's Shadow: Native Americans and Historical Consciousness in the Nineteenth Century.* Conn's is not a "performative" analysis, but his evidence very much supports Fliegelman's theme. Conn points out that at this stage Americans still thought of Indians as being within history, as opposed to, as they would be later, relegated conceptually to natural history or considered largely ahistorically primarily by ethnologists and anthropologists. Many eighteenth-century Americans perceived history as working in continually operating cycles of rise and fall, just as it had been thought of in classical antiquity. This is why Jefferson felt moved to compare the Iroquois war leader Logan to the greatest ancient orators, and why in architecture, place-names, and politics Americans consistently invoked the classical, democratic, but simultaneously slave-owning past. Today, when time is generally thought of in the West as being linear rather than cyclical and ideas about American exceptionalism and triumph over the cycles of history hold sway as well as a pervasive stereotype of the silent or monosyllabic Indian, this respect for Indian eloquence can seem out of place. Yet Jefferson's praise of Indian oratory was in itself a form of boosterism as his new American nation fought to position itself positively in cultural and intellectual terms in relation to the other great powers. The British, for example, also claimed to have discerned a poetry in savage Americans, and Jefferson was keen to argue that such eloquence in fact belonged uniquely to the Republic. "The notion of the 'savage poet' was common in 18th-century Britain," Matthew Lauzon points out, "and those found in North America were a part of the construction of British identity during the colonial period."[10] Jefferson was not alone in referring to Logan as an exemplar of the American trait of eloquence deemed to be characteristic of strong nations; the other Indian voice most often referred to in this context was that of the Six Nations orator and supposed Freemason Red Jacket. Indeed in the antebellum period one of the habitual ways American schoolchildren were encouraged to learn the highly prized skills of oratory and elocution was by memorizing and reciting a variety of such Indian speeches.

It is important to recognize, however, that such elevation of Indian eloquence by non-Indians served very specific purposes, and only very rarely did these include actually reflecting on the import of what Indians had to say. Jefferson venerated Indian oratory but did not hesitate to promote the policies that desecrated Indian land and displaced and dispossessed Indian communities. Anthony Wallace dubbed Jefferson's elevation of Logan's speech following the murder of Logan's family in 1774 "crocodile tears," and in his study *Jefferson and the Indians* makes no bones about acknowledging that the process Jefferson promoted at the time is one known today as "ethnic cleansing." The president's respect for Indians was always mitigated by his desire to advance the new nation; as Wallace puts it, "If Jefferson was guilty of insincerity, duplicity, and hypocrisy in Indian affairs, it must be conceded that this shiftiness, like his political ruthlessness, was a weapon in his struggle to ensure the survival of the United States as a republic governed by Anglo-Saxon yeomen." Tellingly, Wallace points out, by the time Jefferson discovered the elegance of Logan's lament he had also acquired a financial interest in the lands Logan had fought to retain.[11] In sum Indian eloquence could be used as evidence of indigenous American virtue or used, as it was by Indian Affairs Commissioner Thomas McKenney in 1846, as evidence that Indians were "worthy of the Christian teaching and labours, and of the government's protection."[12] It was also invoked nostalgically in memoriam for a supposedly "vanishing race," but when such eloquence referred to Indian dispossession those who invoked it rarely critically reflected upon it. By the nineteenth century Indian eloquence was increasingly seen as evidence of Indian decline, and thus it became a building block of the new narrative of unending American progress. As Conn puts it, "Americans . . . executed a nifty shift in the first half of the nineteenth century: by displacing the historical narrative of the [Puritan] jeremiad, with its sense of declension and repeating cycles of history, onto Native Americans—by making it 'their' narrative rather than 'ours'—Americans cleared a discursive space to be occupied with the much sunnier, linear narrative of progress that would dominate mainstream historical thinking throughout the nineteenth century."[13] It was as if Indians were permitted the quality of eloquence but only as a means to more powerfully articulate their inevitable demise and to starkly contrast with the brightness of the American future. Jefferson may have bemoaned the fact that America had "suffered so many of the Indian tribes already to extinguish," but in the discourse of the time the loss he was really decrying was the loss of Indian languages and knowledge to non-Indian science, not the loss of the lives of Indian peoples themselves.[14]

Even so we must not lose sight of the fact that the American veneration of individual Indian rhetorical skill that characterized the eighteenth century came close to recognizing that Indian peoples had the aesthetic and literary abilities that in Euro-American terms qualified racial groups for nationhood. Skill in language was key to what created nations, and this was especially true in the Renaissance and Enlightenment, in which Freemasonry has its roots. As Benedict Anderson explains, language has the "capacity for generating imagined communities building in effect particular solidarities."[15] John Quincy Adams famously made the point in another form in 1805, referring to the classical era to which his contemporaries were so fond of comparing their own, stating, "Eloquence was power."[16] By the terms of Fliegelman's "elocutionary revolution" Indian rhetorical skill made individual Indian figures appear valid, admirable, and even respectable. As Conn puts it, "The achievement of Indian eloquence might or might not raise the estimation of all Indians, but it had the force to make individual Indian speakers into real men."[17] As eloquent orators, individual Indians allowed early Americans to see the best of themselves reflected in those they considered vanquished and residual. The nineteenth-century archaeologist Caleb Atwater encapsulated this idea especially forcefully when he argued, "Enthusiasm is the secret spirit which hovers over the eloquence of the Indian," an enthusiasm he felt was aroused whenever the selling of ancestral lands was discussed. Then the Indian's "eyes flash fire . . . every muscle is strained . . . and his voice becomes clear, distinct and commanding. He now becomes, to use his own expressive phrase, A MAN." Thus for Atwater at least it was through performance alone that Indian humanity was glimpsed, at the expense of the larger and more obvious way to perceive Indian humanity: through actual connection with and perception of Indian grief, loss, and distress. In sum it was the manner of expression that struck Jefferson's contemporaries as significant about Indian speech, not the message of the words themselves or their implicit or explicit demands for redress.

The period's respect for Indian eloquence was also part of an urge for a return to nature, which Fliegelman connects to the emergence more generally of personality as a concept. It was part of "a revolution in the conceptualization of language, a revolution that sought to replace artificial language with natural language and to make writing over in the image of speaking."[18] Fliegelman quotes the Enlightenment philosopher Thomas Reid, who defined "natural language" as being "like that of dumb people and savages," in that "it has more of nature, is more expressive and is more easily learned."[19] All this was closely linked to the parallel deist ideal of natural rather than revealed religion, an ideal that lies close to the source and heart of Freemasonry. Fliegelman's book shows us how a culture of performance in the revolutionary era provided a way for certain Indians to be incorporated into Freemasonry and thus into a society within society organized by the American elite.

Another wonderful "performative" book not directly about Native American Freemasonry or indeed exclusively concerned with performance studies per se but of relevance to how such work might be approached is Eric Lott's 1993 *Love and Theft: Blackface Minstrelsy and the American Working Class*. Native American Freemasonry may at the outset seem rather far from blackface minstrelsy, the nineteenth-century theatrical form that was mostly urban and northern, in which white men caricatured blacks for pleasure and to make money. After all, Freemasonry is predominantly a middle-class rather than working-class phenomenon, and although the performance of ritual is central to its activities it is carried out in secret rather than in public. Furthermore there is no evidence of ridicule having any overt role in Masonic use of Indian themes. Even so there are aspects of Lott's approach that are both intriguing and instructive, not least because he encourages us to look at the phenomenon of whites dressing up as ethnic Others in new ways. In the Masonic lodge at various times Indians "performed" Indianness as part of Masonic ritual, and Euro-American Masons similarly "performed" as Indians in specific Indian or Indian-inspired Masonic rituals. Lott's analysis provides us with fascinating glimpses of how such a phenomenon might be understood.

Lott is quick to displace and develop some of the older and more obvious ways of understanding white male racial dressing up in the context of minstrelsy. He suggests it was more than simply a means of expressing racial domination or aversion while recognizing that it was in essence nothing less than a form of cultural robbery, in Marx's terms, expropriation. Nevertheless, following the critical theorist Homi Bhabha, Lott emphasizes the ambivalence he senses at the heart of minstrelsy as a practice and the way it evidenced cross-racial desire and white anxiety as much as it did abusive derision. He explores what he terms, following Raymond Williams, the period's "'racial unconscious'—a structured formation, combining thought and feeling, tone and impulse, and at the very edge of semantic availability, whose symptoms and anxieties make it just legible."[20] He is at pains to demonstrate that for all its flaws, minstrelsy was an African American culture. In an analogous fashion I suggest that Native American culture as expressed in Freemasonry served ambivalent functions and that it tapped into sometimes unconscious needs, wants, and desires concerning race within Freemasonry's middle-class, largely white, male constituency.

Perhaps the most elegant and reverberative application to date of the performative approach has been Joseph Roach's 1996 text, *Cities of the Dead: Circum-Atlantic Performance*. Roach looks at what Paul Gilroy terms the "Black Atlantic"—the circum-Atlantic region bounded by Europe, Africa, and the Americas—in terms of live performance, a phenomenon Roach conceptualizes as being highly expansive and experienced not just in theaters but everywhere people congregate. His study focuses on London and New Orleans from the late seventeenth century to the present and explores how the "orature" of those places expresses the interactions of race, class, and gender. Orature seeks to dissolve the usual dichotomy between orality and literacy and stresses that each has always produced the other. Roach's fundamental point is that historic performance survives, and in this sense so too do the dead through the bodies and performances of the living.[21] A key example he gives is the Mardi Gras Indians, African American parade companies who perform Native Americanness through music, dance, and costume and who create new meaning out of a shared circum-Atlantic history of genocide and slavery. Following *The Future of Ritual: Writings on Culture and Performance* by Richard Schechner, one of the foundational figures of performance studies, who suggested that performance could be seen as "restored behaviour," Roach shows how performers have consistently regenerated and revised their history so as to imagine new identities for themselves. Roach unearths a complicated genealogy of performance within which the past is reexamined, reproduced, and reinscribed. A central idea in *Cities of the Dead*, as Roach explained in an interview, is the idea of surrogation or substitution, "where one generation will stand up and stand in for another, and honor the preceding generation by quoting it, but also develop their own ideas and put in their own inventions. It's called repetition with revision, and it resembles jazz in the way it's played out."[22]

Both these significant ideas—of circum-Atlantic performance and of surrogation—provide useful points of access to Native American Freemasonry over time. The performance elements of Freemasonry crossed the Atlantic and joined together Euro-Americans and Indians at key points in the history of each. Masons and Indians used ritual relationships as a vehicle for experiencing connectedness and for generating a satisfying sense of brotherhood and reciprocity. Masonic ritual and Masonic theater are in this sense prime examples of what Roach dubs "circum-Atlantic performance," a co-creation of the peoples who constituted an American "oceanic interculture."[23] Faced with revolutionary circumstances American Masons invented themselves by performing their pasts in the presence of others. Although its extent is impossible to gauge, both Indians and Masons may be thought of as performing surrogation through ritual, enacting cultural memory through substitution. Indians of course had compelling reasons to seek out and maintain places where cultural memory might be retained given both the central social and spiritual significance of ancestors to many Native American communities and the unprecedented levels of death and cultural erosion that beset them in the wake of successive waves of Euro-American incursion and the devastating effects of settler-borne disease and displacement. As Roach points out, black- and Native-informed performance traditions (and here I include Freemasonry) remember the role of "officially forgotten . . . diasporic and genocidal histories of Africa and the Americas, North and South, in the creation of the culture of modernity."[24] Freemasonic "Indian" rituals as well as the significant correspondences between actual Indian rituals, such as that of the Seneca Iroquois Little Water Society and the "traditional history," the final ritual of the Masonic third degree, all served to intermingle things Indian and things Masonic, linking the dead with the living and the past, however constituted, with the present. This performative and, to a lesser extent, literary re-birth of Indian tradition within the Masonic lodge can be seen as a rehabilitation of the dispossessed, an example of what Sharon Holland characterizes in another context as "speaking from the dead," a literature and performance in a space where it was possible for the living and the dead to "converge, mingle, and discourse."[25]

This positive reading of Indian Masonic involvement links directly to Joanna Brooks's argument in *American Lazarus: Religion and the Rise of African-American and Native American Literatures* that Masonic lodges, along with a host of other religious and spiritual fora, became "sites critical to the formation of modern black and Indian political, religious, and cultural consciousness." Brooks shows convincingly that even within a wider social context that deemed blacks and Indians degenerate and socially dependent, "communities of color" were able to "regenerate . . . themselves by forming separate and independent religious bodies." Her main focus is black rather than Indian Freemasonry, in particular the story of the ex-slave Prince Hall, but her overarching point that sites such as the Masonic lodge were sanctuaries where Indian communities might grow links directly to much of what follows in this book. Prince Hall's experience of Masonry contrasts meaningfully with that of Indian Masons. In Boston on the eve of the War of Independence, Hall was initiated by an Irish military regiment and afterward founded a powerful order of black Masonic lodges that promoted the spiritual and political strength of black communities. Brooks looks at the literature of Prince Hall Masonry and, in keeping with her demand that we "rethink our narrow notion of authorship," deems it evidence of black Masons sacralizing a relationship with American community on *their* terms, evidence of a "politically intended protoblack nationalism." "They fashioned," she tells us, "from mystical, biblical, and Masonic texts an *unnatural* history, a counternarrative to eighteenth century empiricisms and 'natural histories' that classified Africa as a cipher, perpetually primitive and unintelligible."[26]

In the same way, by their presence at and to a lesser extent contribution to Masonic ritual, Indian Masons reinscribed Masonic activities so as to centralize and incorporate within them Indian meanings, Indian rituals, and Indian understandings of the past. Indian, or for that matter black, nationalist resistance may not, as Brooks suggests, have originated within Freemasonry (this seems a step too far given the available evidence), but Freemasonry did serve to bring together the respective cultural resources of blacks and Indians, and it isolated a host of noble ethnic exemplars from the Masonic past. In the case of Prince Hall it created a social space uniquely for black people. In the Indian case it created a social and political space where Indians and Euro-Americans could conjoin and interact both at the level of the imagination and within the realm of the sacred. Just as almost every free black male political leader of the nineteenth century was a Prince Hall Mason (with the notable exception of Frederick Douglass), key Indians of the revolutionary era and of the nineteenth century and early twentieth were Masons also.[27] To illustrate this point and to begin to demonstrate how significant Freemasonry was to intellectual ethnic America, consider the following comparative list just in terms of the nineteenth century. On the African American side the evangelist Lemuel Haynes, the African Methodist Episcopal Church founders Richard Allen and Absalom Jones, the Haitian attorney general Prince Saunders, the Liberian president Joseph Jenkins Roberts, the abolitionist James Forten, David Walker, Henry Highland Garnet, William Wells Brown, Josiah Henson, Martin Delaney, Booker T. Washington, and W. E. B. DuBois were all Masons. So too was the first Indian commissioner of Indian Affairs and adjutant to Ulysses S. Grant, Ely S. Parker (1828–95); his great-nephew the New York museum man and anthropologist Arthur Caswell Parker (1881–1955); the anthropologist Francis La Flesche (1857–1932); the Wyandot leader William Walker (1800–74); the Yavapai journalist and spokesperson Carlos Montezuma (1865–1923); the Cherokee leaders John Rollin Ridge (1827–67), Elias Boudinot (1835–90), John Ross (1828–66), Stand Watie (1806–71), and William Potter Ross (1820–91); the Choctaw leader Peter P. Pitchlyn (1806–81); the South Dakota leader and Episcopal priest the Reverend Philip J. Deloria Sr. (1853–1931); the Cherokee humorist Will Rogers (1879–1935); the Tuscarora leader Chief Clinton Rickard (1882–1971); the Kaw Kansas senator Charles Curtis (1860–1936); and the Chickasaw Cherokee U.S. congressional representative Charles David Carter (1868–1929). There was also the mid-nineteenth-century religious nationalism of the Cherokee Keetoowah Society, which was constituted, at least in part, on Masonic terms.

Brooks suggests that what black Masons were doing in their lodges was "passionate research," as Frantz Fanon describes it in his essay "On National Culture," that is, research that is foundational to resisting imperialism, research "directed by the secret hope of discovering beyond the misery of today, beyond self-contempt, resignation, and abjuration, some very beautiful and splendid era whose existence rehabilitates us both in regard to ourselves and in regard to others."[28] Stuart Hall has taken this idea further, suggesting that such research comes in two forms: one "unearths that which the colonial experience buried and overlaid, bringing to light the hidden continuities it suppressed"; another concerns itself with the "*production* of identity . . . not an identity grounded in the archaeology, but in the re-telling of the past."[29] This last type of radical history, one that Indian and black Masons created with their Euro-American brothers, was not about inventing a fixed or static sense of "being" but about encouraging a perpetual and critical process of "becoming." They were reconstituting in

Masonic microcosm what being black or Indian meant socially in the United States. I would add that crucially this was not a straightforward or predictable process and not one where either Indian or Masonic "essences" can easily be isolated; rather it was piecemeal and discontinuous. Masonic ritual exemplifies Renato Rosaldo's depiction of ritual in general as something that most often resembles "a busy intersection" where strange and unplanned meetings may occur. This in turn connects with Rosaldo's more general understanding of culture itself as being open to influence from myriad interlinked sources. He writes, "In contrast with the classic view which posits culture as a self-contained whole made up of coherent patterns, culture can arguably be conceived as a more porous array of intersections where distinct processes crisscross from within and beyond its borders."[30]

Indian Access to History and Freemasonry as Spiritual Sanctuary

At this point one could well ask why the Masonic lodge became an important forum for this mix of identity formation, identity recapitulation, and the reiteration of a usable Indian past. Part of the answer is because being a Mason has always had a great deal to do with history, with its reenactment, with the creation of surrogates, and with the ritual re-creation of mythic past events that are capable of changing form but, as with all myth, are also capable of speaking directly to aspects of the present. The lodge after all, however constituted, was a very special, sacred space whose spatial organization reinforced its unique internal hierarchies and deliberately abrogated outside reality. The Masonic lodge acted as a haven for Indian versions of the Indian past, versions in which the Indian contribution to the story of mankind's development could be emphasized rather than, as occurred outside the lodge, consistently elided and ignored in place of a larger romance about non-Indian triumph. This Romantic aspect to American history, which excluded Indians outside of the lodge, has been fully explored by Stephen Bann in *Romanticism and the Rise of History*. The earliest American historians (Sparks, Bancroft, Parkman), he explains, all told stories of progress, "romances" in which the development of the "New World" seemed preordained. In *Anatomy of Criticism* Northrop Frye defines the romance as being located between myth and naturalism, where myth is displaced in a human direction and where events themselves are conventionalized in an ideal direction. In *Metahistory* Hayden White extends this idea, explaining that the romance, with its hero, quest, redemption, and happy ending, "is a drama of the triumph of good over evil, of virtue over vice, of light over darkness, and of the ultimate transcendence of man over the world in which he was imprisoned by the Fall."[31] Indians were excluded from this drama as culturally developmental entities; they were symbolically cast in stone, for example by Francis Parkman in his 1851 history, *The Conspiracy of Pontiac*: "The Indian is hewn out of rock. You cannot change the form without destruction of the substance." As peoples deemed uniquely incapable of change within history, the only fate available to Indians caught up in the grand sweep of American progress was extinction, a necessary penalty in Parkman's eyes for the recalcitrant Indian, "this irreclaimable son of the wilderness, the child who will not be weaned from the breast of his rugged mother."[32] Crucially, however, Indians could use the very fact of their shadowy and exotic existence apparently outside of history to gain purchase within Masonic communities. Ironically, at points when Indian voices were most violently being silenced, Indian Masons were able to use the tradition of Indian eloquence and prowess as orators to great advantage within the lodge, a place in American society where myth and the oral transmission of shared knowledge still held sway. It is worth recalling at this point Alexander Piatigorsky's point about Freemasonry, that its early internal histories (including Anderson's *Constitutions*, first published in 1723) are, shall we say, highly imaginative, and that in essence the fraternity's most important feature is "a fundamental Masonic historical self-awareness which comprises the idea of a Mason's connection with his past or, more precisely, with the past of a Mason's own particular culture as well as with the past of human culture in general."[33] This historical self-awareness, the fact that from its earliest beginnings Freemasonry has constructed its own metahistory, is as remarkable as its popularity over time. For a number of American Indian individuals such an alternative metahistory was attractive. It offered an alternative space within which to enact history and to perform identity.

The Masonic lodge was never a static cultural forum, but I suggest that at key points it functioned consistently as a sanctuary for Indian tradition, where through ritual Indian spiritual values and the Indian dead could become central rather than peripheral. This takes on its true significance only when we bear in mind that an ongoing assault on Indian ritual and Indian spiritual leadership went hand in hand with the colonizing process in the Americas. The point is recognized by Joshua David Bellin in the introduction to his 2008 text, *Medicine Bundle: Indian Sacred Performance and American Literature, 1824–1932*, the book that began the work of directly applying performance as a paradigm specifically to Indian studies. Bellin sketches the ongoing history of attack on Indian spirituality in the nineteenth century, which one might trace back ultimately to Columbus's confident assertion that Indians had no structured spiritual belief to speak of. In his letter of 1493 Columbus wrote, "They do not hold any creed nor are they idolaters; but they all believe that power and good are in the heavens."[34] His "discovery" of a diverse range of Indian peoples in what was deemed a new world presented a fundamental set of difficulties in terms of the dominant Christian cosmogony of the times, since no mention had been made of them in the Scriptures or in the work of classical authors.[35] One solution to this conundrum was to link Indians with the cultures known previously to Westerners from Old World antiquity: ancient Greeks, Scythians, Tartars, Spaniards, biblical Hebrews, even the peoples of Atlantis. In essence this was to view Indians as weak reflections of a version of the Euro-American self. Neither this nor the larger consensus that developed, of Indians having migrated to the New World via a land bridge, solved the curious problem of obvious and significant cultural diversity in the New World. The answer that fit the classical humanist conception of a Greek and Roman Golden Age and orthodox Christianity's belief in monogenesis was to posit that Indians were a degeneration of mankind following expulsion from the Garden of Eden. Thus Indians were flawed versions of previous civilizations or, at worst, active agents of Satan. In either case Indian religion was perceived as having little or no intrinsic coherence or value; as the English theologian Roger Williams puts it, "The wandring Generations of *Adams* lost posteritie, having lost the true and living God their maker, have created out of the nothing of their owne inventions many false and fained Gods and Creators."[36]

This idea of Indian degeneracy became something of a self-fulfilling prophecy for non-Indians as their encroachment onto Indian lands brought disease, war, displacement, and alcoholism to indigenous communities and as missionizing influences set about actively eroding the spiritual fabric of the successive groups of Native peoples they encountered. In time the idea of Indian degeneracy took root; as Robert Berkhofer explains, "The idea of Indian degeneracy and decay extended far beyond its religious origins of the Renaissance period to become entwined in and with the very foundations of modern social scientific thinking."[37] Indian spiritual leadership became a prime target either for annihilation or displacement as the process of cultural engulfment gained pace and as the twin prongs of religious and political colonization advanced westward. Francis Jennings points out that because an Indian spiritual leader was "one of the strongest unifying factors in any Indian community" he was the figure who "became the object of the most intense hatred of Europeans striving to weaken and dominate his tribe."[38] Puritan missionaries were especially punitive, deeming it imperative that Indian peoples follow the Lord's commandment to worship "none other God but me." Thus John Eliot instructed his Indian converts in 1648 that any spiritual congregation of Indian peoples would incur a material penalty, demanding, "There shall be no more *Pawwowing* amongst the *Indians*. And if any shall hereafter *Pawwow* [Pawwows are Witches or Sorcerers that cure by help of the devil], both he that shall *Powwow*, and he that shall procure him to *Powwow*, shall pay 20 *s*. apeece."[39] Similarly the Puritan minister Cotton Mather convinced himself that the Devil had seduced Indians into occupying the New World to insulate them from the good news of Christ's gospel: "We may guess that probably the devil decoyed those miserable savages hither, in hopes that the gospel of the Lord Jesus Christ would never come here to destroy or disturb his absolute empire over them."[40]

Campaigns against Native spiritual practices developed not only from evangelical ambitions but also from, and at the same time as, the territorial and ideological ambitions of the states active on what would become American soil. The process reached new heights between 1776 and 1838 as the American nation was built. It is important to recognize that this sustained attack on Indian spirituality went on against a background of acute Indian population decline, a decline Ronald Niezen unequivocally calls "ethnocide" in his book *Spirit Wars*. He quotes the Cherokee scholar Russell Thornton's analysis of the U.S. region alone, where Indian population numbers "decreased from 5+ million in 1492 to about 250,000 from 1890 to 1900. . . . Such population decline implies not only that some 5 million American Indians died during the 400 years but that, in fact, many times the approximate figure of 5 million died, as new but ever numerically smaller generations of American Indians were born, lived, and died."[41] Niezen urges us to see the peaceful destruction of Indian communities and Indian spiritual leadership as simply another facet of the centuries-long warfare against Indian existence on Indian terms. "The peaceful termination of indigenous peoples had long been a part, sometimes a pivotal part," he notes, "of colonial enterprises in the New World, often taking the form of missionary efforts struggling for human souls in the midst of the chaotic destruction of human lives."[42] There is of course ample evidence of how intense the attempt to quell Indian spiritual resistance became. Spanish Franciscan cruelty in the seventeenth century to those Pueblo Indians they suspected of generating resistance through messianism or other forms of spirituality is well known. Some of the punishments came directly from the Inquisition and included burning "superstitious" Indians alive and defeating "idolatry" by hanging and other forms of gruesome execution.[43] Fear was also a main missionizing tool for the early seventeenth-century Jesuits working among the Anishinaabe in Ontario, one of whom registered his pleasure in the effect: "The dread of punishment is beginning to gain such an ascendancy over their minds that, although they do not soon amend, yet they are little by little giving up their evil customs."[44] English explorers such as Thomas Harriott even convinced themselves of the reassuring idea that the Indians they encountered were overawed by Protestant Christianity and instantly at pains to adopt it as their own. In *A Briefe and True Report* he wrote, "This is the

summe of their religion, which I learned by having special famil-
iarity with some of their priestes. Wherein they were not so sure
grounded, nor gave such credite to their traditions and stories but
through conversing with us they were brought into great doubts
of their owne, and no small admiration of ours, with earnest desire in many, to learne more than we had meanes for want of perfect utterance in their language to expresse."[45]

Under the catchall word for Indian cultural obliteration,
civilization, the government eventually sponsored a variety of
means whereby Indian spirituality was curtailed or abstracted.
Aside from the work of missionaries, these included the work
of on- and off-reservation boarding schools, the removal and
debarring of Indian peoples from sacred sites, and the general
workings of the anthropological profession itself, intent as it
was on removing, deracinating, and decontextualizing Indian
sacred materials.[46] The second half of the nineteenth century
saw the tentacles of this government quest for Indian "civilization" spread fully across the continent, with the period after the
Civil War until the mid-twentieth century constituting arguably
the worst of times for Indian religion. A key plank of President
Ulysses S. Grant's 1869 Peace Policy was to missionize the reservations, missions that Lee Irwin explains "specifically targeted
Native religions as the bane of all civilized Christian ideology.
. . . Indian ceremonies were banned, religious practices disrupted,
and sacred objects destroyed or confiscated." Courts of Indian Of-
fenses established in 1883 with the specific purpose of obliterating
Indian dances and ritualistic gatherings further augmented the
plan to destroy Native spirituality, as did the 1892 clarification of
the rules of Indian courts specifying fines, prison sentences, im-
prisonment, and the withholding of rations for "any Indian who
shall engage in the sun dance, scalp dance, or war dance, or any
other similar feast so called" and for "any Indian who shall en-

gage in the practices of so-called medicine men, or who . . . shall use any arts of conjure to prevent Indians from abandoning their barbarous rites and customs."[47]

For their part Euro-Americans had very plausible grounds to fear recurrent pan- or intertribal Indian cohesion based on new or renewed forms of spirituality. Messianic movements of the eighteenth and nineteenth century in particular served to bring together Native peoples through ritual practice and to create powerful communication networks between disparate communities. The history of Indian resistance to non-Indian encroachment and of Indian cultural renewal is littered with prophetic leadership: the Munsee leader Papounhan in 1752, the Delaware prophet Neolin in the 1760s, the Seneca prophet Handsome Lake in around 1800, the Cherokee Yonaguska in 1820, the Kickapoo Kenekuk in 1832, the Wanapam Smohalla in the 1850s, and the Paiute Wovoka, a founder of the Ghost Dance movement of 1889. Resistance continued into the twentieth century from figures such as the Creek Chitto Harjo and the Nisqually John Slocum, who established the intertribal and syncretic Shaker Church. Furthermore the revival of diverse Native spiritual practices served to revive Native lifeways that were sometimes but not always at odds with the U.S. government's determination to reorient American Indians away from communalism toward individualism and capitalism. A good example of this was the Northwest Coast practice of potlatch, where status within specific communities lay in what an individual or family might give away or share with the community, in contrast to capitalist society, where status is reflected in what is individually owned and retained for exclusive use.[48] Of course the non-Indian determination not to perceive Indian communities' spirituality and in particular their long-held and sacred relationship to land was bound up with the desire to possess those lands. The concern to break up tribal communities as political, social, and spiritual entities had much more to do with assimilating Indian land and resources than with assimilating individual Indians as anything more than peripheral figures within American capitalism. Full assimilation was the compensation offered to Indian peoples rhetorically in exchange for the loss of their ancestral homelands, but as the twentieth century approached it became obvious, as Frederick Hoxie shows convincingly, that not only were Indians resistant to the process, but their complete acceptance demanded more of the nation's institutions, social values, and cultural life than the citizenry was prepared to grant.[49]

All of this is true, but it is also important to recognize that the widespread denigration of Indian culture and spirituality existed alongside lesser threads of non-Indian reverence, fascination, and even veneration for Indian spiritual life. Niezen points out that the nineteenth-century drive to colonize and control Indian lands had its corollary in a drive to know, classify, control, and explore the deepest recesses of Indian culture. Because the consensus was that Indian cultures were all destined for imminent destruction, for "salvage" ethnologists and anthropologists the drive to know and contain them was an urgent imperative. "American Indian religion in particular came to be understood as a source of exploratory challenge," Niezen explains, "full of esoteric knowledge and fragile secrets. It comprised a vast, differentiated landscape uncharted by the civilized observer."[50] The fact that key facets of the spiritual life of Indian communities were kept secret and that language and its communication were often held to be sacred by Indian peoples added to the challenge. Freemasonry shared a similar veneration for the power of language, especially in ritual, as well as a central veneration for secrecy; this in turn may have served to attract Indian Masons to the fraternity. Niezen provides us with several examples of successful anthropological attempts to prize religious secrets from Indian communities, including the early twentieth-century work of Paul Radin. A recent convert to the peyote faith named Jasper Blowsnake revealed to Radin a version of the sacred Medicine Rite of the Winnebago of Nebraska and Iowa, which Radin published in *The Road of Life and Death*, along with Blowsnake's warning: "This, too, remember. Never tell anyone about this Rite. Keep it absolutely secret. If you disclose it, the world will come to an end. We will all end. We will all die. . . . Only misery and catastrophe would result from such conduct. . . . Into the very bowels of our grandmother Earth, must we protect this information, so that by no possible chance can it ever emerge into daylight. So secret must this be kept. Forever and ever must this be done."[51]

We can only speculate as to how much was revealed by such "revealed rites," especially since many (but not Blowsnake's) were given in exchange for cash or favors.[52] Non-Indian fears that missionizing or legal prohibition would destroy Indian ritual and belief were valid, but it is also true that Indian communities responded strategically to attacks on the sanctity of their beliefs and practice by hiding them from external scrutiny, what Niezen calls "secrecy upon secrecy," so that "nothing was left visible to interest those looking for genuine 'pagan' traditions."[53] Repeatedly we find Indian references to secrecy and the careful guarding of tradition as it gets transmitted across generations. The Ojibwa writer George Copway (Kah-ge-ga-gah-bowh, 1818–69) wrote in 1847, "The *traditions* handed down from father to son, were held very sacred; one half of these are not known by the white people, however far their researches may have extended. There is an unwillingness, on the part of the Indians to communicate many of their traditions."[54] Even so, many commentators over time have remarked on the seeming similarities between the Indian rites recorded around the turn of the century, before the rise of the peyote faith, and those of Freemasonry. These have most often been

Masons, but some have not. Notable among this second group in the late twentieth century was the poet Kenneth Rexroth, who compared the description of Mide-wiwin Society he found in Frances Densmore's *Chippewa Music* directly to the fraternity.[55]

The attack on Indian spirituality began to abate in the wake of the intellectual reaction against the perceived conformity and personality-draining mechanization of industrializing America in the 1920s. Indian ritual performance then found an ally in Indian Commissioner John Collier, who built a degree of respect for Indian ceremony and religious life into the Indian New Deal.[56] However, Indian spiritual expression has remained in need of protection right up to the present day, as reflected in hard-won legislation such as the 1978 American Indian Religious Freedom Act and the 1994 Native American Free Exercise of Religion Act. The 1990 Native American Grave Protection and Repatriation Act went some way toward protecting Indian graves from desecration but did not apply to state lands or private property, leaving Indian peoples to continue to battle to ensure that their dead receive the respect awarded to those in other American communities.

Thus we see that Indian peoples have always had to fight hardest to protect what is most valuable and most sacred. Performance within Freemasonry served as something of a sanctuary for some Indian spiritual ideas, and it gave certain Indians access to how some sorts of history got told. Yet such an emphasis carries with it its own problems and its own pitfalls.

Approaching Native American Freemasonry, Part Two

2

The Pitfalls of the "Performative" Approach

> Performance is about doing, and it is about seeing; it is about image, embodiment, space, collectivity and/or orality; it makes community and it breaks community; it repeats endlessly and it never repeats; it is intentional and unintentional, innovative and derivative, more fake and more real. Performance's many connotations and its varied intellectual kinships ensure that an interdisciplinary conversation around this interdisciplinary site rarely will be neat and straightforward.
>
> —SHANNON JACKSON, *Professing Performance: Theatre in the Academy from Philology to Performativity*

Although it is both possible and appropriate to characterize Indian involvement in Freemasonry positively as a form of cultural adaption and survival in the face of sustained fundamental attack on Indian spiritual and cultural life, this can be taken too far. After all, Masonic Indians, right from the foundation of an American national identity, were taking part in a key social forum for the extension and propagation of colonial interests. Masonry may have allowed for a degree of cultural exchange and on occasion for the co-creation of cultural forms by Indians and

Euro-Americans in the special context of the fraternity, but this was done within what was primarily an elite context, reserved for and heavily policed by those at the heart of American power. Perhaps particularly in the eighteenth century Freemasonry served the interests of a growing state, as did, for that matter, American evangelicalism. While Freemasonry can undoubtedly be legitimately seen as a site of cultural regeneration for Indians, it is important to never lose sight of the fact that this regeneration was reserved for the few and that those Indian few were disproportionately cultural brokers operating close to or within the upper echelons of specific American communities.

This brings us to the question of the extent to which performance as an analytical focus can or should be used generally to recontextualize Indian and non-Indian interaction. The issue merits close scrutiny not least because the approach has the potential to obscure the profound imbalance inherent in colonial cross-cultural exchange. For Bellin, Indian performance (in the nineteenth century at least) is far from uncomplex, but it can be bundled together with that of whites, as his explanation of the title of his book *Medicine Bundle: Indian Sacred Performance and American Literature, 1824–1932* suggests. One of his principal claims is that "there is no *absolute* difference between the performance of medicine by Indians and by whites, that manifestations of Indian and white medicine couple and blur in the words and works of all peoples involved in the encounter." There is, it seems, no opportunity in terms of the lens through which Bellin views Indian performance for it to exist in a discrete sense from that of other forms of performance by non-Indians, even if that performance is perhaps a ribald pastiche or a debilitating travesty of things sacred to specific Indian groups. "The culture of Indian performance," he states, "is a dynamic and inventive arena from which neither party, Indian nor white, can emerge without sharing and shaping the other's medicine."[1]

Such an approach is welcome and enabling in the sense that it puts Indian influence at the heart of, as Bellin puts it, "the constitution of America."[2] It makes Indian peoples active rather than passive agents in the grand narrative of American national development. Generally it draws attention to the indestructibility of certain forms of Indian practice in that it highlights how Indians found ways to incorporate abiding Indian truths into non-Indian performative forms. Furthermore, usefully, the performative turn invokes the inexpressible and brings it into scholarly discourse. Bellin, for example, reminds us that the performance of ritual, oratory, song, or dance transcends the written word and is rooted in a specific context and specific communities. Appropriately he quotes the German traveler Johann Georg Kohl, who in 1860 splendidly captured in language how Indian performance is particularly place- and context-specific. Indian ceremonies, songs, and dances, he wrote, "very frequently resemble polypi and certain molluscs, which, while floating on the sea, have splendid colours and interesting forms, but which, when seized, prove to be a lump of jelly, and dissolve in the hand."[3] This in turn calls to mind Peggy Phelan's recent claim that performance cannot be exactly repeated (ritual is of course repeated, but each performance of it is unique and irreplaceable): "Performance cannot be saved, recorded, documented, or otherwise participate in the circulation of representations: once it does so, it becomes something other than performance. To the degree that performance attempts to enter the economy of reproduction it betrays and lessens the promise of its ontology. Performance's being . . . becomes itself through disappearance."[4]

Other specific benefits accrue in the Indian context as a result of the performative approach. As an analytical lens it places emphasis on identity as being relational and the fact that a meeting of separate cultures is in itself a prerequisite for difference to emerge. As James Clifford puts it, "Difference is an effect of inventive syncretism."[5] At the same time, for Bellin, as indeed for Roach, performance is a phenomenon that transcends time itself and belies the Western obsession with locating points of origin.[6] Viewed positively this emphasizes the indestructible and infinitely adaptable and morphological nature of many Indian traditions, traditions that have survived repeated onslaught and in many cases have made very successful transitions from oral to print form. Here one is reminded of the Laguna novelist Leslie Marmon Silko's work *Ceremony*, in which a part-Navajo shaman, Betonie, reminds us that Native ceremonies have always been a dynamic and fluid cultural force: "At one time, the ceremonies as they had been performed were enough for the way the world was then. But after the white people came, elements in this world began to shift; and it became necessary to create new ceremonies. I have made changes in the rituals. The people mistrust this greatly, but only this growth keeps the ceremonies strong."[7] Aside from this emphasis on the indestructible and changing nature of Indian ritual, the performative approach also moves us from any bounded sense of the "middle ground," to use Richard White's term, away from the idea that intercultural interaction ceased with the War of 1812 or with the American Revolution, the point when "Indians ceased to have the power to force whites onto the middle ground" and were thereafter forced to live with an identity imposed upon them externally.[8] Instead through performance we get a strong sense, as we did with Bellin's first book, *The Demon of the Continent*, of what he terms the impossibility of measuring in any meaningful way the process of "mutual acculturation" that went on before and after watersheds such as 1812.[9]

It is this ability to move us intellectually away from the binary oppositions inherent in ideas of race and manifest destiny that is among the most attractive things about the performance paradigm. Rather than viewing ethnic groups as discrete and unlinked phenomena it allows us to track how they are marked or contested irrespective of whether the culture or tradition in question passes on information generally by oral or literary means. It takes the locus of analysis away from dominant or central groups and into the interstices of relationships between cultures and groups, and we are able to respond intellectually to Mikhail Bakhtin's injunction that "the most intense and productive life of culture takes place on the boundaries."[10] This is an awareness imported from postmodern ethnography and the work of authors such Dwight Conquergood, James Clifford, and Renato Rosaldo, in which the contingent, the borrowed, and the developmental elements of culture are emphasized.[11] Conquergood tells us, "Meaning is contested and struggled for in the interstices, *in between* structures. Identity is invented and contingent, not autonomous," and Clifford describes "organic culture reconceived as inventive process or creolized 'interculture.'"[12] Clifford in particular has been keen to posit colonial or neocolonial identity as almost infinitely malleable and regenerative, writing, "Groups negotiating their identity in contexts of domination and exchange, persist, patch themselves together in ways different from a living organism. A community, unlike a body, can lose a central 'organ' and not die. All the critical elements of identity are in specific conditions replaceable: language, land, blood, leadership, religion. Recognized, viable tribes exist in which any one or even most of these elements are missing, replaced, or largely transformed."[13] In part this reinforces and extends previous work in American history on the interconnections between American ethnic groups, in particular the change of direction heralded by Gary Nash's 1995 presidential address to the Organization of American Historians ("The Hidden History of Mestizo America") and the work of Jack D. Forbes in *Africans and Native Americans: The Language of Race*.[14]

However, readers familiar with debates in Native American studies will feel a sense of unease at Clifford's notion that all the elements of identity are replaceable given the long history of Indian efforts to assert the opposite, that elements such as land, language, and the ability to freely practice religion are essential to the survival of specific Indian identities in specific, sacred places. Indeed Clifford eventually concludes that all identity is infinitely fluid and contextual, an intellectual position that removes certain well-worn bases for political action since it becomes impossible to argue for the rights or sovereignty of a group if its cultural identity is deemed to be invented or relational. This in turn leads us to consider problems in general with the emphasis on "middleness," on the interstitial and the seemingly reciprocal nature of cultural borrowing. Some of the same critique that has been leveled at Richard White's characterization of the "middle ground" can be applied to performance as an analytical lens. Cohen in "A Mutually Comprehensible World? Native Americans, Europeans, and Play in Eighteenth Century America" and Herman in "Romance on the Middle Ground," for example, have thoroughly unpicked the suggestion they find inherent in the idea of a middle ground: that racialized hierarchies were in any way or at any point assuaged by the very fact of two cultures meeting. Rosemarie Bank has issued a similar warning against falling for the romance of performance as a phenomenon that can somehow sidestep the asymmetrical power relationships that have characterized Indian–non-Indian interaction over time. She suggests that the performative approach "in its insistence that from the beginning red and white cultures acted upon, influenced, and appropriated each other, erasing the possibility of a return for either race to an untouched ('originary' or 'real') condition, is perilous if it is assumed that the cultural stakes for red and white peoples in the internal imperialist scenario were the same."[15] One is reminded of the forthright warnings concerning just such elision of asymmetrical relationships of power once given by older anthropologists such as Stanley Diamond. Diamond wrote in 1974, "Civilization originates in conquest abroad and repression at home. Each is an aspect of the other. Anthropologists who use, or misuse, words such as acculturation beg this basic question. For the major mode of acculturation, the direct shaping of one culture by another through which civilization develops, has been conquest."[16]

In stark contrast to Bellin and Roach, Diamond argued that any diffusion of cultural traits is evidence of struggle and to view it in any other terms is false, if not dangerous. He cautioned, "When—as generally happens-this diffusion is traced as an abstract exchange, somehow justified by the universal balance sheet of the imperial civilization, the assault by civilized upon primitive or traditional societies is masked, or its implications evaded."[17] The danger is that the performance paradigm attracts historians because it appears to offer a means of locating within the Indian record a usable version of the past that elides or assuages the specifics of cultural assault and of selective co-optation. Performance then becomes nothing more than a means of sidestepping the conundrum once articulated by the Oxford University Regius Professor of History Hugh Trevor-Roper when speaking about African history. A conventional historian committed to the primacy of archival documentation, he said in 1963, "Perhaps in the future there will be some African history to teach. But at present there is none; there is only the history of Europeans in Africa. The rest is darkness . . . and darkness is not a subject of history."[18] Confronted with Africa's indigenous oral traditions, Trevor-Roper, like Hegel before him, could find no version of history amenable to his method, and so he simply decided that African history per se did not exist. The question remains as to whether performance as an analytical approach appeals because it allows us a means of incorporating the history of indigenes and non-Europeans into a largely Euro-American story of America, a story that remains largely Euro-American because the parameters of history as praxis remain Euro-American in constitution. Yet for a number of writers working in modern ethnography it is precisely the potential of the performance paradigm to move analysis beyond the text that is most attractive and subversive. Writing in opposition to Clifford Geertz's influential textual model of culture, "Deep Play: Notes on the Balinese Cockfight," Conquergood suggests that performance can transform the ethnographer from detached observer into intimately involved co-performer. "The performance paradigm," he argues, "can help ethnographers recognize 'the limitations of literacy' and critique the textual bias of western civilization." While it is possible that performance could, as Conquergood suggests, "decentre" texts within analysis it is hard to see how performance in itself is necessarily subversive or resistant to dominant ideologies.[19] As Conquergood's critic W. B. Worthen puts it, "The authority of writing and other performances as modes of cultural production is determined as much as that of speech acts is: within an elaborate, historically contingent, dynamic network of citational possibilities."[20] The same larger context of power holds true irrespective of the extent to which performance is considered to be co-created by the ethnographer and those studied.

Diamond, it is worth remembering, also pointed out that imperialism *always* strives to take the guise of mutuality, to appear as a joint enterprise, as a collaboration of cultures because such a collaboration feeds into the old idea of Western cultural superiority and progress.[21] Admonitions like Diamond's cannot necessarily be fully refuted when considered in relation to the performance paradigm, and we can only remain vigilant that while performance as an approach brings with it multiple benefits, the old but valuable critiques of inclusive history still have purchase. With this in mind it is perhaps useful to remain aware of the provenance of the concept. Like Freemasonry, performance has English roots.[22] The genesis of the word *perform* stems from transgressions in English law over property and land seizure; thereafter the word migrated to other parts of culture such that both contracts binding in Elizabethan law and plays in the theater came to be talked of as being "performed."[23] Given that both the word and the idea are alien to Indian culture and given that their origins lie with the European obsession with property rights and ownership of land, scholars of Native American history are well advised to proceed with caution. Any simple conflation of the interests of Indians and Masons within or outside of the Masonic lodge risks reinscribing some of the most pernicious and false colonial myths about the mutual benefits brought by the "civilizing" forces on American soil.

In terms of Freemasonry as an area of study in itself, performance cannot replace other extremely valid and established approaches such as viewing the fraternity through the lens of gender or class or as part of the history of association, just as it cannot do away with structural or cultural inequalities of power. I argue that although certain Indians found positive intercultural space in the Masonic lodge, this does not mean that what went on in lodges was necessarily "pure" in terms of intercultural representation or that the balance of power between the dominant culture and Indian cultures was wholly refigured by the Masonic context. There is much to suggest that the non-Indian attraction to Indian Masons and to versions of Indian ritual over time can be linked meaningfully and directly to contemporary phenomena such as Robert Bly's men's movement, with its use of "Indian" practices to unburden contemporary middle-class males of the stresses and inhibition that can accompany modern life. Also it is essential that we recognize that whenever ritual is practiced in inappropriate contexts or by those without appropriate cultural authority or knowledge it is rarely anything less than crass cultural theft, liable to empty spiritually significant ceremonies of coherence and sacred purchase. The Mohawk Irish scholar Christopher Ronwanièn:te Jocks has likened cultural theft of this sort to the deepest forms of physical desecration: "For Indians, these ceremonies and the knowledge they express are like our skin. That's how close to us they are. When people we don't know, or people we do, pretend to use these ceremonies away from their proper setting, it really is like stealing the 'skin off our backs.'"[24] Similarly one could argue that because "Indian" elements of ritual as practiced in the Masonic lodge were available for replication within the Masonic community their development could be construed as a form of commercialization of Indian spirituality, something much more akin to contemporary New Age cultural co-optation than to intercultural co-creation. Here one is reminded of the activist Russell Means's take on such practices. "When they wanted our land," he said, "they just announced that they had a right to it and therefore owned it. Now, being spiritually bankrupt themselves, they want our spirituality as well."[25] The dangers of mixing ritual practices from disparate cultures has perhaps best been expressed by the controversial figure Ward Churchill, who warned, "To play at ritual potluck is to debase all spiritual traditions, voiding their internal coherence and leaving nothing usably sacrosanct as a cultural anchor for the peoples who conceived and developed them, and who have consequently organized their societies around them."[26] As Vine Deloria Jr. explains in his wonderful end-of-life examination of old accounts of incidences of Indian spiritual power, such records, wherever found, should not be read solely in terms of magical trickery or of performance but as real manifestations of Indian spirituality at work. This involves a respect for ritual, spirits, powers, and ancestors that the non-Indian contemporary world generally finds difficult to grapple with, but that for Deloria and others have always been real and alive.[27]

If we look closely we find that the fundamental question at the heart of Indian–Euro-American performance is that of ownership and reciprocity, specifically the extent to which Euro-American adoption of Indians themselves within performance may have had an impact beyond what was originally intended. Using Roach's terms, Bellin suggests that Euro-Americans sought to "embody and to replace" Indians, to conjure themselves "into illusory fullness of being by acting out what they think they are not."[28] Crucially for Bellin, in the process Euro-Americans became not possessors of "Indian medicine" but possessed of it. Somehow the identity of each became constitutive of the other such that "Euro-Americans and Native Americans remained locked in a struggle for the meaning, control, and use of Indian sacred performance, a struggle in which both parties grounded their being on the absent presence of the other."[29] I would suggest that such a reading of the early performance traditions of Indians and Euro-Americans is too close to the perfect colonial fantasy, in which the asymmetrical power relations inherent in assimilation to a dominant culture are masked by a rhetoric of mutuality and unforced exchange. In truth too often Euro-American adoption of Indian performance traditions was nothing more than what Philip Deloria terms "playing Indian," that "characteristically American kind of domination in which the exercise of power was hidden, denied, qualified, or mourned."[30] However, to ascribe ultimate power to Euro-American activities runs the risk of reinscribing another persistent myth, that of the omnipotent state capable of erasing all vestiges of indigenous culture. We risk reiterating the kind of thinking that informed early nineteenth-century ethnology, in which Indian culture was deemed to be the opposite of wily, indeed entirely fragile, incapable of agency, and in dire need of salvage. Thus to the grandfather of American ethnology, Lewis Henry Morgan, civilization was an all-encompassing, unstoppable force and Indian culture was paper-thin. It was a view he explained in 1851 in his book *League of the Iroquois*: "Civilization is aggressive, as well as progressive—a positive state of society, attacking every obstacle, overwhelming every lesser agency, and searching out and filling up every crevice, both in the moral and physical world; while Indian life is an unarmed condition, a negative state, without inherent vitality, and without powers of resistance."[31] Interestingly even exemplars of such thinking felt the need to act it out in a fraternal context. Morgan led a proto-Masonic organization, the Grand Order of the Iroquois, that allowed its young initiates, temporarily at least, to take on a new identity, to dress up as they understood Indians dressed, to "speak Indian" and to give each other Indian names. Morgan took on the "warrior" name Skenandoah, was the group's supreme chieftain, and formulated all the fraternity's rules and rituals.[32] As with Freemasonry, entry to the group involved ritual, in this case "In-Indianation," in which the spirits of long-dead Indian "fathers" required of initiates that they make recompense by keeping alive "lost" Indian traditions. The fiction was kept up that Indian agency was in the past (Indians were "declining races") and Indian retribution for Euro-American wrongs likely to come only from Indian ghosts. Reassuringly the initiatory ritual offered candidates "complete redemption and a new life through mystic rebirth as an Indian child."[33]

The question remains as to where and when Indian traditions can be said to begin and end and at what point they can be said to have been destroyed, debased, or irrevocably travestied. If, as in Bellin's analysis of nineteenth-century Cherokee politics, Indian tradition is deemed to be infinite in form, encompassing both the heartfelt enemy of Cherokee removal, John Ross (a Mason), and the assimilationist Buck Watie (aka Elias Boudinot, probably also a Mason), a removal treaty-signer eventually executed by fellow Cherokee as a traitor, then the question is moot.[34] Similarly if we dispense with the customary means of positioning Indian leadership as existing at some point along a spectrum ranging from outright resistance to almost complete assimilation in relation to the dominant culture, and instead go along with Bellin's suggestion that "one might better recognize that all were engaged in comparable, if not identical, acts involving the renewal of the sacred/traditional through the invented/imitated," the question arises as to what then happens to cultural politics.[35] Indeed what happens to basic moral questions of right and wrong in terms of the respect normally deemed to be owed to symbols and practices linked to cultural sovereignty? Can performance adequately replace or supersede politics in this sense? Although several important scholars have urged persuasively that we re-vision subaltern "signifying" and dispense with or learn to suspect any simplistic notion of the genuine or the "real," to view all Indian action in history primarily as performance carries with it inherent dangers.[36]

The performative lens can drain politics from the past and suggest inappropriate and unsubtle bases for comparison. Take, for example, Bellin's linkage of the Ghost Dance with Buffalo Bill's Wild West Show, where he urges us to see both phenomena as positive intertribal performative adaptations. "For however different their acts were in form and intent," Bellin writes, "both orchestrated performances that helped to consolidate an intertribal Indian identity centred on the costume, ritual, and dance of the Plains, an identity that persists, in the eyes of Indians and whites alike, to this day." For Bellin, both phenomena "fused Indian sacred performance with the performance of Indianness" and thus "gave birth to a new authenticity that could be (re)produced only *through* performance."[37] Such a comparison is misleading since the Ghost Dance as a political and sacred intertribal movement of cultural resistance and resurgence was by no means equivalent to a desacralizing, homogenizing pastiche of multiple Indian cultures undertaken to make money under conditions of wider Indian cultural oppression, such as Cody's Wild West Show. It is essential to keep continually in mind the ways performance, for all its syncretic and comparative complexity, is still as subject to and redolent of political and cultural imperatives as any other social phenomenon. To the extent that the mantle of performance obscures those imperatives and the unlovely realities of colonialism and neocolonialism, it is to be distrusted. While it is of course entirely possible, as Bellin suggests, that a culture might revitalize its own traditions by imitating another's, such imitation is never without political context.[38] Power still operates when aspects of culture are borrowed, and such exchanges have very different meanings depending on the balance of political and sovereign agency operative between each respective culture. Thus it is difficult to accept Bellin's suggestion that both Indian Ghost Dancers and Wild West "Indian" performers were "'show Indians,' who not only showed their Indianness through intercultural performance but also constructed Indianness through that show."[39] To reduce a spiritual and political phenomenon, the Ghost Dance movement, to performance in this way is to devalue its historical significance.[40] The ways dominant cultures have required subordinate cultures to perform an invented identity have generally been held to be a fantasy, indeed a pathology of the colonial mind. The colonized have been forced to become performers when faced with ongoing, overwhelming cultural incomprehension, but this does not mean that identity, resistance, or cultural representation within capitalism can be adequately understood in terms of performance alone.[41]

It is only if we conceive of culture as being essentially imaginative that performance as an analytical paradigm fully functions. This is how Robert Cantwell conceives of culture in his 1992 book, *Ethnomimesis: Folklife and the Representation of Culture*. Cantwell argues that cultural presence is expressed through *ethnemes*, signifiers like music, costume, and speech that may be divorced from their indigenous community but that are compatible with some prejudice or stereotype held by their audience. For Cantwell, within the "cultural ecosystem of stereotype" a "resolving synthesis" can be arrived at whereby relationships of power are destabilized and the performer can dissolve the space between himself or herself and the audience.[42] But even here questions that are political and economic rather than primarily imaginative impinge. Performance cannot fully disguise or supplant hierarchy. As Andrew Scheiber puts it, the issues still remain: "Who is looking, and who is performing? And under what duress, or with what privileges?"[43] The larger political hierarchies that bear down upon culture and its presentation isolated by Rosaldo still apply. In all performance it matters who makes themselves visible and in what ways such visibility is made permissible by the dominant culture. Rosaldo points out that culture in itself is a phenomenon recognized or not recognized at the whim of those who dominate, and those who have culture have also tended to occupy subordinate positions within nation-states. He writes, "Full citizenship and cultural visibility appear to be inversely related. When one increases, the other decreases. Full citizens lack culture, and those most culturally endowed lack full citizenship." Culture and the permitted expression of culture he links directly to "imperialist nostalgia" in dominant cultures, "the process of yearning for what one has destroyed."[44]

In sum performance as an analytical stance in Native American studies is liable to many of the same critiques that have been leveled at the free-flowing circulation of signs described by post-structuralism and at ideas of syncretism and hybridity more generally. The former has been deemed uncomfortably close to a perfect notion of capitalist exchange, and the latter, because they deem identity to be re-creatable and invented from multiple sources, as making identity seem similarly infinitely interchangeable. Perhaps the main problem with performance analytically is that it has been used as an indiscriminate and blanket term. The same problem has been isolated by Ella Shohat and Robert Stam with reference to all forms of syncretism in general:

> A celebration of syncreticism and hybridity per se, if not articulated with questions of historical hegemonies, risks sanctifying the fait accompli of colonial violence. For oppressed people, even artistic syncreticism is not a game but a sublimated form of historical pain, which is why Jimi Hendrix played the "Star Spangled Banner" in a dissonant mode, and why even a politically conservative performer like Ray Charles renders "America the Beautiful" as a moan and a cry. As a descriptive catch-all term, "hybridity" fails to discriminate between the diverse modalities of hybridity: colonial imposition, obligatory assimilation, political co-option, cultural mimicry and so forth. Elites have always made co-optive top-down raids on subaltern cultures, while the dominated have always "signified" and parodied as well as emulated elite practice. Hybridity, in other words, is power-laden and asymmetrical. . . . Hybridity is also co-optable.[45]

The boundaries of performance's utility within Indian studies can be said to lie with the extent to which what is being performed represents a positive and generative intercultural sharing and, at the other end of the spectrum, the extent to which it might represent yet another example of colonial appropriation and greed. The specter in this regard is that of cultural cannibalism, a phenomenon with a long and slippery history in colonial relations.[46]

After all, the subject of loquaciousness with which we opened our discussion of Masonic Indians of the eighteenth century was an attribute not only ascribed to those deemed potentially capable of citizenship; it was also ascribed to the bogey man of the New World: the indigenous cannibal. Deemed to be present in America right from "discovery," the cannibal was in great part a projection of the all-consuming European invader. It would be the invader's insatiable appetite for all things Indian that would dominate the succeeding centuries, and our challenge today is to remain alert to that long and ongoing history of appropriation. Deborah Root in *Cannibal Culture* warns against seeing cannibalism as a phenomenon limited to the past. "It is also useful," she suggests, "to extend the definition of cannibalism to forms of consumption that occur beyond the physical body of the individual or even the community. It is possible to consume somebody's spirit, somebody's past or history, or somebody's arts and to do so in such a way as that the act of consumption appears beautiful and heroic."[47] As we approach the phenomenon of Native American Freemasonry over time, deciding which examples of fraternal performance were indeed positive intercultural co-creations and which were in fact examples of conscious or unconscious cannibalism will be our foremost challenge.[48]

At the very least, however, the incidences of "Indian performance" in American Freemasonry do centrally upset older understandings of the relationship between Indians and the trajectory of American drama. In Walter J. Meserve's widely accepted 1977 reading of the issue, he explains that Indians were invoked dramatically by Euro-Americans, then erased, only over time to be reinvented as "ideal characters," so that Indian spiritual authenticity could be tapped into without having to deal with the reality of actual, living autochthonous Indians.[49] This supported a triumphalist and largely blameless version of the American past that could be readily consumed by the American public. Although Meserve's analysis is no doubt generally true, within the Masonic context specifically it is not. Indian Masons and Indians dramatically represented within Masonry revoked this staged story of manifest destiny and instead presented a Masonic version of the past that included rather than sidelined the Indian contribution to the story of mankind and, just as important, the Indian contribution to the future of America. While the role of the nineteenth-century dramatic Indian was to vanish (repeatedly!) so as to allow non-Indians to indulge in a wistful nostalgia, in Masonic dramas such reassurance was forgone and instead Indian Masons performed as active and ongoing agents representing their people positively. In Masonic drama the powerful tropes of Indian death and extinction (as in *Last of the Mohicans*, *Logan*, *The Last of the Race of Shikellemus*, and *Metamora; or, the Last of Wampanoags*) were set aside and at points replaced by Masonic ritual dramas that gave Indians an ongoing, even timeless role as Masons and as active, contemporary civic agents.

Indian Masons: Locating the Unexpected

With all of these reservations borne in mind, performance can still be a useful context in which to examine Native American Freemasonry. But at a core level work in this area owes most to another body of work, that of the historian Philip J. Deloria. In fundamental ways that performance studies cannot address, Deloria has reoriented Indian scholarship and shown Indians over time to be active agents whose involvement in American social life was formative and reciprocal. In books such as *Indians in Unexpected Places* and *Playing Indian* he has unearthed histories that have been overlooked because they failed to accord with powerful sets of expectations about Indians that have their roots in stereotype and the rhetoric of American triumphalism. Particularly when we examine Indian Masonic involvement in the nineteenth and twentieth centuries we discover exactly the type of unexpectedness Deloria describes, Indian figures reveling in the brotherhood of success and enjoying the relaxed company of other men of status. Indian Freemasonry thus forces us to join Deloria's project of reexamining how American history has tended to view Indians, that is, as being generally outside of the narrative of success and outside of the organizational engagement that has characterized so much of the American past. It forces us to reassess the view that Indians are culturally static, peoples who somehow have persisted but at the same time not been part of modernizing America. As Deloria notes, when it comes to Indians, all too often our expectations "tend to assume a status quo defined around failure, the result of some innate limitation on the part of Indian people. Success is written off as an anomaly, a bizarre little episode that calls up a chuckle." To the contrary, the truth is that "the entire world of the modern belonged—and belongs—to Indian people, as much as it does to anyone else." To flesh out that truth we need to seek out the secret histories of the unexpected, just as Deloria has done, to look, as he exhorts us to, for "the complex lineaments of personal and cultural identity that can never be captured by dichotomies built around crude notions of difference and assimilation, white and Indian, primitive and advanced."[50] The importance of performance is that it may hold one of the keys to help us examine that complexity by dispensing with long-held binaries and encourage us to seek out Indians who retained various forms of status within multiple communities even as their communities suffered unprecedented loss.

An example of modern Indian success in this regard is Deloria's ancestor, the Episcopal priest, community leader, and Freemason, the Reverend Philip J. Deloria (Tipi Sapa, Black Lodge, 1853–1931).[51] In 1890, having qualified as a deacon, he became an inspiring superintending presbyter of the Episcopal Church's work at Standing Rock reservation, land that straddles the western boundaries of present-day North and South Dakota. He qualified as a priest in 1892 and worked at Standing Rock for forty years, using his skills as an orator to guide his people through some of the most tumultuous times, including the height of the Ghost Dance movement.[52] He became a Freemason in Aberdeen Lodge No. 38 in South Dakota in 1911, the same year he joined the fledgling pan-tribal Indian assimilationist group the Society of American Indians, an organization that contained a number of prominent Masons and eventually its own subfraternities.[53] Deloria went on to gain one of the degrees that culminate the teachings of the Scottish Rite, the thirty-second. As with so many important Indian men, it is not known exactly how Freemasonry figured in his life or how it fit into his Christian faith. Many ministers of the time were Masons, and, as we have seen, there was nothing about Freemasonry's spiritual journey that precluded a Protestant minister from taking part. Indeed Tipi Sapa's son, the Reverend Vine Deloria, continued both the Episcopal and Masonic traditions. He was initiated in 1934 at Pioneer Lodge No. 219 in Martin, South Dakota, and served as Grand Chaplain of the Grand Lodge of South Dakota in 1946. According to Vine Deloria Jr., his grandfather was a Mason primarily as a means of educating non-Indians about Indian ways: "Tipi Sapa became a Mason and participated in their ritual, recognizing that these kinds of relationships were a big help in influencing white society to understand his people."[54]

According to the Ella Deloria scholar Susan Gardner, in his daughter's opinion Philip J. Deloria's spirituality was principally pragmatic, a strategic response to conditions of unprecedented cultural attack. His membership in the Masonic lodge may have been for the same reasons. Three years after her father died Ella wrote, "He knew that the race, as a race, was doomed, insofar as they failed to adjust to conditions brought on by European civilization."[55] When we wonder at Deloria's decision to adopt an alien faith, Christianity, so completely and an alien society, Freemasonry, up to the thirty-second degree, it is perhaps worth bearing in mind the psychological burdens he bore as his family's first Euro-American-style intellectual, as someone who fought consistently against terrific odds for his people's welfare in the wake of shock waves caused by generations of conflict between tribes and with the U.S. military. Having survived brutal, forced migration, adrift in a sea of endemic corruption, bereft of their homelands, and forbidden the web of spiritual practice that sustains traditional Dakota culture, the Deloria family turned to institutions that offered some semblance of the spiritual solace and kinship they had lost: the Church and the Masonic lodge. Certainly two of Freemasonry's abiding characteristics, fraternity and the absence of sectarianism, were important to Deloria, because soon after his conversion he helped found an indigenous organization that gradually spread to all the Sioux reservations, the Planting Society, later known as the Brotherhood of Christian Unity. It remained active until the early 1940s. Just like the Masons, Deloria's fraternity made charity key to their activities, and though it encouraged assimilation its primary function was to foster kinship and community among a people in spiritual and social peril.

The burning need to replace the beauty of what had been lost in Indian communities in the postfrontier era is perhaps too easy to underestimate. American expansion left Dakota society coldly empty, bereft of energy, with no available spiritual architecture to cling to. Gardner quotes Ella Deloria's comment: "What good was it now anyway, in pieces? The sun dance—without its sacrificial core; festive war dances—without fresh war deeds to celebrate; the Hunka rite of blessing little children—without the tender Ring of Relatives to give it meaning; who would want such empty leavings? . . . But it left him ['the' Indian] lonely, with an ache in the heart and an emptiness of soul. And then the church came and filled the emptiness to overflowing."[56] Philip Joseph Deloria, although a zealous eradicator of traditional practices, especially in the early days of his conversion, also remained nostalgic for the joy and fellowship of his pre-Christian life. Just six years after his Masonic initiation as an Entered Apprentice and some nineteen years after qualifying as a priest, he said he had "a terrible longing for it": "It is very hard for a people to change their whole mode of life. Now, we just sit in camp and talk back and forth. There is nothing to do in the way of amusement, and no fun for anybody."[57] For Indians like Deloria as much as perhaps for Euro-Americans in a modernizing America, Masonic life may well have offered the levity, pleasure, and camaraderie that had been ripped away by the migration and inexorable processes of individuation that characterized the era. Masonry was an allowed means whereby "spiritual brokers" like Deloria could maintain practices in sympathy with the old tribal life, luxuriate in expanded social ties reminiscent of the kinship networks of their own communities, and undertake spiritual journeys on their own terms. The Indian men welcomed into the Masonic lodges of the nineteenth century and early twentieth were special people, who may have sought compensation for the enormous price they paid in adopting an alien culture in the unique and assured promotional structure of the Masonic lodge.

For their part Masons embraced Indians because, particularly at times of accelerated social change, they too sought a means whereby they could reintegrate into their lives those things that seemed to be slipping away—such things, to paraphrase Stanley Diamond, as custom, traditional leadership, kinship in social and economic organization, diffuse social and economic functions assigned to each individual, and ritual for individual and group expression.[58] Not only were versions of Indian identity constructed by Masons and Indians, but Indians and Masons also co-constructed versions of the Masonic, predominantly Protestant, Anglo-Saxon identity. Individual Indians were attractive to Freemasons, who were keen to use them to legitimize their claims to having access to arcane and essential truths, since the idea of a culturally authentic Native American identity strengthened Masonic claims to ancient and spiritually potent knowledge. Individual Indians meanwhile used Masonry to insert an Indian identity into a subculture that has remained at the heart of American community power until relatively recently. While Freemasonry allowed Euro-American elites to bolster certain concepts of masculinity and to literally act out narratives of pure origin and heroic versions of a glorious past, it also allowed certain Indians to perpetuate versions of oral tradition, to perpetuate ritual and secrecy, and to maintain tribal ideas about hierarchy. Uniquely it provided a context for Indian individuals to assimilate into the dominant culture without sacrificing their individual claims to essential difference.

American Freemasonry had deep personal meaning for key Native leaders over time, for the other ethnic groups who sought to make connection with it, and for the bulk of its American membership, those drawn from the ranks of the white, Anglo-Saxon Protestant middle class. It was and remains an expressive as opposed to instrumental form of association, functioning as an end in itself, meeting the specific and dynamic social and personal needs of those involved. This theme of an essential responsiveness to the changing needs of its membership can be traced across the three most significant periods of Masonic strength in the United

States: the revolutionary era, the last third of the nineteenth century, and the years following the First World War.

As we approach the detailed history of Freemasonry in the next two chapters it is worth first sketching the bare bones of Indian involvement in Freemasonry across time so as to get a basic sense of its form. It developed along regional or tribally specific lines that reflected the course of European American intrusion, namely in the Northeast (especially among the Iroquois), the Southeast (continued in Indian Territory after removal), and the Great Lakes area. In the Northeast Freemasonry was an important form of power play for leaders in the revolutionary era such as Joseph Brant and in the nineteenth century Ely S. Parker. It is connected with the rise of American ethnology, in particular with professional Native American anthropologists such as the Seneca Iroquois Arthur C. Parker (1881–1955), Francis La Flesche (1857–1932), and John Napoleon Brinton Hewitt (1859–1937). It played a very important role in Indian Territory politics, with many key Indian political figures of the late nineteenth century and early twentieth being Masons in good standing. By 1848 there was a regular lodge of Cherokee Indians in Oklahoma, chartered by the Grand Lodge of Arkansas (Cherokee Lodge No. 21). Masonry was again especially significant during Cherokee removal, and in the years succeeding removal policy the Cherokee Keetoowah Society, with its clear Masonic connections, fostered a unique form of pro-abolitionist religious nationalism. The turn of the twentieth century saw Freemasonry closely associated with a key development in Indian life: the rise of urban Native American fraternal organizations. Groups such as the Loyal Order of Tecumseh and Descendants of the American Aborigine (both created within the first intellectual pan-Indian group, the Society of American Indians, in 1912) as well as hybrid organizations such as the Tepee Order of America (1915) and the Indian Council Fire (1923), all had

Masonic links. Such an outline may whet the appetite, but what is really needed to understand Native American Freemasonry is first to understand Freemasonry in general in the United States in historical context, in particular its deeper principles and guiding philosophy. We must also see it as a transatlantic phenomenon at the heart of the colonizing process.

A History of Freemasonry   3

From Europe to the United States

What follows is a history of Freemasonry that explores the story of the fraternity's birth and development with an eye toward how it eventually became so central to so many often well-known individual Native Americans. It is an analytical genealogy of Masonic origins in Foucault's sense, rather than a conventional narrative history.[1] This in itself does not get us out of the problem of the vast number of competing historical narratives on the topic of Masonry's origins and historical significance, but it does allow us a specific purchase on these issues, and it focuses our attention on how historical consciousness changed as Freemasonry was born in Scotland and England, developed across Europe, and then spread with empire across the globe to find arguably its greatest strength in the United States. The focus here is on what has been called Anglo-Saxon Masonry, shared by Scotland, England, and the United States. Anglo-Saxon Masonry split from the Grand Orient of France in 1877, when it rejected the tenet, or in Masonic terms *landmark*, of belief in God. Masonry in France, Spain, Italy, and South America is significantly different from the Masonry discussed here. This chapter begins with the debate over the fraternity's origins in Scotland and England, traces its development transnationally, and then explores

1. Oklahoma Indian Masonic Degree Team, ca. 1955. Curt Teich and Co., Chicago. Scottish Rite Masonic Museum and Library, A/96/066/4333.

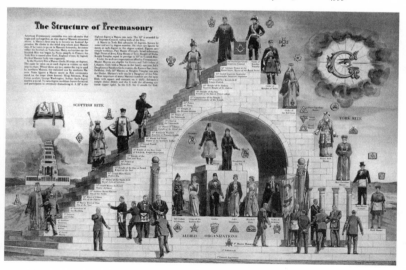

2. A chart by Everett Henry of the organizations in Freemasonry. From "Busy Brotherly World of Freemasonry: The Ancient Fraternity Is Thriving in America," *Life* 41, no. 15 (October 8, 1956). Courtesy of Macoy Publishing.

3. The murder of Hiram Abiff, "floorwork" of the third degree. From Jabez Richardson, *Richardson's Monitor of Free-Masonry* (New York: Dick and Fitzgerald, 1860). Courtesy of the Livingston Masonic Library, New York City.

4. The council of animal familiars restores the life of the Good Hunter. Watercolor by Sanford Plumber (Seneca). Buffalo Museum of Science.

5. Portrait of Joseph Brant
(Thayendanegea), 1865. From *Life
of Joseph Brant (Thayendanegea)
including the Border Wars of the
American Revolution* . . . (Albany
NY: J. Munsell, 1865). Scottish Rite
Masonic Museum and Library, gift
of Lloyd M. Brinkman, RARE E99.M8
B88 1865.

6. Prince Hall Freemason, ca. 1860.
Scottish Rite Masonic Museum
and Library, 85.41.

7. The rescue of Colonel McKinstry by Chief Joseph Brant of the Mohawks. Painted by C. E. Ohleson. Owned by J. Fairbairn Smith. Courtesy of Macoy Publishing. Given to the author by Jim Tresner, The Masonic Fraternity of Oklahoma, Guthrie.

AE 2041 Masonic silver brooch; Tribe--Seneca; Col. by--A. C. Parker. Masonic; exterior bars plain; inner bars at bottom engraved with dot and leaf; diamond center cut; quadralateral and quadrangular cuts; diamond cut at bottom; engraved with dot, leaf, line.

ht.-5. cm.   w.-4. cm. th.-.1 cm.

"Do you like it? Cost me a squaw and two of my best horses."

8. (*Opposite top*) Masonic silver Iroquois brooch, no. AE 2041, purchased through A. C. Parker, State Museum, Albany, New York, December 28, 1923. From Elizabeth H. Van Horn, *Iroquois Silver Brooches (As-ne-as-ga)* (Rochester NY: Rochester Museum and Science Center, 1971). Courtesy of the Rochester Museum and Science Center, Rochester, New York.

9. (*Opposite bottom*) Albert Pike, ca. 1880. Photograph by Alexander Gardner. Washington DC. Scottish Rite Masonic Museum and Library, 86.2.

10. (*Above*) Masonic "Indian" joke. From Stewart M. L. Pollard, *Tied to Masonic Apron Strings* (Richmond VA: Macoy Publishing and Masonic Supply Co., Inc., 1974), 4. Courtesy of Macoy Publishing.

11. Program: Levant Lodge observes Indian Night, October 22, 1946 (Levant Lodge No. 967, Third Erie District, New York). From the collection of the author.

PROGRAM

RECEPTION OF PRESENT AND PAST GRAND LODGE OFFICERS
PRESENTATION OF COLORS
RECEPTION OF INDIAN MASONS
INVOCATION
SOLO . . . . BROTHER CEDRIC MATTHEWS
MESSAGE . . . . CHIEF RICKARD
ORGAN MUSIC . . . . BROTHER KEN ALLAART
SPEAKER . . . . BROTHER CHARLES A. NEUMANN
INDIAN HYMNS . . . . JOHN WATERMAN
MESSAGE . . . . DISTRICT DEPUTY GRAND MASTER
BENEDICTION
SOLO

INDIAN MASONS

Chief Clinton Rickard
Cornelius Seneca
Frank Beauvais
Carlton Jemison
John Button
Ira Mitten
Harry Patterson
John Waterman

Clifford Shongo
Wyman Jemison, Sr.
Wyman Jemison, Jr.
William R. Longboat
Nelson Mount Pleasant
Edgar Parker
Arthur Parker
Perry Mount Pleasant
W. Henry Watso

Noah Henry
Melvin Johnson
Harold Johnson
FRANKLIN Patterson
TITUS J. Patterson
DAVID Patterson
CLARK Rickard
WILLIAM Rickard

*"Freemasonry knows no nationality, but its kingdom
is in the hearts of men."*

12. Levant Lodge observes Indian Night, October 22, 1946 (Levant Lodge No. 967, Third Erie District, New York). From the collection of the author.

13. Clinton Rickard (*right*) honored by fellow Masons. From the collection of the author.

14. Clinton Rickard (*center*) in old age honored by the Grand Lodge of Free and Accepted Masons of New York. From the collection of the author.

in depth its eventual transplantation and phenomenal growth within the United States.

One useful starting point for such a history is to view Freemasonry from the outset from an Atlanticist perspective, as a conduit for cultural exchange between the peoples linked by the Atlantic Ocean. It has always been a supranational phenomenon, a transoceanic network with a role transcendent of nation-state boundaries whose importance during the age of empire is only now gaining recognition through work such as that of Jessica Harland-Jacob. Although our overall focus will ultimately be the United States, it is as well to recognize at the outset that as Freemasonry spread, so spread a British institution and with it British influence overseas. It was, one could say, an aspect of British (and ultimately American) imperial "soft power" long before Joseph Nye invented the term and persuaded us of the importance of what he calls "the complex power of interdependence" in world politics.[2] Furthermore the ritual at Freemasonry's heart was fundamental to the politics it facilitated.[3]

Earliest Origins

Before delving into Freemasonry's transnational and Atlanticist character it is as well to begin properly with its origins, a question that has dominated historical discussion of the fraternity over time and that has fascinated writers of every hue.[4] Thomas Paine even suggested that it was in Freemasonry's mysterious beginnings that its real fascination and deepest secrets lay. He wrote, "Their real secret is no other than their origin, which but few of them understand; and those that do, envelope it in mystery."[5] The debate over roots continues to predominate even when we separate out the poorer Masonic histories and the long legacy of fictional accounts of Masonic origins from the accounts put forward by respected academic and nonacademic historians. Such sifting is essential given the sheer volume of underresearched and fantastic depictions of the fraternity that continue to find a market. This is a point worth making early on not least because it is likely that anyone seriously interested in Freemasonry beyond the confines of this book will have to wade through swaths of hokum and salacious exposé before arriving at what is a relatively contained and consequently precious kernel of reasoned and supported research and analysis. As Brother Douglas D. Knoop, one of the earliest historians of Masonry, put it in 1947, "[Masonic history is] a department of history which is not only obscure and highly controversial, but by ill luck the happiest of all hunting grounds for the light-headed, the fanciful, the altogether unscholarly and the lunatic fringe of the British Museum Reading Room."[6] Added to this is the sheer enormity of material and its formidable, underresearched character. As John Roberts explained when he bemoaned the absence of scholarly attention paid to the topic in 1969, "The sheer bulk of secondary material is immense and its content repellent: no one who is not a devoted freemason is likely to have the resilience to sift the mass of matter generated by such arcane debates as those over the Royal Arch, or legitimacy or illegitimacy of 'Scottish' degrees."[7] Be that as it may, it is essential that we understand how Masonry began and something of what accounted for its early spread so that we can begin to understand the power it held over generations of men from the early eighteenth century up until the beginnings of what would appear to be its terminal decline following the First World War. Furthermore the core paradoxes and unique characteristics of the fraternity have not substantially changed over time, and it is important to grasp how and why they were generated before we consider what happened when the fraternity was transplanted across the Atlantic.

Freemasonry's many origin myths, theories, and legends, including the central "Hiramic legend" concerning King Solomon and his murdered favorite, Hiram Abiff, were described by Noel P. Gist in 1940.[8] I will return to these subsequently, but a more concrete starting point is the formation of the first Grand Lodge of England, in London in 1717.[9] David Stevenson has shown that when the earliest origins of Freemasonry have been considered, a great deal of Scottish Masonic evidence has been ignored even though Scotland played a major role in the organization's development. However, his *Origins of Freemasonry: Scotland's Century 1590–1710* and *The First Freemasons* make an overtly nationalistic case and are not concerned with how or why Freemasonry began and prospered. Rather their point is primarily to redeem speculative Freemasonry (in contrast to the operative Masonry practiced by working stonemasons) from the English.[10] Stevenson argues that a Scottish phase was the decisive, generative phase of Freemasonry beginning around 1600, sandwiched between two English phases. Its earliest roots, its craft organization and legends he traces to the medieval period, but its lodge structure and rituals and the secret means whereby Masons recognize each other—the Mason Word—he locates in late Renaissance Scotland. The word *freemason* itself, Stevenson suggests, may have come from the medieval English term for a mason skilled enough to work in the fine-grained freestone that could be cut and carved in any direction, or it may simply have denoted a skilled as opposed to a rough mason. A master mason in a trade guild would be made "free" of his guild or town and be given certain privileges, thus becoming a "freeman mason" or "freemason."[11] By the time of the official establishment of the Freemason's Grand Lodge in 1717 this older, "operative" Freemasonry had given way to a "speculative" Freemasonry only symbolically rooted in masonry as a craft.

The point where Freemasonry evolved into a system of societies Stevenson links to William Shaw, James VI's Master of Works, who in 1598 codified older craft regulations that became known as the Old Charges. These linked masonry and geometry to La-mech, who is mentioned in Genesis, to Hermes Trismegistus, a great-grandson of Noah, and to Euclid. Stevenson stresses the Renaissance contribution to Freemasonry, especially the last school of ancient pre-Christian religion that swept through Europe, Neoplatonism. Here it is possible to trace correspondences with aspects of many Native American spiritual traditions, especially the shared ideas of kinship between the animate and the inanimate and an emphasis upon unity between matter and spirit. During Renaissance Neoplatonism "instead of being regarded as an inanimate mass, the Earth itself was deemed to be alive. The universe was peopled by a hierarchy of spirits, and thought to manifest all kinds of occult influences and sympathies. The cosmos was an organic unity in which every part bore a sympathetic relationship to the rest. Even colours, letters and numbers were endowed with magical properties."[12] Stevenson explores how, particularly in the decades surrounding 1600, magic and alchemy were linked to this quest to understand the myriad interconnections deemed to make up the world. He explains that Masonic secrecy was in part a legacy of the medieval period but also was connected to a Neoplatonist passion to keep occult truths secret in the era when the lodge system was born. Furthermore Neoplatonism esteemed symbolism, especially hieroglyphs and emblems, and revered the visual, which Stevenson links to Masonic ritual, with its codified gestures, rehearsed action, and deep symbolism. All of this connects with a Renaissance desire to eschew the recent past and to connect instead with the distant past as a means of finding knowledge, an impulse exemplified in the Renaissance veneration of the magical mystery religion of Hermeticism (linked to Hermes Trismegistus).

In 1599 Shaw issued a second set of Masonic statutes, which required Masons to become skilled in a Hermetic art, that of memory. This again fashionably linked Masonry to the Renaissance and to the arts of rhetoric that were so valued by the ancient world. Fittingly the Mason's method of developing his memory was architectural; he was to link the themes in his speech to a large and complicated building he envisaged in his mind. The Masonic lodge thus in itself became a "real" mnemonic, a useful means of carrying secret information and all information not communicated through the new medium of print.[13] Although Masonic symbolism cannot be exclusively linked to the Renaissance art of memory, Stevenson argues that "the seventeenth century Masonic lodge may have been in one sense a memory temple, an imaginary building with places and images fixed in it as aids to memorising the secrets of the Mason Word and the rituals of initiation."[14] The various degrees of induced physical or psychological stress that accompanied early Masonic initiation rituals Stevenson also associates with memory and with a contemporary belief that discomfort of this sort could serve as an aid to the retention of information. Equally fashionable in the sixteenth century was the idea of the architect as chief among all artisans and as a scholar-practitioner of some of the burgeoning new forms of knowledge, including mathematics. Stevenson makes the useful point that this new concept of the architect helped to solidify the Masonic idea that social rank was irrelevant within the confines of the lodge. The lodge was deemed to be a unique forum where the craftsman could learn from those above him and vice versa, such that both the gentleman philosopher and the architect could be united in the quest for deep knowledge.[15]

From its beginnings the Masonic lodge was unique in another sense that connects directly to our larger theme of performance as an avenue for interconnection between Indians and non-Indians. Freemasonry's growth in the Reformation, Stevenson suggests, was itself a reaction against the Reformation, a means of filling a vacuum created by the advent of Protestantism. After all, Protestantism placed heavy restrictions on the performance of the old craft plays and on ritual generally, including the celebrations of saints' days. As Stevenson puts it, "In effect the church eventually suppressed all drama, both because of 'papist' or pagan influences in traditional plays and through moral objections to the whole idea of actors 'pretending' to be other people."[16] By comparison Freemasons were able to venerate their patron saint, St. John, on his feast day and to develop the elaborate, participative, and responsive system of ritual that to this day characterizes regular Masonic activity. Masons were also able to continue venerating the power of specific words. Their rituals of identification and initiation were called the "Mason Word," connecting their activity to the almost magical qualities ascribed to God's word in John's gospel and in the Apocrypha, specifically to the Wisdom of Solomon. This veneration for language connects with a number of Indian traditions in which language has transformative spiritual power, as do symbol and thought. In the words of the Kiowa Pulitzer Prize-winning author N. Scott Momaday, in Indian oral traditions "language bears the burden of the sacred, the burden of belief."[17] Masonic veneration for the Word connects to the necromancy at the heart of the key Masonic legend and ritual concerning Hiram Abiff, the master builder of Solomon's temple.[18] The secret knowledge that medieval and Renaissance magic held to be obtainable from the dead once they were ritually summoned or revivified was called "words"; these words were exchanged when Masons made their five-point embrace of fellowship.[19] The Hiram ritual involved the Masonic candidate in the symbolic enactment of death and rebirth, a ritual "death" followed by a "raising" from the dead through the power of brotherhood into the warmth of the five-point fellowship embrace.

One of Stevenson's most welcome contributions is the fact that he stresses the fraternity's essential nostalgia and the way it has always invoked the past and had anachronistic attributes right from its birth:

> If the strange (to outsiders) rituals of freemasonry seem out of place in the Age of Enlightenment, consisting of superstitious mumbo-jumbo with dark overtones of necromancy, this was because at heart the movement was not an Enlightenment but a Renaissance phenomenon. That the Age of Enlightenment was nonetheless the great age of freemasonry is a seeming paradox indicating that for all the eighteenth-century's appeal to reason, many still hankered after elements of mystery, ritual secrecy, and the quest for hidden truth. They found a framework for indulging such tastes, as well as sociability, in organisations and rituals of Scottish Renaissance origin, combined with Medieval mythical craft history.[20]

If we accept Stevenson's characterization of Freemasonry as a revitalization of forms of belief and practice already deemed out of place in seventeenth-century Europe, it makes the fact that aspects of it remained attractive to Native Americans over time more understandable, since various Indian spiritual, philosophical, and intellectual traditions have more in common with pre-sixteenth-century than with post-Newtonian Europe.[21] The impulses toward quantification and measurement that characterized European societies as early as the fifteenth century in fact developed from a prior set of impulses much less rationalist in nature. Admittedly a shift in Western mentality toward a more mechanized understanding of nature was in place by 1700, but the antecedents of that change had a stronger connection with aspects of indigenous American Indian thinking than is perhaps generally recognized.[22]

Of course not everyone agrees with the perceived nationalist thrust of Stevenson's work, but even his most robust critic, Margaret Jacob, concurs that a non-Christian spiritual core lay at the center of the radical tradition of early Freemasonry. Jacob's work has tended to reorient what is significant and characteristic about early Freemasonry back to England, specifically to the city of London. She writes, "The Scottish lodges may have been the first to admit non-masons and to take on a philosophical direction, but it is the London lodges that created the eighteenth-century phenomenon so central to enlightened discourse."[23] Elsewhere she holds that not only is Freemasonry English in its essentials, but so too is the Enlightenment per se: "In both its moderate and radical forms, [the Enlightenment] began in England but achieved intellectual maturity in Europe."[24] Although she has been accused of overenthusiastically making claims about both Freemasonry and the sociability of the Enlightenment from limited archival evidence, her research is among the most intellectually vigorous, the most rewarding, and the most groundbreaking in its import within the field.[25] Her work provides a wonderful platform for understanding Freemasonry in the European context, and unlike much other writing in this area it directly addresses the issue of why early Freemasonry enjoyed such a broad-based appeal. Her "Masonic" book that has attracted particular ire is *The Radical Enlightenment: Pantheists, Freemasons and Republicans*. Here she divides the Enlightenment into Newtonian and Radical traditions, with the Newtonian tradition, because it emphasized a "providentially guided polity," serving to enhance the power of elites and advance the prevailing Christian orthodoxy and the monarchy. The "Radical Enlightenment," in comparison, was keen to retain aspects of the new science but sought to escape the ideology that went with it by turning to pantheism and materialism, a shift Jacob argues stemmed from the disillusionment of some Whigs in the aftermath of the social upheaval accompanying the Glorious Revolution of 1688–89 in Britain. Such pantheism denied the Christian separation of God from creation and the separation of matter from spirit; instead it held that all people—and their environment—were simply part of the same great "Is." These radicals saw nature in a way that was directly linked to the older magical and Hermetic traditions, as being alive and infused with spirit. This was a pantheism, Jacob argues, that was highly compatible with republicanism—it "could constitute the philosophical foundations for democratic belief" in that "this pantheistic materialism proclaimed the equality of all people through nature as well as the usefulness of the popular sciences—alchemy, astrology, herbal medicine and the magical arts."[26] Masons institutionalized religious respect for a sort of third religious entity, the "Grand Architect," in essence the God of Newtonian science, who could be worshipped by both Christians and deists. Thus Masonry held within it both the capacity to reinforce the establishment and the capacity to radically subvert it on religious and political grounds. One of its particular attractions in an age of disaffection with both Church and chapel was its highly social nature and the way it could bind men together through ritual and secrecy.

Jacob is at pains to highlight Freemasonry's inherently political nature in the Radical and Newtonian traditions, but her detractors ask for further evidence and suggest she makes too much of what was essentially a very small band of radicals.[27] Instead they stress simply that Freemasonry could be many things to many men at different times, something Jacob does acknowledge by stressing Masonry's inherently protean and multivalent nature. On the one hand, official Freemasonry was deeply faithful to the status quo, echoing in form and style the ordered, harmonious universe under God's providence connected with Newton's theories. Thus Masons presented themselves as good, urban merchants who replicated the harmonious and stable Newtonian vision of society within the lodge. However, there was also a substratum of radical subversion within Freemasonry, which Jacob argues was "intent upon subverting the prevailing order in church and state."[28] The Masonic lodge was also a unique forum where men were encouraged to educate and develop themselves, particularly in mathematics and the associated fields of architecture and geometry. This, Jacob argues, promoted equality at least within the confines of the lodge. She cites European lodge records that describe Freemasonry as an "institution which has as its object to recall men to their primitive equality and to reassert among Masons the bonds of society and humanity by undercutting the distinctions of birth, rank and occupation."[29] Thus Freemasonry may have taken on a predominantly conservative Whig and Newtonian texture after 1717 in England, but it also exported to Europe and beyond a form of socializing that went against the hegemony of the aristocracy and that of an absolutist monarchy. For Jacob, the radicalism of the Enlightenment was social and, as an international culture, Masonic in nature. Masonry thus had a subversive and republican strain that in great part explains the fears it consistently generated within religious and political authorities in Catholic and continental countries.[30]

Freemasonry's Indigenous Pantheism and Republican Heart

If we accept Jacob's argument that there is a link between republicanism. which began in the 1690s in England and then spread to northern Europe, and pantheism, which she argues is at the heart of the more radical tradition of Freemasonry and at the core of the radical tradition within the Enlightenment, that link may provide a key to understanding the fraternity's subsequent attraction to Native America. Masons could be seen to have transplanted a set of republican ideals and pantheistic values that had meaningful correspondences with certain traditions within Native American thought. Of course Native faith traditions cannot be simply mapped onto any other tradition, including pantheism, but this does not preclude there being elements of each that were shared and thus capable of constituting a conduit for exchange, for example the emphasis on ritual, symbol, and community and ideas of communalism. Although a preponderance of Native American Masons were Christian, some also practiced traditional religions. Further, although Freemasonry may appear to be a Judeo-Christian organization because its rituals center on the story of King Solomon and the building of the temple of Jerusalem, the organization itself has always been at pains to stipulate that it is nondenominational and its membership dependent only on avowed belief in any one system of faith. This nondenominationalism marks Freemasonry as part of the onward sweep of secularism in the West, a move away from the idea that religious affiliation is all-consuming and the only prism through which the life of an individual may be experienced. Even so Masonry's ritualistic pageantry, Christian motifs as the self-styled "handmaid to religion," and emphasis on transcendence of creeds made it especially attractive to liberal Protestants, especially in the years following the American Civil War. Although it is important to recognize Freemasonry's nondenominationalism and its pantheism, Ruth Benedict was essentially right when she wrote in 1942 that all secret societies in America overwhelmingly reflect the acceptance of Christian ideology.[31] Even so both Catholic and Protestant Churches have at points reacted extremely strongly against Freemasonry's naturalistic, deist, and pantheistic teachings.

It is worth looking at the argument for a pantheistic and republican core to Freemasonry in greater depth, not least because over time it consistently reoccurs in discussions of the fraternity, especially following its transplantation to the United States and at the points when anti-Masonry sentiment rears its head. Central to Jacob's claim to a pantheistic Masonic radicalism is a man from Inishowen, in the north of Ireland, the philosopher John Toland (1670–1722), and his publications, including *Pantheisticon* (1720). His aim was to reclaim an indigenous pantheism through Freemasonry and with it a new political and religious reality.[32] Toland, Jacob tells us, was part of a wider eighteenth-century urge to return to indigenous spirituality as a means of eclipsing the religious troubles that resulted from the English Revolution. He sought "a universal religion complete with a new community and a new ritual," and his *Pantheisticon* was "used or intended to be used as a ritual for Masonic meetings, the seedbed for just such a change."[33] Toland sought to go forward by looking backward, to the indigenous Anglo-Saxon and Celtic religion of the Druids, whose worship of nature and reverence for the sun Christianity had supplanted.[34] Equally significant, the political analogue of Toland's religion had real meaning for seventeenth-century English revolutionaries, who believed the original Anglo-Saxons were free-born and self-governing before the onslaught of the Norman Conquest.[35] According to Jacob, "If the institution of a republic of Druids seems a little far-fetched it should be recalled that Anglo-American radicals until well into the late eighteenth century held the Druids in high regard. Thomas Paine, quite possibly a freemason himself, argued that Masonry was derived from 'the religion of the ancient Druids who like the magi of Persia and the priests of Helipolis in Egypt, were priests of the sun,' while radical republicans in the new American republic were known to set up Druidical lodges."[36] Pantheism, because it held that spirit was contained in matter, was in these circles "the philosophical foundation for republican and even democratic philosophies of government." Why? Because if all things were sacred, then systems of government that ultimately justified their authority on supernatural anointment were invalid and people could in turn revolt without having to step outside of their own religious framework.[37]

There is evidence to support Jacob's link between republicanism, Freemasonry, and aspects of pantheism. Founding father Thomas Paine was convinced that the fraternity was a surviving remnant of the Druids following their persecution in the wake of the spread of Christianity. In his 1805 essay "Origin of Freemasonry" he argues that both Christianity and Masonry derived from the worship of the sun, with Christianity having morphed into a "parody" of sun worship by replacing Christ with the sun, while Masonry remained true to the Druids, "that wise, elegant, philosophical religion . . . the faith opposite to the faith of the gloomy Christian Church." For Paine, the Druids were wise indeed, worshippers of "this great luminary, as the great visible agent of a great invisible first cause, whom they styled 'Time without limits.'"[38] Toward the end of his life Toland shared Paine's fascination with the Druids and, considerably ahead of his time, emphasized a radical, person-centered commitment to reason. He is often considered the first intellectual of the Left in part because he urged his fellow men to think critically and to retain within themselves the responsibility for making judgments about things spiritual and material. He held this ability to be universal and too precious for anyone in any walk of life to give up.[39] Toland had much in common with Masons and, following Giordano Bruno (1548–1600), placed great value on memory and mnemonics, believed in the essential unity of all matter, and stressed the metaphysical power of those actions "ensouled with" secrecy.[40]

Perhaps, however, we should not swallow whole Jacob's linking of Toland, Paine, pantheism, and Freemasonry given that Toland's foremost analyst, Stephen H. Daniel, has disputed her suggestion that Toland, or indeed pantheists per se, can be directly linked to Freemasonry at all. On the contrary, Daniel argues, "to conclude that Toland's pantheists were Freemasons is to confuse *Freemasons* with *freethinkers*." He also suggests that some of the material Jacob cites linking Toland and Freemasonry was actually written in jest and caricature.[41] Another scholar, Frederick C. Beiser, has also been at pains to separate Toland entirely from pre-Christian spirituality. Instead he stresses that the radical religion of both Toland and freethinkers was in fact continuous with the radical Protestant tradition. Toland, Beiser argues, had as his primary concern the facilitation of civil liberty and religious tolerance, and he naïvely believed that reason and faith could never be in conflict.[42] Whatever the case, there is undoubtedly evidence that English deism and French skepticism of various sorts survived transplantation to the New World and that the revolutionary era saw a number of prominent regional figures, especially clergy, who were either Freemasons, Druids, outspoken deists, or a combination of all three. Organizational examples of this phenomenon included the Druid Society, an offshoot of a Masonic lodge in Newburgh, New York, in 1788–1800, and its sister organization, the Deistic Society, also of New York. However, because on an organizational level at least such developments were closely associated with anti-Federalism and perceived Federalist support for clericalism, following the election of 1800 these groups were left without a cause. G. Adolf Koch describes the transition: "The religion of the republican millennium fell with the religion of deism. In its place there arose a curious and most irrational belief in a millennium associated with the end of the world."[43] In sum one could say that a deist interlude flourished in the last three decades of the eighteenth century, when intellectual cosmopolitanism served as a spiritual counterpart to revolutionary politics.

Though we may well balk at the breadth of linkage Jacob suggests, between pantheism and republicanism and between Freemasonry and the revolutions of the late eighteenth century, her contextualization of Freemasonry in *The Radical Enlightenment* and the ways she further develops these ideas in her subsequent book, *Living the Enlightenment: Freemasonry and Politics in Eighteenth-Century Europe*, cannot be dismissed. Even the title of the latter suggests our own performative theme: the lodge allowed people to act out on a private stage ideas then circulating within enlightened thought. One of the most significant things they acted out, Jacob argues, was constitutional government, with all its forms and structures, such as elections, constitution writing, oratory, and voting. To back her claim she cites Habermas, who argues that the Masonic lodge, along with the philosophical society and the scientific academy, was key to the transformation of the modern public sphere.[44]

Jacob does not delve into the issue, but Habermas also provides a way of approaching Freemasonry's most obvious inherent paradox: its claim to inclusivity while at the same time operating as an exclusive club. It is, after all, an organization that holds merit and not birth is what constitutes a good Mason and therefore what constitutes a good member of civil society, yet as an organization it always has been highly selective. Only those accepted as Masons and capable of paying the required dues, and only men, can continue in the fraternity and partake of the special context of equality operative within the lodges. So although Freemasonry may have encouraged the spread internationally of certain ideas, from constitutional government to natural philosophy to science itself, as well as arguably ideals such as equality, it did so at the same time that it excluded large segments of society from public culture. Women are the most obvious example. Admittedly there were women in some European lodges, but it is easy to detect a long history of disparagement of female sensibility in Masonic writing.[45] Freemasonry was a key part of a much wider ongoing process of the time, the crystallization of separate public and private spheres. This in turn entailed, as Paul Elliott and Stephen Daniels explain in a recent discussion of the limits of the spread of science by Freemasonry, "an expansion of a masculine associational culture as a counterpart to domestic life."[46] Habermas provides a useful perspective on some of these mutually contradictory impulses in Masonry; he argues that as an arena of discursive rather than market relationships the public sphere demands that certain inequalities of power and rank are put aside, or "bracketed," in order for it to function. Of course as writers such as Nancy Fraser have pointed out, such bracketing usually "works to the advantage of dominant groups in society and to the disadvantage of subordinates." Freemasonry was in fact one of a number of voluntary associations of the eighteenth century, a network, Fraser explains, that eventually became "the power base of a stratum of bourgeois men, who were coming to see themselves as a 'universal class' and preparing to assert their fitness to govern."[47] In this sense Masonic paraphernalia and practices were markers of what Pierre Bourdieu calls "distinction"; that is, they were a means whereby men could differentiate themselves.[48] And of course almost from the earliest beginnings of the Masonic Grand Lodges throughout Europe leadership fell to the aristocracy; in form lodges thus replicated older versions of hierarchy. In this sense Freemasonry contained both current and countercurrent; it both elided social divisions with all its talk of harmony and the ideal society while at the same time affirming social divisions through its exclusivity.

This brings us to the questions of just how republican and how revolutionary early Freemasons were, questions that have occupied the minds of a number of historians. The strongest voice implicating eighteenth-century Freemasonry in what he saw as the totalitarian impulses of the 1790s and by implication Jacobinism and the Terror of the French Revolution is that of the French historian François Furet in *Interpreting the French Revolution*.[49] Jacob, in contrast, dubs Furet right wing and his approach flatly anti-Masonic and grounded in dated scholarship.[50] She links Furet's conclusions to the long line of anti-Masonic conspiracy that suggests it (and perhaps the Enlightenment also) caused the French Revolution, that it was and remains inherently subversive, a line of continental thinking that she argues stretches at least as far back as the Nazi persecution of Freemasons in the 1930s.[51] To Jacob, the Masonic ideology that involved men rising within their fraternity by merit (even though Masons have always sought aristocratic leadership) owed a great deal to the English republican tradition, and it made lodges into schools of a sort for democratic and constitutional government. After all, as they developed across Europe (Jacob claims there were fifty thousand European and American Masons by 1750) lodges taught and developed their forms of governance, from the payment of dues and the giving of oaths to orating before one's peers, setting the terms of officers and elections, instituting constitutions, individual voting (sometimes by individual ballot), and majority rule, and even proffering prescriptions for civic life and the policing of social mores through Masonic courts.[52] In a sense this was what was truly political about Masonic lodges; they taught men new methods of discourse and a secular (albeit spiritually oriented) means of identifying themselves as ethical, if self-interested, civic contributors. As Jacob explains, "The importance of the lodges lay in their ability to teach men identified by their supposed merit how to integrate enlightened values with the habits of governance. The lodges sought to civilize, to teach manners and decorum, to augment the order and harmony of civil society. They taught men to speak in public, to keep records, to pay 'taxes,' to be tolerant, to debate freely, to vote, to moderate their feasting, and to give devotion to other citizens of their order."[53]

But just how much overt politics went on within early lodges is another matter, given that, ostensibly at least, all discussion of politics was strictly forbidden. Indeed when the official Masonic *Constitutions* were published in 1723 in London they expressly forbade "any quarrels about religion, or nations, or state policy. . . . We . . . are resolved against all Politicks, as what never yet conduc'd to the Welfare of the Lodge."[54] Jacob is careful to explain that at the time such an aversion to politics was a way out of the maelstrom of political dispute raging in the wake of the Revolution Settlement of 1688–89 in Britain and that it did not in any sense point to a denial of the civic by Freemasons, who on the contrary idealized it. However, eschewal of discussion of politics within lodges has remained at the core of Masonry over time, and in the American context, rhetorically at least, the maintenance of lodges as apolitical spaces has always been upheld. Jacob and later Lynn Hunt in *Politics, Culture, and Class in the French Revolution* have been careful to differentiate early European Freemasons from revolution, but it is still the case that many Freemasons were involved in politics of various hues and that the governmental practices that went on within lodges provided a perfect seedbed for new forms of civic relationships beyond those associated with monarchy. Jacob is among those keen for us to perceive Freemasonry as a conduit for an English form of egalitarianism, quoting Paul Langford on English relationships between masters and servants in the period and a general national "consciousness of rights."[55] It is certainly the case that, in their earliest incarnations at least, craft guilds in general were designed to foster equality among their members in the sense that they sought to limit competition to ensure an independent relationship between the craftsman and the great merchant entrepreneurs who employed him. As Antony Black explains in his in-depth study of early guilds, they were "one of the several models upon which modern 'democracy' was fashioned. In particular, they were a seedbed of fraternity as a political belief."[56]

Yet it is perhaps most appropriate to give the final word on this matter to an older voice, that of Eric Hobsbawm, who pays serious attention to how important ritual brotherhood was in all its forms from 1789 to 1848 in terms of social and world history in general. He points out that ritualized secret brotherhood was a key agent of change that in all its variety was clearly descended from the Masonic pattern. "Throughout the period of the three French Revolutions," he notes, "the secret revolutionary brotherhood was by far the most important form of organization for changing society in Western Europe, and it was often ritualized to the point of resembling an Italian opera rather than a revolutionary body."[57] On Freemasonry specifically Hobsbawm is at pains to point out that because it was so amorphous and much more a complex of groups rather than an organization, theories of conspiracy linked to it directly rarely stand up. Yet Masonic lodges remained a refuge for revolutionaries of all sorts, with many Masons prominent in both the French and American revolutions and many lodges associated with Irish radicalism. What Jim Smyth calls the "political muscle" of Irish Masonry was evident in the United Irishmen of 1798 and especially strong in Toland's county, Ulster.[58] According to Hobsbawm, "The very sympathy of Masons (or other bodies formed on their model) for the ideas which found expression in the American and French Revolutions, made many of them revolutionaries, and Masonic organization made it easy for lodges or higher groupings to turn into political centres or pressure groups, to hatch or protect revolutionary brotherhoods, and to be in turn 'infiltrated' by them."[59]

Even so the extent to which such fundamental questioning of existing structures was a stance unique to early Freemasons is another matter. As Kant points out, all things were open to examination and adjudication during the age of Enlightenment; it was an age imbued with the impulse to criticize.[60] At the very least when considering this question we must recognize that whether or not Freemasonry can be deemed revolutionary, its genesis and growth across Europe was intertwined with the development of a meaningful public sphere as Habermas defined it, that is, of a new social reality in the wake of England in the 1690s and the birth of parliamentary government and constitutional monarchy. Black dubs early European guilds such as Masonry "the counter-culture to civil society," but it is perhaps more apt to think of the fraternity operating as the political nation-state in microcosm.[61] Equally important, in a general sense Masonic involvement allowed individual men to imagine themselves as cosmopolites, as elite representatives of all of humanity. The lodge may have been a place of play and leisure, but it was still the case that within it men were playing at living under constitutions and creating space for their own utopia based on harmony, order, fraternity—and of course exclusion. By 1789 there were more than one hundred thousand Masons or members of Masonic-type organizations in Europe.[62] As key constituents of Western civil society they had an ideological, civic, and spiritual organizational framework in Freemasonry from which to set forth across the globe as its vanguard. And as Masonic lodges spread, so too did empire.

Freemasonry as a Transatlantic and Transoceanic Phenomenon

Masonry has always been protean in shape, capable of changing its makeup according to circumstances and the wishes of local membership, but at its core cosmopolitanism, nationhood, and a sense of global family have been part of its rhetoric from its early history. Conceptually brotherhood in Freemasonry linked the individual man to a great family of man spread across the globe, as one of the most cited Masonic orations of 1740 explains: "The earth itself is only a great republic, of which each nation is a family, and each particular a child." Another Masonic commonplace was the idea that the fraternity "spread over the surface of the earth" and that Masonic friendship could transcend both battle and national boundaries.[63] As Jacob explains in discussing the organization's origins, "Masonic rhetoric captured the moment in the development of Western hegemony when European secular culture could be imagined as being everywhere." At a practical level the fraternity made traveling the world and trading across continents easier.[64] Indeed from its earliest, "operative" origins it has always been associated with travel and mobility; beginning in the Middle Ages "the mason often led a life of movement and unpredictability."[65] In this sense early masons were ahead of their time; they were mobile craftsmen working in groups of varying sizes in a world most people still experienced as local, with production bounded by family ties. In contrast masons were sent out from their homes to work on particular buildings; they became part of ad hoc working groups and as such often found that they needed a lodge, or temporary home. Compared with other medieval craftsmen the mason needed to be able to quickly make specific associations, and he needed an especially flexible organizational framework within which he might thrive. Thus Masonry was and is cosmopolitan at its core. Its cosmopolitanism maps exactly Amanda Anderson's definition of the term as denoting a "cultivated detachment from restrictive forms of identity" and the articulation of "ethical ideals for the cultivation of character and for negotiating the experience of otherness."[66]

Masons themselves have from earliest records recognized theirs as a potentially global institution, and from its inception the organization's structure and administration were designed to facilitate and encourage growth. Since the founding of the Grand Lodge in London in 1717 and the subsequent founding of the Grand Lodge of Ireland around 1725 and the Grand Lodge of Scotland in 1736, there has been a formal, centralized administrative structure whose purpose was to generate and circulate Masonic rules and thinking, to arbitrate on matters of membership and good practice, and to issue warrants to allow the setting up of new lodges. These central lodges did the important work of keeping a record of the processes and actions of the lodges peripheral to them. Finally, they ensured their own perpetuation and that of their subsidiary lodges through the organized collection of initiation fees, various other fees, and dues. Thus by 1841 Masons could characterize their fraternity as "a vast chain extending round the whole globe."[67] As a well-organized vehicle for the spread of ideas among the like-minded wherever they found themselves, Masonry taught its members attributes key to the larger phenomenon that successfully spread its tentacles across the globe alongside it: capitalism. Masons were taught the value of organization, of systems, of record keeping, and of hierarchy; paradoxically they were also taught a commitment to fraternity and universal brotherhood within an internal structure devoted to the delineation of levels of hierarchy generally achievable only at considerable individual financial cost.

A key factor that allowed British Freemasonry to spread across the globe and become "coterminous with the empire," as Ronald Hyam puts it, was the development by the Grand Lodge of Ireland after 1728 of the concept of a Masonic "travelling warrant."[68] As Harland-Jacobs explains, this made Masonry mobile, freed it from ties to specific localities, and allowed military lodges to hold meetings anywhere in the world.[69] Just as important, these peripatetic military lodges tended to seed permanent new lodges in their wake, allowing Masonic values to take root in whatever colony was exposed to them. A good example of a military lodge that very successfully marketed Freemasonry across two continents is the Irish Lodge of Social and Military Virtues, which prompted new lodges to be formed in both Australia and Canada.[70] Emigration and the readiness of the Grand Lodges to give warrants to new colonial lodges abroad also speeded Masonry's proliferation, as did the fact that beginning in the mid-eighteenth century British Grand Lodges appointed representatives with their own powers to constitute new lodges. These provincial Grand Masters, rather like colonial governors, had the authority to act on behalf of the central organization back home. Such expansion was seen by Masonic leaders as a means whereby the organization could act as the servant of empire. "Wherever our flag has gone we are able to say there Masonry has gone," the Grand Master of the Grand Lodge of Scotland said of British Masonry in 1888, "and we have been able to found lodges for those who have left our shores to found fresh empires."[71] It would appear that this was a link with real meaning for individual Masons. As one New Brunswick member put it, "All Masons were proud of having descended directly from the Mother Grand Lodges of Britain. These were no mean heritages, for they created and maintained a unity of Brotherhood and Empire which no international upheavals could sever."[72]

By the 1880s there were 1,200 lodges across the globe; a lodge in The Hague was the first outside of England to officially adopt the Freemasonry of the Grand Lodge of London. Their form and practices were essentially expressive, serving men's needs within a particular ritualistic framework that was adaptive to those needs. They were designed to please, but Masonry's potential in the far-flung reaches of the empire to meet men's material needs also played its part.[73] To an extent Freemasonry always existed to help its members materially given that a commitment to helping a brother in need is enshrined in Anderson's Charges of 1723. Masons were instructed to aid a "strange Brother" and were told, "If he is in want, you must relieve him if you can, or else direct him how he may be reliev'd: You must employ him some Days, or else recommend him to be employ'd." Furthermore a Mason was required to prefer a fellow Mason "before any other poor People in the same Circumstances."[74] For soldiers, merchants, emigrants, and imperial servants of every ilk far from home, the safety net of a familiar organization transplanted abroad, that could in extremis save a brother in need and his family, was an attractive insurance worth paying regular dues for. That said, Masonry's foremost attraction has perhaps never been exclusively or even primarily material; rather it has been social and spiritual. More will be said about the power of Masonic ritual in another chapter, but here it is worth noting that its repetition abroad would have served to comfort men and to remind them of the culture and traditions of their homeland. As a commentator published in 1885 put it, the sound of the Master's gavel and the old familiar ritual takes Englishmen in a distant colony "back many thousands of miles, and they rejoice to do something which strengthens the tie which binds them to the land of their fathers."[75] Masons could also be proud that whatever was required of them as figures at the forefront of colonialism, as Masons they were signed up to a commendable ethical and moral code. In a real sense Masonry was a global extension of the British public school, with which it shared numerous links. Just as the British elite took succor from the bonds generated from their old school ties and their gentlemen's clubs, the Masonic lodge, wherever constituted, offered a known and welcome haven, where the ritual they experienced as schoolboys was reassuringly replicated in foreign climes.[76] Their organization transcended religious divisions; in the nineteenth century it would style itself the "handmaid of religion" because it was always fundamentally spiritual in nature. It shared all the paraphernalia of religious practice, from special clothing invested with spiritual significance to celebrated feast days, along with ritual, rites, sermons, and mystic symbolism. Anglophone Freemasonry has remained dedicated to its spiritual roots over time, even splitting in the late 1870s with the Grand Orient of France over that body's decision to admit atheists. Although ritual and spirituality are key, what really caused fellow Masons to congregate in the past is what most often causes them to congregate today: the sense of social inclusion, relaxation, and bonhomie and the food and drink that dominate lodge life. As John Hamill puts it, "As a fellowship or brotherhood the social side of Freemasonry is almost as important as the principles and tenets which are taught in the formalized setting of the meeting."[77] Freemasonry was and for many still is fun, and the consecration of the lodge meant the consecration of a place of conviviality and relaxed good humor.

There is evidence that Masonry's structuring as a global family served to encourage genuine inclusion of indigenous Others into what in the United States was primarily a white, Anglo-Saxon, and Protestant organization.[78] Harland-Jacobs explains that the language of kinship and the metaphor of the family has been fundamental to Freemasonry, and the same aspects of Victorian ideology that applied to interlinked families applied to the brotherhood: loyalty and duty, mutual support, affective bonds, and patriarchal authority.[79] Masons all over the world were "brothers" and able to draw on Masonic patronage especially during hard times. Masonic membership created a supranational kin network which, as the *Freemason's Manual* spelled out, required a Mason to express "sentiments of beneficence" to "those who are bound to him by the ties of kindred," such that "a Mason, destitute and worthy, may find in every clime a brother, and in every land a home." Such beneficence was said to "form . . . the basis of the Masonic Institution," with Freemasonry having "especial regard to the three stages of destitution—infancy, unavoidable misfortune, and extreme old age; for all these, when proved worthy, relief is at hand."[80] Such brotherly love was put forward, rhetorically at least, as being capable of transcending racial and religious boundaries. For example, John Grant, freshly back from India, told Londonderry Freemasons in 1850 (whose city was then reeling from the effects of the Irish famine and where sectarianism was rife) about the group's commitment to the "principle of universal love" and its faith in "universal brotherhood," a faith shared by new members all around the world, including "the Jew, the Gentile, the Nomadic Arab, and the wild Indian."[81] The imagined global republic of Freemasonry was, it seems, capable of encompassing the most profound contradictions of the age: the impulse for brutal, nationalist expansion and a deep-seated yearning for worldwide kinship.

Freemasonry as Ornamentalism

4

Class, Race, and Social Hierarchy

As the previous chapter suggests, Freemasonry is a quintessentially British institution, and, as with so much of the British way of exercising and maintaining power overseas, it owes a great deal to performance. That Britishness should be performative during the country's reign as an empire was perhaps inevitable given the vast swaths of territory it controlled for so long. Even though British superiority in arms was an inescapable fact, it was still the case that, as Paul Rich explains, "the ability to enforce politics by force was limited. The British used ceremonies as a substitute for gunboats."[1] Though it is difficult to go as far as Harland-Jacobs and agree that "the British empire was a fraternal enterprise," it is true that Freemasonry was a key part of that delineation of superiority on which an all-important Native dread of a seemingly omniscient colonial power was based.[2] A self-proclaimed moral force for good, it provided not just good-hearted comradeship for the British overseas but also spectacle, wherein empire builders could enact their worth ritually again and again. Freemasonry was part of the mask worn by white men and some indigenes of rank, a mask that Hyam with great acuity describes (inverting Frantz Fanon) as being of "apparently incontrovertible omniscience and infallibility."[3]

Examination of Freemasonry in this light prompts us to view colonialism through British eyes and to follow the advice of historians such as Karen Ordahl Kupperman and David Cannadine, who argue that in English colonial relationships rank in fact mattered much more than race. To the extent that Freemasonry perpetuated a focus on rank rather than race in the United States it can be said to have provided a sanctuary for a British approach to colonialism. This in turn allowed Native Americans to find an avenue for equality of status and personal advancement beyond racially inscribed limits. After all, Freemasonry always centrally concerned itself with hierarchy and with the achievement of costumed grades or degrees of merit, an obsession with the display of rank graded downward from the sovereign that also characterized British activity overseas from the seventeenth century into the twentieth. In her provocative study *Settling with the Indians*, which unusually for such studies takes an overview of a range of English relationships with Native American peoples, Kupperman concludes that for the English of the sixteenth and seventeenth century "the really important category was status."[4] Status was fundamental to all other categories, and therefore when the English encountered Native Americans they evaluated them according to their existing standards of social hierarchy rather than according to any collective notion such as race. This is a radical idea given that so much has been written since the late 1950s about the primacy of racial hierarchies in governing social relationships, particularly in the United States. Undoubtedly racial hierarchy did triumph on American soil after the 1850s, but prior to that and within Freemasonry for many succeeding decades a separate form of evaluating status persisted, and it provided a window for individual Native American fraternity with their social equals. The Masonic version of the ideal social hierarchy retained its resonance within both American and British cultures, and as Cannadine usefully reminds us, individual social ordering often took precedence over collective racial othering. Using freemasonry in a sense not specific to the organization, he explains, "The traditional, pre-Enlightenment freemasonry based on the shared recognition of high social rank—a freemasonry to which Martin Malia has suggestively given the name 'aristocratic internationalism'—both trumped and transcended the alternative and more recent freemasonry based on the unifying characteristic of shared skin colour."[5]

Cannadine's *Ornamentalism* is a repost to Edward Said's *Orientalism*, calling our focus back to class as opposed to Said's emphasis on racial difference and inequality.[6] Cannadine's book was much criticized, primarily because of its focus on elites, because of political desire among intellectuals never to see race subordinated to class, and because Cannadine puts forward the idea that there was a consensual, Burkean notion of hierarchy in operation within Britain and across its empire.[7] In fact, however, *Ornamentalism* never attempts to elide racism either within empire or in Edmund Burke himself. Instead it suggests very plausibly that empire makers were desirous, nostalgically, to replicate abroad the sort of authentic, harmonious social world they felt was being eroded by the Industrial Revolution back home. Even though Cannadine ignores Freemasonry altogether, it can nonetheless, with its tidal ebbs and flows in terms of influence and vigor in the United States, be seen as an indicator of this tension between antihierarchical and pro-hierarchical impulses within empire. However unpalatable the idea might appear to some, after 1776 the desire for graded hierarchy and for the vision of gracious social harmony put forward by that British invention Freemasonry remained. There persisted within American society a widespread male desire to flamboyantly assert ritual and to regularly make extravagant displays of symbolic rank and precedence. Freemasonry in the United States and elsewhere fulfilled a desire to see tradition and a reassuringly layered version of society perpetuated.

The reassurance provided by the visible display of hierarchy within Freemasonry was important and had its corollary in the unprecedented growth in honors within the British Empire in the nineteenth and twentieth centuries. Hierarchy of either sort homogenized, as Cannadine points out, "the heterogeneity of empire" such that the British at least created "one integrated, ordered, titular, transracial hierarchy that no other empire could rival."[8] As Rich explains, in order to perpetuate the ritual that kept colonized millions in their place, British imperialists became impresarios, directing a worldwide extravaganza. As has been noted, ritually reinforcing British cultural hegemony was vital because the great scope of the empire limited the British ability to secure politics by force.[9] Just like American Freemasons, many of those honored found it possible to be honored more than once, gaining membership in multiple fraternities of rank in what were often spectacular costumed displays. "The most successful British proconsuls and imperial soldiers," Cannadine explains, writing of the early decades of the twentieth century, "were knights and peers several times over, veritable walking Christmas trees of stars and collars, medals and sashes, ermine robes and coronets who personified the honorific imperial hierarchy at its most elaborate."[10] Something similar could be said about American fraternal men. For example, only partially exaggerating, Walter B. Hill wrote in *Century Magazine* in 1892 about the "thousand and one Societies that have State and national organizations [with] an enormous supply of official positions . . . commensurate in territorial magnitude with our great country." For Hill this was a reassuring means for America to avoid festering collective dissent. "Here then we have the great American safety valve—we are a nation of presidents."[11]

What the British habit of ennobling and the American propensity for ennobling within fraternities both shared was a concern to isolate affinities and delineate status on an individual as opposed to a collective level. A man earned his degrees as a Mason by individual achievement rather than by virtue of any collective identity, such as race. As such and as a uniquely British institution, Freemasonry supported Cannadine's claim that "in certain contexts and situations, the British *did* regard the dark-skinned members of their empire as more admirable, more important and more noble than white men. This is not the whole truth of things. But it is a substantial, a significant and neglected truth."[12] In the same sense the inclusion of key Native American individuals in American Freemasonry was evidence of just this sort of emphasis on a man's achieved rank as opposed to his supposedly inherent race. American Freemasonry therefore can be seen as a survivor of America's colonial past, a sanctuary for a vision of tradition and ordered social harmony based on rank that Americans had rejected politically in 1776, when they embraced the revolutionary idea that "all men are created equal." Of course just as with the honors system created as a bulwark of the British Empire, there was much about American Freemasonry that always was made up, fanciful, and self-deceiving. Thus it is perhaps not coincidental that Freemasonry in the United States reached an all-time low in terms of social respect at the same time as the British Empire ceased to hold together in the 1960s. At this point Western culture generally felt able to heap scorn and ridicule on all established forms of hierarchical display and the ornamentalism attached to status in society more generally. Freemasonry suffered painfully from the decline in deference that characterized that age.

American Freemasonry: American "Antients" and a New Egalitarianism

One of the most interesting things about early American Freemasonry is the fact that culturally it was undoubtedly part of the glue that held the new republic together. Indeed the Masonic "imagined community," with its own alternative "ancient" history, was eventually perceived as so powerful that it sparked a reverberative anti-Masonic movement within the fledgling nation in 1826.[13] Overall, American fraternalism can be divided into two century-long cycles, the first beginning in 1730 with the advent of organized Freemasonry on American soil in Philadelphia. Membership remained limited to the elite of commercial cities until 1760, when a grand expansion began that lasted until the 1820s, when the anti-Masonic movement caused a hemorrhage in numbers and put a stop to growth, especially in the North. Steven C. Bullock's exceptional book *Revolutionary Brotherhood* echoes earlier scholarship in characterizing the revolutionary years and immediately after as Freemasonry's high point in terms of prestige, its "First Golden Age." The foundational (but by no means canonical) Masonic document, the first edition of Anderson's *Constitutions of the Free-Masons*, appeared in the United States at the same time as the first lodge, commonly thought to have opened in Boston in 1723. It was published by Benjamin Franklin, an active Mason from his own initiation in 1730. Structurally and it would seem philosophically American lodges saw themselves as an elite segment of British ranked colonial culture, not least because they were organized under a structure of Provincial Grand Lodges that operated under the authority of the Grand Lodge of England.

Sometime in the 1740s Masons began to agitate for a fuller form of egalitarianism within their lodges. Figures such as the Irish immigrant Lawrence Dermott wrote against Masonic elitism and in favor of the artisan, the tradesman, and the small merchant as well as reasserting the centrality to Masonry of the universal religion of nature.[14] A split resulted, and "antient" or "Scottish" Freemasonry was born. (Confusingly it was not particularly Scottish and it was new rather than ancient, but adherents used the term because they claimed to have a firmer grasp of authentic ritual tradition.) By the 1760s most of the American lodges were "antient" and thus not directly tied to London and the jurisdiction of its Grand Lodge. Because of its more inclusive nature both in terms of racial hierarchies and in terms of class, the Ancients, spurred on by the inclusive impetus of their Irish brethren, played a key role in spreading Freemasonry globally. It is in fact possible to trace a strong thread of Irish influence in the story of how Freemasonry came to be seeded across the globe, from Toland's influence to the invention of traveling warrants in Irish military lodges and the popular and adaptable work of the Ancients. American "antients" included many urban artisans and inland elites politically mobilized by the Revolution. Part of Masonry's attraction was the way it was able to sell itself as revolutionary by emphasizing its rationalism and (limited) universalism. Added to this was the fact that it could trumpet the large number of Masons who had served in the Continental Army, including George Washington and many of his generals.[15] Freemasonry was to become more elaborate in 1801 with the creation beyond the first "Blue Lodge" three degrees of the Ancient Accepted Scottish Rite with its thirty-three degrees and then American Rite or Masonic Knight Templary, which conferred thirteen. These exotic, chivalric extensions of Masonry would prove directional in terms of the style of American fraternalism as the century progressed.

Bullock places a responsive revolutionary-era Masonry (but one he sees as largely devoid of spiritual or ritual emphasis in the colonial period) at the heart of various transitions in American life: from a world of patronage and gentry politics to a more commerce-driven Jacksonian democracy; from a world of hierarchy and public impassivity epitomized by Washington to a world of private sanctuary and a new emphasis on the self, and with it a preparedness for emotional display epitomized by Emerson. In sum Masonry thrived after the Revolution because of its unique ability to combine contradictory impulses for both equality and elitism; with its educational potential it claimed to foster a nobility of true virtue, the natural aristocracy that would be Jefferson's vision for the United States. As an institution Masonry embodied the merit and morality seen as key to the effective functioning of the republic, and it articulated the respected Enlightenment ideals of sociability and benevolence. Its moral authority was also used to attack the injustices of the era by educated women (such as Hannah Mather Crocker, as Bullock explores) and by ex-slaves.

Prince Hall Masonry

One of the best known freed slaves was Prince Hall of Boston. In 1775 he fell in with Irish Regimental Lodge No. 441, which added him along with fourteen other elite blacks to its ranks. Here again we find the Irish at the root of a bold attempt to democratize the fraternity. Once the Irish lodge had moved on, Hall set up his own "African Lodge," and after around eight years, in September 1784, it was issued a warrant as Lodge No. 459 by the Grand Lodge of England, the last warrant issued by the moderns to a group of American Masons. Hall and his fellow Mason, the black Methodist minister John Marrant (who had lived with the Cherokee for a time), used Freemasonry strategically to advance their cause of antislavery and as a platform from which to speak for their communities. Prince Hall Masonry made much of the principle of universal brotherhood enshrined in Masonic rhetoric and attempted to insert black people into the Christian past and into a positive narrative of mankind's overall development. Hall did so by claiming that as descendents of the Queen of Sheba, African Masons had been received by King Solomon and were closely associated with the Masonic forerunners the Knights of Malta.

Scholars such as Joanna Brooks have made a powerful case for black Masonry as a "counterpublic strategy," a means of "reconstructing black identity oppositionally within the refuge of black-only corporations and collectives."[16] How successful such a strategy may have been is another matter. Certainly black Masons in American Masonic thinking occupied a wholly separate fraternal space and time than did Native American Masons, whose selective inclusion in terms of ritual, Masonic history, and physical presence in the lodge was not only possible but welcomed. In the imagined kinship of international Masonry blacks, it seems, were not an acknowledged part of the fraternal family. Mainstream American Masons were to keep their black counterparts at arm's length, segregated, frequently ridiculed, and despite repeated appeals to the English Grand Lodge denied institutional legitimacy.

Overall Freemasonry's ability to make a positive contribution to eliminating America's fundamental hindrance to brotherhood—racial oppression and racial segregation—has been limited. Even today, excepting Alpha Lodge No. 116 in New Jersey, conventional Freemasonry remains predominantly white.[17] As Loretta J. Williams wrote in 1980, "The legitimation of social intermingling between black and white Masons has remained an anathema in mainstream Freemasonry."[18] This is exemplified in the number of legal suits pursued by black and white lodges against each other over time, usually citing the misuse of Masonic names, symbols, and rituals. The racism of Albert Pike, the doyen of nineteenth-century American Freemasonry, is also worth noting in this regard. Pike aided Prince Hall Masonic development, even allowing black lodges access to specific rituals, but always maintained that in keeping with other key American institutions Freemasonry must remain strictly segregated. Masonic history and the strength of the institution in the twentieth century would undoubtedly have been very different had the fraternity's commitment to inclusion and universality been extended to black Americans. Over time in both the North and the South they have been avid voluntary organizers or "superjoiners," as Skocpol and Oser put it, echoing Gunnar Myrdal.[19] Myrdal explained in 1944 that even though disproportionately lower class, black Americans were much more inclined than whites to join associations.[20] In this sense they were "exaggerated" Americans and a vast untapped reservoir of membership that Freemasonry, especially in the twentieth century, chose to ignore to its ultimate cost.

The Morgan Affair

The history of black exclusion from Freemasonry highlights the different roles separate ethnic identities occupy within the Masonic imagination, but Masons themselves have also suffered from the roles imposed on them by their wider communities. Like Indians, American Freemasons have at times occupied a particular and fanciful space in the American imagination, becoming stalwarts of the periodic dramas concerning conspiracy and subversion that pepper the American past. American versions of Masonic conspiracy were able to draw on a long history of such fears, documented in books of the 1790s by John Robison and Abbé Augustin de Barruel and later expanded in the famous hoax publication *The Protocols of the Elders of Zion*. Freemasons joined a list of American figures occupying the twilight zone of fear within the American imagination, linked to what Richard Hofstader called the "paranoid style" in American politics and to the apocalyptic millennial beliefs of the early Protestant settlers. At points in American history Indians and Masons alike seemed to threaten private property, established order, and Christianity. Indeed for some early colonists, the political and social freedoms both Indians and Masons represented were traps set by the Devil to destabilize the New American Jerusalem, part of what Robert Alan Goldberg describes as "conspiracies of Indians, dissent and witches."[21]

Conspiracy fears have always been politically useful phenomena, and in the early nineteenth century American clergy were able to use the anti-Masonic claims of Robison and Barruel to garner support for the anti-immigrant Federalist Alien and Sedition Acts. George Washington, who was both a Federalist and a Mason, joined with President John Adams to defend Freemasonry, but attack could not be held off for long. Then in the 1820s a deeper and stronger anti-Masonic movement sprang up and had lasting effects. It was in response to an incident that in itself was a giant overreaction, and as with so many paranoid, politically reverberative events it was made much worse by the subsequent attempt to cover it up.

In 1826 a New York Mason named William Morgan was kidnapped and, it was supposed, murdered because he threatened to expose secret Masonic words and signs, in particular those of the York Rite degrees. Forty-five at the time, Morgan had become disillusioned with Masonry and had taken steps with a journalist friend to publish a hostile exposé entitled *Morgan's Illustrations*, a title similar to that the Masonic writer William Preston produced forty-four years earlier. Unfortunately for Morgan, upstate New York at the time was something of a hotbed of both pro- and anti-Masonic feeling. The official Masonic version of events reported, "Some ineffective attempts were made to procure his silence; he was then removed [accounts vary as to whether he went willingly or not] to Fort Niagara. The rest is silence, but a rumour of his murder gave rise to an anti-Masonic movement."[22]

Morgan, it was claimed, was taken first to Canandaigua, where he was hidden by Indians before being murdered. The aged Red Jacket (1751–1830), thought to have been an Entered Apprentice, was said to have counseled those on the reservation against taking Morgan in, although this seems unlikely since he was based at Buffalo Creek reservation at the time. According to Red Jacket's descendent Arthur Parker, Red Jacket lived near Morgan near Batavia, New York, and shunned him as a traitor. Parker did claim in print, however, that soon after the Morgan incident "a furtive stranger appeared to the Parker home near Tonawanda Falls and begged to be allowed to store a package which he said evil men were after." The parcel was "reluctantly hidden" on a bookshelf by William Parker, Arthur's great-grandfather (1793–1864).[23] William Denslow's 1956 publication quotes Parker adding credence to the hoary rumor that Morgan met a grizzly end at the Tonawanda reservation.[24] Masonic reports from 1883 even suggest that Joseph Brant, as a Mason and renowned warrior, was charged with the task of dispatching him.[25] Yet other reports claimed that Morgan had himself "become an Indian chief."[26]

It was commonly thought that Masonic influence had allowed the perpetrators to get away with the crime of Morgan's murder, in particular that the legal authorities and local media had helped to cover it up. After a decomposed body washed up on the shores of Lake Ontario over a year later, public feeling intensified that Morgan had been ritually murdered as part of a pervasive conspiracy. Masonry was deemed to be both immoral and antidemocratic, and the anti-Masonic movement that resulted spread to New England and the Midwest. Print was key to anti-Masonry, and newspapers, books, and periodicals provided its lifeblood; 130 anti-Masonic periodicals were in existence by 1830. Anti-Masonic candidates ran for office in a number of states, and in 1828 the movement gave birth to the first third party in the United States, the Anti-Masonic Party. An anti-Masonic candidate even ran for president in 1832. After this the political impetus behind the party was gradually absorbed into the developing Whig Party, but it could be argued that the apex of the movement came in the mid-1850s with the formation in New York of a nationwide group known as the Order of the Star Spangled Banner (also known as the "Know Nothings" since this secretive group claimed they "knew nothing" when queried about its operations). In 1854 Massachusetts candidates backed by the Know Nothings controlled the state legislature, governed the state, and held all the state's seats in the U.S. House of Representatives.

The Morgan incident was peculiar on two fronts. From a Masonic standpoint, given the number of readily available exposés of the first three degrees in existence since the mid-1700s, the allegedly violent response of his fellow Masons to Morgan's actions was entirely disproportionate. Admittedly Morgan was prepared to reveal the newer York Rite rituals and the Royal Arch secret name of God, but again this was hardly a serious threat to the fraternity overall. If the alleged crime is in itself difficult to explain, so too are the exact contours of the anti-Masonic response to it. Dorothy Lipson has provided evidence that there was a groundswell of anti-Masonic feeling even before 1826 in New England because it was perceived as a threat to Calvinism, but there is no conclusive answer as to why Freemasonry became so socially unacceptable beginning in the late 1820s until feelings subsided after 1840.[27] Whitney Cross's work has until recently dominated thinking on the topic; he suggests that the reaction against Masonry was actually the lower classes revolting against the village and urban aristocracy.[28] Scholars who have taken a closer, county-by-county look at places in western New York that were dominated by Masons in key positions of political and civic affairs, such as Genesee County (home, incidentally, to the elite Indian and Masonic

Parker family), more or less concur. They argue that the anti-Masonic response sprang from a genuine concern for republicanism and justice.[29] For writers such as Steven Bullock, the anti-Masonic interlude represents a watershed, when Freemasonry lost its mystique and centrality in American culture, a point when American society became fundamentally more liberal and democratic and multiple private spheres separated off from public life.[30] In a real sense anti-Masonry gave special interest politics a new purchase in American life; it brought morality and conscience into political discourse in a new fashion as well as prefiguring a number of other democratizing changes of the nineteenth century. From a political perspective, it brought the national nominating convention to presidential politics and contributed to the development of the Whig Party. According to Clawson and others, women allied to evangelical Christians were especially prominent in the anti-Masonry of this period, but when Freemasonry reasserted itself it entrenched gender and race on its terms as the appropriate categories for collective identity.[31]

Bullock argues that Freemasonry responded to anti-Masonry after 1826 by increasingly emphasizing its Christian dimensions and by retreating into a more privately oriented symbolism. With the reverence the fraternity had inspired around the time of the Revolution dissipated, it simultaneously sought a new public context while retreating inward in spiritual terms.[32] Yet opinion on Freemasonry's religious status and spiritual direction has always been both vexed and ambiguous. Certainly as far as Roman Catholicism is concerned, the fraternity has more or less always been a dangerous leveler of all faiths, intent upon returning mankind to a pre-Christian understanding of the world. Papal condemnation started as early as 1738 largely because of the organization's perceived threat to order and monarchy expressed in its fondness for holding elections. Jacob describes how Catholics were urged to view Freemasonry as evidence of that English disease, incipient republicanism. "This society," it was claimed, "imitates an aspect of the government of Republics. Its leaders are chosen, or dismissed, at its will."[33] Successive popes kept up the attack, convinced the fraternity's ultimate aim was "the utter overthrow of the whole religious and political order of the world which the Christian teaching has produced" and its replacement with human reason, human nature and "Naturalism."[34]

American Freemasonry may have taken on a more Christian hue following 1826, but there is much to suggest that Masonic spirituality was and remains nondenominational. As James Anderson's *Constitutions*, a founding codification of Masonic practice, made clear in 1723, "A mason is obliged . . . to that Religion in which all men agree, leaving their particular opinions to themselves." If a Freemason "rightly understands the Art, he will never be a stupid atheist, nor an irreligious Libertine."[35] Thus the fraternity requires of men only that they have some form of spiritual awareness, not that they swear allegiance to any one specified definition of faith. Freemasons are required only to affirm that they believe in a supreme being, referred to in Masonic circles as the "Great Architect of the Universe." Just as religious freedom has always been vouchsafed within Masonic lodges, so too has political freedom, with overt discussion of politics forbidden. Thus Masonic charge VI, part 1 reads, "We are . . . of all Nations, Tongues, Kindreds, and Languages, and are resolv'd against all Politicks." Masonic lodges were by formal agreement to be sanctuaries of harmony and pleasure. There was to be no talk "of anything impertinent or unseemly" and "no private Piques or Quarrels . . . brought within the Door of the Lodge, far less any Quarrels about Religion or Nations, or State Policy."[36] This commitment to the maintenance of Masonic lodges as sites of political and religious sanctuary was not dissolved by the anti-Masonry of the early nineteenth century; neither did the need for such contexts disappear. In fact the most significant spiritual developments to grow out of the anti-Masonic era owed a great deal to Freemasonry and shared its impulse to transcend sectarianism. That new religion was Mormonism.

Mormons, Masons, and Indians

Mormonism and Freemasonry have significant correspondences, especially in terms of their origins.[37] Like Freemasonry, Mormonism has its roots in the urge to transcend sectarian strife. Joseph Smith, who first received the Book of Mormon from the angel Moroni in 1827, was disgusted with the interdenominational conflict that so beset the American spiritual landscape. By transplanting a sacred narrative to America (as opposed to the Middle East) he created a uniquely American faith that sidestepped the whole issue of biblical interpretation. Furthermore, like Masonry, Mormonism was linked controversially with magic, especially treasure divining, fortune seeking, and, for Smith particularly, various occult practices. Indeed Mormonism can be seen as a development from Freemasonry, an outgrowth that occurred just when it seemed that Masonry in the United States would never recover. At the time Masonry was, as one biographer of Smith puts it, the subject of "delirious hatred":

> So it happened that Joseph Smith was writing the Book of Mormon in the thick of a political crusade that gave backwoods New York, hitherto politically stagnant and socially déclassé, a certain prestige and glory. And he quickly introduced into the book the theme of the Gadianton band, a secret society whose oaths for fraternal protection were bald parallels of Masonic oaths, and whose avowed aim was the overthrow of the democratic Nephite government. "And it came to pass that they did have their signs," he wrote, "yea, their se-

cret signs, and their secret words; and this that they might distinguish a brother who had entered into the covenant."[38]

A significant number of those who converted to Mormonism in the 1830s had been Freemasons before the rise of anti-Masonry, and Smith was able to get the help of more than thirty former Masons when he established a lodge at Nauvoo, Illinois, in 1842.

Furthermore there is much to suggest that Smith's main interest in Masonry lay in its ritual. Indeed a long list of Masonic ritual practices correspond with aspects of Mormonism, from the use of tiny white aprons for the actors who represent Adam and Eve to the use of "keys," handshakes, and passwords alongside secret names by which each man would be known in heaven. Much Masonic symbolism reoccurs in Mormonism, including the all-seeing eye, the beehive, the two clasped hands, and the point inside a circle. The sun, the moon, and the stars, the "lesser lights" of Masonic symbology, are also embedded in the new Mormon cosmology of the three heavens. Smith taught that Masonic ritual was simply a corruption of the ancient ritual of Solomon and that his own rites were a restoration of the ancient Hebrew legacy.[39] Even prior to his becoming a prophet Smith and his family had had much exposure to Masonic influences, including the Masonic legend of a lost sacred word at one time engraved upon a triangular plate of gold. His family were known to be treasure hunters, and Smith claimed he had translated the Book of Mormon using a seer stone from a set of gold plates he found near his home in Palmyra in upstate New York. He believed that Masonry was divine at its core but had been corrupted by man; the task of restoring what was called at the time "pure Masonry" was key to his religious mission. This may explain his eventual plural marriage to Lucinda Morgan, the widow of William Morgan, the Royal Arch Mason whose threat to expose Freemasonry's higher degrees had so incensed his peers.

However, this is not to suggest that the arguments in Clyde R. Forsberg's *Equal Rites: The Book of Mormon, Masonry, Gender, and American Culture* are necessarily valid. Forsberg makes the blanket assertion that the Book of Mormon is in essence "a well-crafted defense of Christian Masonry" and argues that what Smith hoped for was "the restoration of a beleaguered Masonic political order (looking backward and forward) that promised to end sectarian rivalry, reestablish social harmony, guarantee economic equality, and avoid racial discord through a carefully monitored system of polygamous mixed marriages."[40] Even though the links between Masonry and Mormonism are tangible and deserve further study, Forsberg does not provide us with enough in terms of Masonry or of Mormonism to support such all-encompassing claims. We would do better to follow Douglas Davies's suggestion, following conservative Latter Day Saints thinking, and to think of Mormonism as a movement intending to restore to mankind rites as old as Eden, known in outline by Masonry but authentically and fully revealed to Joseph Smith.[41]

As custodians of such sacred wisdom, Indian peoples were another preoccupation of Joseph Smith's prior to his taking on the role of prophet. Both Indians and Masons had a central place in his spiritual imagination. "In the course of our [family's] evening conversations," his mother remembered, "Joseph would give us some of the most amusing recitals which could be imagined. He would describe the ancient inhabitants of this continent—their dress, their manner of travelling, the animals which they rode, the cities that were built by them, the structures of their buildings, with every particular of their mode of warfare, their religious worship as particularly as though he had spent his life with them."[42] As Dan Vogel's thoroughly researched *Indian Origins and the Book of Mormon* explains, Smith was neither unusual nor alone in his fascination for things Indian, and the ideas he received from the angel Moroni were symptomatic of the intellectual, popular, and theological culture of the time. The theological conundrum posed by the presence of Indian cultures in the New World and the mounds built by their ancestors had long been a favorite topic at several levels of society. The Indian presence had not been prefigured in the Bible, and dominant thinking characterized them as degenerate and incapable. How, then, had such major feats of engineering as the Great Serpent Mound of Ohio been achieved (now associated with Adena culture prior to 1700 CE)?

If anything Mormonism's Indian underpinnings are stronger than its Masonic ones given that the presence of Native Americans is put forward as evidence of the Book of Mormon's veracity and the task of redeeming Indian peoples is central to the Mormon mission. Quite simply the Book of Mormon is an Indian history, a record appearing in 1830 that explains how Indians fit into the story of mankind and how they will play a pivotal role in the future. It argues that once redeemed by Mormons, Indians (a Lamanite remnant of ancient Hebrews) will take the lead in building a New Jerusalem, the site of the Second Coming of Christ. According to Mormon theology, Indians are a lost tribe of Israel, the people to whom Jesus ministered when he came to the United States after resurrection. Descendents of the tribes of Ephraim and Manesseh, they traveled by boat to America around 600 BCE and split into two: the nomadic, cursed, and dark-skinned Lamanites and the righteous, city-building Nephites. The Lamanites annihilated the fair-skinned Nephites and in so doing destroyed Christianity in America. It was only with Joseph Smith's revelation of the Book of Mormon (revealed to him by the angel Moroni, the last Nephite scribe) that Indians, these Lamanite descendents, "remnants of Jacob," and kin to the Mormons, would take on their true role in world history as saviors. Only Mormons would survive the Apocalypse, along with a mighty, crushing army of redeemed Indians, who by this stage would have regained their glory and with it, remarkably, their fair skin. The Mormon role was to bring Indians hope in the form of the gospel of Jesus Christ, thus removing the "scales of darkness" from their eyes and restoring them to a state that was both powerful and "white and delightsome."

This does not mean that interconnections among Masons, Mormons, and Indians in this period are uncomplex. Even though the later Mormon leader Brigham Young's claim that it was easier to feed mid-nineteenth-century Indians than to fight them is often quoted, in fact the history of Mormon-Indian relations is as complicated (some would say as sullied) as is much other interaction between Indians and non-Indians, not least because both communities often found themselves competing for the same resources. An example is the postmassacre conversions in 1873 of many of the Northwestern Band of Shoshone of Bingham City, Utah, conversions that were an alternative to starvation and forced removal to reservations for most of the survivors of that Indian community. Ultimately, in a process greatly accelerated in the 1970s, Mormons ended up owning the majority of what had been Shoshone land in the area. For his part, Smith did make various attempts to realize the destiny of Indians in relation to himself and to Mormons more generally right from the beginning of his role as Mormon prophet: he attempted to locate a new Mormon "centre place" in Missouri, "on the borders of the Lamanites," what was then the newly created Indian Territory. But his plans for Indian missionizing largely failed, and over time Mormon plans to include Indian peoples in their religious and society-building schemes have proved inconsistent. As Jared Farmer puts it, there has been "tension in Mormon thought between Indian-as-brother and Indian as other; between sympathy and contempt, belief and doubt."[43] Right up until his death by lynching in 1844 (when he used the

Masonic sign of distress to no avail), Smith held out hope for a coordination of Indian and Mormon interests and for the fulfillment of his prophecy.

Mormonism, as a home-grown American faith, is a reminder that not all Americans in the nineteenth century thought in the same way about indigenous America. In this instance at least, a mixture of revelation, Christianity, and Masonry allowed one settler religious group to envisage a homeland on American soil imbued with spiritual significance, to have a way of conceptualizing human relationships to land that was more akin to certain traditional Indian ways than those of contemporary Euro-Americans. It also allowed Mormons to imagine not just a central but a preeminent spiritual and social role for Indian peoples in an apocalyptic and postapocalyptic future. Whatever failings occurred in terms of the relationships forged between Indian and Mormon communities on the frontier, in terms of Mormon doctrine at least they shared a fundamental kinship and were brothers in arms as mankind lived out its days until the Second Coming. If we think about Mormon doctrine against the backdrop of the generally negative image of Indians that was predominant at the beginning of the nineteenth century, a legacy both of the colonizing impulse itself and of its Puritan antecedents, then Smith's attempt to identify Indians with the lost tribes of Israel was in one sense positive and inclusive. It was at least, as Roy Harvey Pearce points out with reference to other, similar attempts of the time, "part of a last-moment revivalist effort to find a secure place for the Indian in a civilized, Christian world."[44] Furthermore Mormonism has always been practiced and received in complex ways. Although its theology is replete with colonial metaphors and racially charged symbolism, its central text has been subject to wide interpretation, and in spite of its racialism the church continues to be able to attract healthy numbers of nonwhites.[45]

Yet the obvious still holds true. The idea that the Indians who were Smith's contemporaries were degenerate versions of a previous race of talented white-skinned Hebrews was a convenient and invidious myth. It removed responsibility for the state of dispossessed Indians from Euro-American settlers and reinscribed the racial thinking of the time, including the pernicious idea that civilization characterized only white peoples, those at the vanguard of human development. The Book of Mormon purported to be about the spiritual redemption of Indian peoples (its title page states that its purpose is to show Indians "what great things the Lord hath done for their fathers; and that they may know the covenants of the Lord, that they are not cast off forever"), but in fact it was about the psychological redemption of non-Indians. By imagining Lamanites, a set of Indian ancestors that had all the loathsome characteristics associated with the savage and the non-Christian, Mormonism figured Euro-American settlers as redeemers and absolved them of responsibility for the theft of Indian land. It explained away evidence of centuries-long occupation by Indians of the American environment and performed the all-important trick of making Mormon Americans heroes, placing them on the same side as a coming vengeful army of reformed, spiritually dominant Indian warriors. It is a larger process of legitimation analogous to how Utah Mormon boosters used the Indian-sounding name Timpanogos to give authenticity and antiquity to their chosen mountain landmark at the expense of the actual location's landmark, Utah Lake, central to the spiritual geography of the Ute peoples they had displaced. Both the creation of the Timpanogos landmark and the doctrine of the Latter Day Saints served the same purpose: the redirection of collective historical memory away from an awkward past of cultural displacement toward a new history of heroic Mormon pioneering and attachment to place.[46]

Perhaps in essence what really connects Masonry, Mormonism, and aspects of Indian spirituality is what all three share with Hermeticism, in particular the respect for ritual and for ideas about the coequality of spirit and matter. Mormonism distanced itself from its Hermetic origins after the 1850s, but as John L. Brooke has shown, Joseph Smith's thinking can be linked directly to the Radical Reformation in Europe, to roots in the positive and inclusive philosophy that saw the divine in mankind, Hermeticism.[47] Smith's followers were a "prepared people," as Brooke puts it, already predisposed by a sectarian, perfectionist transatlantic heritage to accept the spiritual wonders Smith revealed. Such an approach links to one of this book's overarching themes, that there were points of spiritual interconnection between indigenous and settler early America whose significance has been underplayed.

After the Morgan affair and the birth of Mormonism, in the 1840s Freemasonry's numbers again began to grow, and Masonic ritual and language served as a template for the growth of voluntary organization in the United States generally. The Scottish Rite ballooned in numbers, as did eventually a host of other fraternal groups as well as Masonic-inspired mutual insurance groups, labor unions such as the early Knights of Labor, and political groups such as the Grange and the Grand Army of the Republic, made up of Civil War veterans. Between 1885 and 1900 more than 150 new American fraternal organizations were formed; by 1820 thirty million, around half the adult population, were attached to one or more of eight hundred secret orders.[48] Up until the Civil War fraternal growth was mostly Masonic and in an analogous group, the Independent Order of Odd Fellows, but then between the mid-1840s and mid-1880s a host of new fraternities were born, all modeled on the Masonic pattern. It is possible that in a basic sense men were looking, as Arthur Stinchcombe suggested in

1965, to reestablish an essential American brotherhood that had been sundered by the war.[49] But as I explain in the next chapter, a host of other factors also came into play. Certainly the acute fraternal upswing between 1870 and the turn of the twentieth century was to cut across class lines and to give those involved precious organizational experience.[50]

In 1900 the two largest organizations, Freemasons and Odd Fellows, had one million members each out of a total male population of thirty-nine million, with at least four other fraternal orders together having more than thirty-nine million.[51] Expansion started to slow in the 1920s, just before fraternalism was to take a body blow during the Depression era. Masonry revived in the 1940s, but other groups, such as Odd Fellows, never really recovered. By the 1960s more than four million American men and two million women belonged to Masonic lodges, but the decline that began in the 1960s resulted in Masonry's numbers falling to around two million by 2000.[52] By the late nineteenth century Freemasonry was deeply respectable for middle-class American men, and many women worked behind the scenes to support their men in creating and maintaining formidable Masonic buildings. Generally speaking Masonic structure in the United States had the following pattern. A man gained the first three degrees of Freemasonry—Entered Apprentice, Fellowcraft, and Master Mason—from an ordinary lodge, often called a "Craft Lodge" or "Blue Lodge." After becoming a Master Mason he could seek additional Masonic degrees from the Scottish Rite or the York Rite. In the York Rite a chapter confers Royal Arch degrees numbered four to seven; a council of Royal and Select Masters confers the eighth and ninth degrees of Cryptic Masonry, and a "commandery" confers the three additional orders through which a man may be created a Knight Templar. However high a man proceeds through Masonic degrees of whatever sort, there is much to suggest that, spiritually at least, it is the third degree, the Master Mason qualification, that is most significant. Given that Masonic ritual is repeatedly performed or watched by attending Masons, one could say that the third degree ritual, to paraphrase Clifford Geertz, is the primary story Masons as a group tell themselves about themselves.[53] The values it encapsulates concerning fidelity, loyalty, secrecy, and hierarchy and the spiritually symbolic lessons it exposes initiates to are fundamental to Freemasonry as a practice. That said, while a strict hierarchy applies in terms of the payment of dues and adherence to rules dictated by the central bodies or Grand Lodges within Masonry, there has always been variation in how the rituals are performed for each Masonic degree from state to state and from lodge to lodge. It is perhaps a failing of this book that I tend to speak in general terms about Masonic practice even though it has always been diverse and particularly responsive to wider changes in society. However, variations in practice, though significant, do not substantially mitigate my arguments. It is reasonable to view American Masonry as more or less fixed by the early nineteenth century, with ritualized initiations as the core lodge activity. Its various degrees and orders, however, should not be thought of as a cohesive, progressive integrated system. Instead the qualifications beyond the Craft and Royal Arch level are simply continuations, emphasizing morals and principles initiates have already encountered earlier.

In academic writing on Freemasonry the fraternity has too often been written off as racist. But it is simply not the case that the only unmediated brotherhood with nonwhites that fraternal men could stomach was with the dead, an *esprit de corpse*, as Dana Nelson wittily terms it.[54] Even though writers such as Clawson are correct in stating explicitly that "racial exclusion was a hallmark of mainstream American fraternalism throughout its history," this does not provide the whole story.[55] Others have suggested that Free-masonry's "moment of relative inclusiveness"—the period when it allowed indigenous elites access to lodges—did not outlive the 1700s. Loretta J. Williams in *Black Freemasonry and Middle-Class Realities*, for example, states, "Native Americans were not considered worthy of the brotherhood by most mainstream Masons"; she argues that hostility to Indians among Masons especially increased in the nineteenth century.[56] Harland-Jacobs holds that at the beginning of the nineteenth century "colonial subjects [were no longer] permitted to enter the lodge and use its language, symbols and rituals to lay claim to Enlightenment ideals of liberty and equality."[57] Harland-Jacobs's and Williams's statements may be true in the largest sense, yet the story of nineteenth- and twentieth-century indigenous inclusion in American Masonry suggests that there is more subtlety to this history and that the Indian Masons who were accepted into lodges sought more than simply Enlightenment equality from their brotherhoods. Key indigenous figures, from Hawaiian royalty to Cherokee politicians in the midst of removal, all took part in "the politics of the sacred," to use the historian Steven Bullock's phrase, and used Masonic ritual for their own diverse ends.[58] Exploring how this came about and why is almost as fascinating as the fraternity itself.

The Attractions of Freemasonry to Indians and Others, Part One

5

As ethnohistorians have long been at pains to point out, for explanations of cultural change within American Indian societies to be truly meaningful, they must come from within those societies themselves. Each member of an Indian community who joined Masonic fraternities did so for his own reasons, and each individual Indian who sought admission did so, as far as Freemasonry was concerned, based on his own merit. Yet there are aspects of Freemasonry that may have made it amenable to individual Indians and a larger social, spiritual, cultural, and political context to Indian engagement with the fraternity that clearly bear scrutiny.

Magic, Its Persistence and Influence

Chapter 1 explored the European origins of Freemasonry and suggested ways in which aspects of Freemasonry may have interlinked with what are commonly discussed as "traditional" elements within Native American lifeways. We have become accustomed, partly as a result of the long history of writing on American exceptionalism and triumphalism, to thinking of Indian traditions since contact as being radically and indissolubly different from those of European colonists; in fact there were significant correspondences. Although non-Indian writers, especially those with

Puritan roots, have tended to stress Indian spirituality as wholly alien to European lifeways, in fact settlers reacted so negatively to what they perceived as Indian "magic" and "heathenism" because it reminded them of suppressed aspects of themselves, in particular their own resurgent histories of non-Christian spiritualism. To the extent that American Freemasonry carried within it kernels of these non-Christian traditions in its Neoplatonic and Hermetic roots it corresponded with certain Indian traditions and Indian ways of perceiving. In particular Freemasonry perpetuated a sense of the essential kinship between all things and preserved cultural space for ritual and symbolism. Indeed part of the reason we tend to think of magic and religion in the ways we do, with the one involving ritual that is coercive and to do with practice and the other involving ritual that is intercessionary and to do with belief, is in great part a result of the Protestant Reformation, a movement that was determined to prioritize the individual's faith in God as opposed to the matrix of supernatural and social awareness invoked by "magic."[1] It is as well to recognize that the condescension (in E. P. Thompson's sense) we may feel toward what is deemed irrational, whether we perceive it in Indian cultures or in the European past, is in itself a symptom of this specific shift.[2]

Perhaps the best book to help us understand just how un-Christian sixteenth- and seventeenth-century England, where Freemasonry took root, was is Keith Thomas's *Religion and the Decline of Magic*. Thomas is keen to compare his subject negatively with contemporary "primitive" practices in Africa and elsewhere, but if we leave to one side this anachronistic and hierarchical approach to global systems of belief, we are left with a fascinating and unique exploration of "astrology, witchcraft, magical healing, divination, ancient prophecies, ghosts and fairies"—all those things Thomas describes as "now all rightly disdained by intelligent persons [but] taken seriously by equally intelligent persons in the past." One of the great contributions of Thomas's sizable book is the way he brings to life just how magical the medieval Church was in England and how blurred the line has been between religion as it is commonly understood and magic. He explains, "The medieval Church appeared as a vast reservoir of magical power, capable of being deployed for a variety of secular purposes. Indeed it is difficult to think of any human aspiration for which it would not cater."[3] As Jon Butler explains in his book on the process whereby the American people became Christianized, early modern supernaturalism in fact underwrote Christianity, and the occult thrived in it.[4] American land teemed with rival, interconnected systems of belief, including "cunning folk" capable of magical healing, "wise men" and "wise women" who could keep away disease, those who understood omens, prophecies, portents, dreams, thief-magic, witchcraft, and astrology, and those for whom supernatural sightings of all sorts, including ghosts and fairies, were not uncommon. Many knew little or nothing of established religious dogma, and it was a frequent refrain in the late seventeenth century that the remote and the poor were as ignorant "as the savages of America."[5]

Neither was a belief in what is now deemed magic confined to the uneducated. The Neoplatonism that swept though Renaissance Europe revived notions of the Earth as alive, of the universe peopled by spirits, and of the world governed by fundamental correspondences and relationships between all things. Admittedly by the end of the seventeenth century most scientists were moving toward belief in a more mechanistic world. Magic and science originally advanced side by side, but as Thomas explains, although elements of magic survived within orthodox religion even after the Reformation, eventually a rejection of Neoplatonism marked the end of magic's whole intellectual basis. The idea that nature was subject to immutable laws took away the validity of miracles, and the "Cartesian concept of matter relegated spirits, whether good or bad, to the purely mental world."[6] Yet another blow came from the commitment to experiment that characterized the burgeoning new science, a commitment antithetical to belief in a world governed by enchantment. It has been suggested that part of the decline Thomas charts in magic belief during the late seventeenth century and early eighteenth was linked to general improvements in living conditions, or that it may simply have been the case that toleration for magical belief increased and so mention of it decreased in the court records on which social historians in this period rely.

Certainly for the Protestants who were so instrumental in settling America, the practices and ideas of "cunning men," witches, and astrologers were actions done "without understanding" and therefore deeply suspect before God.[7] Protestantism took away from the Church its countermagic, its relics, sacraments, and benign workings, and left people desperate for a spiritual defense against "black" witchcraft.[8] In response to that came the successive waves of articulate opinion and action against magic that characterized early modern Europe. When European Protestants landed in the New World it seemed to them that the very practices and beliefs they had wrestled with in their homeland lurked behind every twist of landscape, and in particular in the hearts of "heathen" Native America. This was augmented by a general fear in the seventeenth century that what would eventually be identified in the nineteenth century as secularism might in fact win out in the New World. Because magic and occultism had also made the journey alongside Christianity, there was an awareness, as Butler explains, that "colonisation both retarded and reinforced religious expressions that church leaders found as troubling in the New World as they had in the Old." The 1692 witch trials in Salem and the more than two hundred witch episodes that preceded them are just one indicator of how prevalent occult practice was in New England and of how fearful early American religious entities were of its power. Sympathy for the occult straddled the social spectrum, but according to Butler, when magic became "folklorised" in the eighteenth century it then also became confined to the poor and the more marginalized in society.[9] Seventeenth-century popular New England was, as David Hall puts it, a "world of wonder," where paradoxically the "popish superstitions" that were so heavily disparaged were also integral to colonial systems of belief. Wonder at the paranormal and over portents, dreams, and visions testified to a communal respect for ideas and beliefs transplanted from the European past, ideas that included classical meteorology, medieval scholasticism, and Hermeticism.[10]

Lest we think that such an emphasis on what is, after all, a British influence on American colonialism is overdone, it is worth remembering just how British America is in its cultural origins. As David Hackett Fischer explains, key cultural "folkways" in the United States came from Britain, and in terms of its core as a voluntary society, America can be said to have germinated from "Albion's Seed."[11] As chapter 3 explored, the seed that became American Freemasonry was British with medieval and sixteenth-century roots steeped in magic and "primitive" religion. A great deal that is central to Freemasonry and its practice, from the idea of orientationally sacred space to the idea of ritualized language having power in itself, ideas about power being seated in objects, and the link between pre-Christian mythology and "Masonic time" as expressed in the fraternity's almanacs, all share these medieval roots.

It is worth giving real consideration to the shift away from magic that was in progress in the West at the same time as the "discovery" and settlement of the New World. Thomas's analysis of the decline of magic in Britain invokes Malinowski's famous, highly ethnocentric dictum that magic is "to be expected and generally to be found whenever man comes to an unbridgeable gap, a hiatus in his knowledge or in his powers of practical control, and yet has to continue in his pursuit."[12] It is impossible to seriously suggest that British or European magic is directly comparable with the rich diversity of spiritual belief practiced in Native America, but it is reasonable to assert that certain European beliefs in the nonrational and supernatural corresponded strongly and meaningfully with aspects of Native American spiritual and social traditions. Furthermore, in both contexts, the phenomena that get subsumed under the name *magic* served (and continues to serve in some communities) many more functions than those Malinowski observed. However, as Max Weber pointed out long after Malinowski, the magic that stubbornly persisted in Europe was indeed "one of the most serious obstructions to the rationalisation of economic life," and some combination of Christian and other interests brought about in the West a "disenchantment of the world."[13] According to Weber, this drove certain values into the realms of either fraternity or mysticism. As he explained in "Science as a Vocation," "The fate of our times is characterized by rationalization and intellectualization, and, above all, by the 'disenchantment of the world.' Precisely the ultimate and most sublime values have retreated from public life either into the transcendental realm of mystic life or into the brotherliness of direct and personal human relations."[14]

Weber's point, that with the onset of modernity fraternalism became the sanctuary of an enchanted worldview, is much more generative than some other approaches that have stressed binary oppositions when it comes to magic and its meaning in history. Until relatively recently, for example, Euro-American historians have confidently asserted that the "magical" spiritual beliefs within their own cultural past, which they also suggest characterized "primitive" societies elsewhere, were uniquely connected with an agrarian lifestyle. Christopher Hill, for one, explains a decline in magic in sixteenth-century England by stating simply, "Magic is agrarian," the idea being that because an agricultural life is governed more by the vicissitudes of nature than an urban one, man at an agriculturalist "stage" was readier to believe in a nonrational world.[15] This idea is obviously flawed, not least because what is deemed "magical thinking" still persists and flourishes within urban environments globally. The term *magic* also connects with a number of worldviews that, as with so many terms rooted in Christian history, belie enormous diversity of belief that have shown remarkable persistence over centuries.[16]

I suggest it is more useful, following Weber, to think of Freemasonry, born in the early eighteenth century and reaching what would appear to be its declining years after 1960, as an indicator of a larger, ongoing Western shift away from irrationality toward the secular (admittedly a word Weber is careful to avoid). This shift is difficult to separate intellectually from the growth of modernity or, as recent scholarship would have us think of it, the various onsets of multiple, alternative modernities.[17] Certainly Freemasonry's origins and growth correspond with the end of Western peoples' belief in an enchanted world; instead people looked for spiritual "fullness" from sources (including science) that do not involve or that at least mitigate the influence of God.[18] Masonry thus can be seen simultaneously as both evidence of the decline of such an enchanted world and as evidence of its persistence in a very specific form within Euro-American and Native American cultures.

The late seventeenth century and early eighteenth saw a shift in Western elite cultures toward deism, toward anthropocentrism, toward the idea of impersonal order and the idea of a true, natural religion. As polite society developed and, as Hume put it, "the ideas of men enlarged on all sides," people developed what Charles Taylor calls a "buffered identity" arising from this disenchantment.[19] Most important, their new take on the life of the spirit removed them in part from their communities; it involved "disintricating the issue of religious truth from participation in a certain community practice of religious life, into which facets of prayer, faith, hope are woven."[20] Freemasonry both advanced and assuaged this lack because it reconstituted community but in a newly enlarged and specific way that encapsulated a refined set of spiritual beliefs at once both respectful of God and freed from the sectarianism and rigidity associated with the early Church.

In sum, Freemasonry can be seen as a development arising from the growth of capitalism, providing essential forms of brotherliness that by the late 1950s were available to the mass of American and European males. Freemasonry universalized the religious ethic of brotherliness, creating the potential for community, in terms of rhetoric at least, to become global, interdenominational, and cross-racial. It filled a gap pinpointed by Weber, who wrote, "The more the world of modern capitalist economy follows its own immanent laws, the less accessible it is to any imaginable relationship with a religious ethic of brotherliness. The more rational, and thus impersonal, capitalism becomes, the more this is the case."[21]

It is important to recognize that Freemasonry as a sanctuary for enchantment, for specific aspects of magical thinking, and for ritual developed in form and function at a time when all these things were being forcefully suppressed. To carry out this suppression, to replace, as Taylor put it accurately, "one constellation of implicit understandings of our relation to God, the cosmos, other humans, and time . . . by another in a multifaceted mutation," required violence both spiritual and physical.[22] Such suppression was zealously perpetuated by early Protestantism in the United States, and every effort made to ensure that religion displayed "no bodily ecstasies . . . no mortifications of the flesh, no demonic agency, and no hallucinatory provocations."[23] Indeed part of the reason Freemasonry has been so attractive to American conspiracy theorists may well have less to do with Masonry per se and more to do with a national cultural propensity that stems from this impulse and this period, a propensity to search out conspiracy whether it exists or not. As Robert Alan Goldberg and others have recently suggested, the urge to escape malevolent conspiracy (perpetuated by the English monarch, by the established Church, or by occult forces) can be said to lie at the very heart of revolutionary and Puritan America.[24] Furthermore, as the Shawnee-Lenape scholar Steven Newcomb has recently pointed out, the cognitive map that surrounded Christian settler language, with its binary demarcations contrasting "heathens" and "pagans" from Christians, was key to how settler communities justified Indian displacement and oppression and informed precisely how federal Indian law took shape.[25]

Contemporary sociologists and theorists are now returning to the idea of enchantment as something of continuing valence, with thinkers such as Zygmunt Bauman writing of a postmodern "re-enchantment of the world."[26] Yet in one sense magic never went away in Western-influenced cultures. As Marshall McLuhan explained in 1951 in his scathing critique of advertising, *The Mechanical Bride: Folklore of Industrial Man*, the economy of desire that underpins our current market system actually depends on the continual invention of newer and ever fancier forms of magic and enchantment. For eighteenth-, nineteenth-, and twentieth-century Masonic initiates, however, the magic of the Masonic lodge was more immediate, tangible, and real. Within the darkened recesses of the lodge they knew they were entering a separate reality. Deprived of literal and, they were told, metaphorical light, they would wait, surrounded by the hypnotic, low sound of men's voices chanting, singing, or reciting ritual language until their brothers deemed them ready to receive the sacred word, and with it perhaps the capacity to comprehend man's greatest secret, his own self.

Behind the Ritual

> It's Heaven to me, sittin' in Lodge again. It's all comin' back now, watching their mistakes. I haven't much religion, but all I had I learned in Lodge. . . .
>
> Then I realized for the first time what word- and gesture-perfect Ritual can be brought to mean. We all applauded, the one-footed Corporal most of all. It was a revelation.
>
> —RUDYARD KIPLING, "In the Interests of the Brethren"

> There is a strange and powerful attraction for some men in the mysticism of the ritual. There is a peculiar fascination in the unreality of the initiation, the allurement about fine "team" work, a charm of the deep potency in the unrestricted, out-of-the-world atmosphere which surrounds the scenes where men are knit together by the closest ties, bound by the most solemn obligations to maintain secrecy as to the events which transpire within the walls.
>
> —W. S. HARWOOD, "Secret Societies in the United States"

The difficulties for the modern reader of grasping the deep-set attractions of Freemasonry and its rituals have been much discussed. Jacob advises that to comprehend eighteenth-century Masonic life "the historian must assume a willing suspension of disbelief. . . . How else are we to understand why women and men would devote many hours a month, spend lavishly in the process, and covet the opportunity to participate formally in quasi-religious, yet secular ceremonies that we can only imagine as meaningful and satisfying?"[27] Her words perhaps apply equally as we look back over the nineteenth and twentieth centuries and the primarily petit bourgeois engagement of American males with the nation's preeminent fraternity.[28]

It is worth bearing in mind that the blossoming of Masonic rituals happened relatively quickly; by the mid-eighteenth century a system of thirty-three degrees was in place in continental Europe. The process whereby the original London Masonic degrees were adapted and developed as Freemasonry spread globally began very early on, but perhaps the overall high point of creative Masonic ritual complexity and proliferation came between 1840 and 1860 in the United States. This was a period of massive social and economic change, when men felt especially keenly the need for the compensatory feelings of control and self-mastery that ritual offered. After all, in ritual reality everything except spiritual boundaries is clear-cut and comprehensible. In this sense Masonic ritual offered "pure space," a calming sanctuary from a world that was increasingly changing and hybrid. Here we might usefully invoke Mary Douglas's characterization of ritual as generally working to contain fears of social formlessness, as offering an unsullied and abstract arena where participants might feel noble and unpolluted.[29]

Such an approach helps explain the Masonic ritual emphasis on death and symbolic rebirth and the fact that within the lodge a man was reminded of death's cold and ever-watchful hand and was "reborn" ritually into the warm embrace of fraternal community. Repeatedly Masonic rituals confronted initiates with death's degradations, surrounded them with its tools and symbols, and encouraged them to think hard on its inevitability and humbling spiritual message. Hiram Abiff's death and resurrection in the centerpiece of all Masonic ritual, the Third Degree, was a touchstone for the repeated figurative and spiritual death and resurrection of the fraternal member as he progressed through Masonic and certain other fraternal degrees. The deeper the initiate was plunged into the world of death and the more he was exposed to the funereal, to skeletons, daggers, and gruesome tools of execution, the more restorative and enabling his eventual symbolic rebirth would be. Thus the third degree candidate and his fellow lodge members repeatedly partook in a sort of theater of necromancy, with candidates "dying" as Hiram and being "reborn" as newly enlightened versions of themselves. It was a ritual tradition that invoked a seventeenth-century Western obsession with the recuperation of lost knowledge and other biblical traditions concerning raising the dead. As Vine Deloria Jr. points out, quoting Ake Hultkranz's work on shamanic healing and North American Indian concepts of the soul, a concern with reviving the dead and with the soul's relationship to the physical body also permeates a great number of Indian spiritual traditions.[30] Contemporary scholars of ritual have explained such an emphasis on death and violence by suggesting that it is a way of "mortgaging death" in uncertain times. Others, following René Girard, argue that incidences of contained ritualized violence may serve to inoculate the larger society involved against the outbreak of bigger, more destructive anarchic violence.[31]

Masonic rituals are constitutionally set (arguably in the American context since the publication in 1797 of Thomas Smith Webb's *Freemason's Monitor or Illustrations of Masonry*), but they are responsive to and, on occasion, capable of developmental change. Like certain Native American rituals they may alter and develop as their communities do. According to one Masonic historian writing in the 1920s, they were most "fluid" prior to the early nineteenth century.[32] Perhaps the obvious larger difference is that in many Indian cultures ritual roles are often inherited, whereas in the Masonic tradition ritual status is intended to reflect only individual merit. This individualism at the heart of the Masonic tradition to some extent conflicts with its fraternal ethos, but it points to a less obvious but more important contrast with aspects of many Native traditions. As Vine Deloria pointed out in 1973 in *God Is Red*, much about traditional Indian life is communitarian; ceremonies are undertaken not for personal spiritual advancement but for the good of the group, so that "the people might live," as the Lakota Sun Dance saying goes. Masonic ritual also binds together individuals, but it is as individuals that Masonic "work" is embarked on, and each Mason's journey is his own. Another key difference between Masonic ritualized dramas, especially in the twentieth century, and those practiced in a number of Native traditions is that Native ritual dramas tend not to have observers. Instead everyone participates. As Alfonso Ortiz reflected in 1972 of ritual drama in San Juan Pueblo and among Pueblo communities in general, "There are, ideally speaking, no observers, only participants. . . . The larger dramas, at whatever time of the year, are carefully orchestrated performances which require sustained action at several levels of society for their success, as well as the expenditure of many resources."[33]

How, then, can we make a new attempt to approach ritual, something most historians have found impossible to explain? After all, it has remained resolutely at the heart of Masonic practice over time, and the attempt to comprehend it seriously is both essential in this context and formidable. In anthropology the quest to understand ritual as a human activity has been fundamental to the field since its inception. It has been at the core of the work of anthropologists such as William Robertson Smith, Emile Durkheim, and James Frazer. In France it has preoccupied Arnold van Gennep and Claude Lévi-Strauss, in Britain Bronislaw Malinowski, Alfred Radcliffe-Brown, and Mary Douglas, and in the United States Roy Rappaport and Clifford Geertz. Yet understanding ritual is in fact impossible, because as Catherine Bell suggests, the conceptual tools we pick up to address the issue preclude us from arriving at an answer. Bell tells us that the very category "ritual" contains within it a dualism (thought versus action) that betrays the term's development as a category in Western intellectual life during a period when reason and science predominated.[34] Victor Turner, the anthropologist Mark Carnes drew upon in his analysis of Freemasonry, argues that ritual is not even a bounded phenomenon, that it is more a process than a set of events, that it is dialectical and performative, a vehicle for unfolding social dramas that express the deepest values of a culture.[35] What is certain is that ritual simply cannot be ignored; it is too important. According to Rappaport, it is humanity's "basic social act," the thing that gives life what he calls middle- and higher-order meaning. Echoing Durkheim, he has pointed out that now, in the information age, we need ritual more than ever because it alone is what makes us social, it alone transcends daily life and puts us into contact with realms of experience and feeling that unify the self with the Other.[36] Ritual broadly defined is the only thing, he argues, that creates the conditions for a social world as opposed to one that is purely governed by often grubby human self-interest.

To rephrase our initial question: What was really happening when Indians and non-Indian Masons undertook ritual activity and *made society* in the sense Rappaport suggests? In Malinowski's terms, ritual is primarily a means of generating optimism in the face of the inexplicable and the potentially insurmountable. Because Malinowski noticed that indigenous ritualists were generally highly practical people, he argued that the effort they put into ritual must be their way of reducing anxiety. This may be part of the truth, but Eric Hobsbawm probably set us on a more productive path when he highlighted the acute emotions fraternity as a phenomenon could conjure, its impact "uniting something like the sentiments of kinship, friendship and love in the heightened atmosphere of something like religion."[37] Certainly ritual has its own subjectivity and cannot reasonably be evaluated in the same way nonspiritual human activities are.

This becomes even more evident when we look at the nature of Masonic ritual specifically from the perspective of theater. Masonic ritual is "secret" in the sense that it is a theater for the self and only secondarily a performance for other Masons. In this way it is an inversion of the regular way of acting and of theatrical performance. As Alexander Piatigorsky points out to the would-be Mason, "Instead of playing other people's lives for other people (theatre imitating life, so to speak), you will be playing for yourself on the scene of your own life, acting in the play which is real only for you and not to an audience consisting of other people (life imitating theatre)." For example, in the Hiramic ritual of the third degree the initiate experiences the drama as himself in his own person, but also *as if he were someone else.* "He becomes another in the process of the ritual," Piatigorsky explains. "Thus, the candidate is 'tortured' as if he were Hiram, dies as Master Hiram died and, as a result, he becomes the Word and figures as Master Hiram from then on."[38] Or, to put what may actually be inarticulable another way, the Third Degree initiate is a performer acting as his soul is simultaneously suffering and developing. This is the critical difference between aesthetic theater and ritual: actors on stage must always seem to be the characters they play or they have failed; ritualists need only be what they are, as Victor Turner puts it, "frail human beings playing with those things that kill us for their sport." Thus ritual drama can have an immediacy and an all-encompassing personal impact that far outweighs anything theater acting can generate. This is because stage drama, as Turner writes, "is about the extrapolation of the individual into alien roles and personalities; ritual drama is about the complete delimitation, the total definition of person."[39]

Perhaps no Mason better summed up this complexity than the renowned nineteenth-century actor Edwin Booth, who wrote, "In all my research and study, in all my close study of the masterpieces of Shakespeare . . . I have never, and nowhere, met tragedy so real, so sublime, so magnificent as the legend of Hiram. . . . To be Worshipful Master, and to throw my whole soul into that work, with the candidate for my audience and the Lodge for my stage, would be a greater personal distinction than to receive the plaudits of people in the theatres of the world."[40] In the Masonic lodge Booth was not acting; as he makes clear, his whole identity, his very soul was engaged in "work" in a wholly separate category. It was this utter transformation that supposedly accompanied the enactment of Masonic ritual and justified the heavy theatricality employed by the Scottish Rite at the turn of the century. As one Michigan Mason explained in 1886, costume and solemnity were a requirement when men were in the process of embodying ancient patriarchs because, once engaged in ritual,

> the Worshipful Master is no longer simply the Master of a Lodge. The lofty teachings of the Order link him to the awful seat of Solomon, King of Israel. The Senior Warden is no longer there; it is Hiram, King of Tyre, the friend and bosom companion of King Solomon, the mighty builder.
>
> . . . A want of proper care and conformity in regard to clothing and ceremony detracts incalculably from the solemnity and impressiveness of the work in every degree, in every place, and at every time, and no eloquence of the ritualist can supply the lack or entirely atone for the incongruity.[41]

The specifics of Masonic ritual dramas, whether or not they invoke Indian themes or involve Indian initiates or officiates, are thus not completely amenable to the performance paradigm. After all, part of the intellectual attraction of viewing culture as the giving of performances is the fact that in doing so the researcher, historian, or theorist is repositioned to a place much closer to the action: he or she can legitimately draw up a chair before specific cultural events confident that his or her presence is a reciprocated and required part of what is being generated. If, however, what is being performed is primarily internal and spiritual, the observer is shut out. When applied outside specific Western contexts performance is fundamentally an analogy and a metaphor, useful for describing but not a passport to comprehending what can be understood only through experience. This connects to the problem Western theorists have come up against when encountering Indian ritual in general. Often indigenous participants believe that ritual will directly affect powerful spiritual and material forces such as harvests, disease, or enemies, but this is a belief most performance theorists, steeped as they are in rationality, however close they may become to the performance itself, cannot share. Masonic ritual claims only to make changes to the interior life of those involved, but this is still work that the observer cannot necessarily fully comprehend. In a real sense this is Masonry's greatest "secret," that the knowledge or awareness it possesses can be accessed only through the experience of ritual initiation, and as such, if it exists, it is uncommunicable.

We need to acknowledge therefore that we cannot confront the ritual act itself without experiencing it, but this does not preclude consideration in the broader sense of what is actually going on as ritual is enacted or created. Because the spiritual is inaccessible, a number of theorists have turned to its psychological aspects, arguing that it is a means of mitigating social conflict and of taking away the perceived need for violence. According to Turner, in ritual "norms and values, on the one hand, become saturated with emotion, while the gross and basic emotions become ennobled through contact with social values. The irksomeness of moral constraint is transformed into the 'love of virtue.'"[42] This aspect of ritual is obvious when we consider Indian and Euro-American interaction within Freemasonry, given that the need to find common ground to communicate without violence has always been important in settler history. A shared focus on a ritual reality and a mythologized Masonic past was one of only a limited number of ways whereby an Indian and a Euro-American elite could positively formally interact. While they were engaged in such cross-cultural activity conflict was averted and specific relationships and perceptions reinforced. As Steven Lukes explains, ritual in general "helps to define as authoritative certain ways of seeing society: it serves to specify what in society is of special significance, it draws people's attention to certain forms of relationships and activity—and at the same time, therefore, it deflects their attention away from other forms, since every way of seeing is also a way of not seeing."[43]

Ritual practice has this sort of political importance because, unlike adherence to written laws, it is very flexible. As Bourdieu and Douglas have pointed out, in one sense ritual requires a great deal of consensus for it to be undertaken, but at the same time it serves to cloak fundamental social conflict because it repeatedly affirms that larger, more significant loyalties are beyond question.[44] It is easily possible to engage in ritual without necessarily internally accepting its values as being exclusively legitimate (as was the case with so many early colonial Indian structural conversions to Christianity). In itself ritual is a form of power, but of a particular sort, one that can be appropriated by the individual. Masonic ritual was in all probability as diversely practiced in form and import as tribal ritualizations were and have been. No reasoned analysis can make blanket claims to ritual's universality, but it is possible to characterize Masonic ritual and ritual per se as a less encompassing or dominating form of social interaction and control than many other forms of power. As Catherine Bell explains, "In terms of scope, dependence, and legitimation, the type of authority formulated by ritualization tends to make ritual activities effective in grounding and displaying a sense of community *without* overriding the autonomy of individuals or subgroups." Ritual activity acknowledges larger, intangible forces than that possessed by any single sovereign nation, and its purpose, if we are to believe Bell, is essentially to reproduce itself, to create people who act in a ritualized fashion in relation to power.[45] Indians and Masons engaged in shared ritual were interrelating on a separate plane, one that generated and inscribed relationships that contained the potential for a degree of freedom. This is where ritual transcends performance, because ritual has the ability to create political relationships. Theater, for example, may comment on social relationships, but ritual has the capability, within limits, to actively develop them. As Rappaport explains, "If performatives are understood to be conventional acts achieving conventional effects then ritual is not simply performative, but meta-performative as well, for it not only brings conventional states of affairs into being, but may also establish the very conventions in terms of which those conventional effects are realized."[46]

The most useful theorist for thinking about Masonic and Masonic Indian ritual in this context may well be the anthropologist Gregory Bateson, who wrote on Balinese ritual prior to 1942. Bateson saw Balinese ritual as tending to create a certain kind of character that centered on a "steady state," as one critic recently put it, "a model of a living, thinking culture that survives via continual strategic re-organizations of non-progressive change."[47] Symbols were at the heart of Balinese performance just as they are at the heart of Masonic ritual, and I would argue that, as in Masonic ritual, the symbols invoked provided a platform for understanding all sorts of relationships. Within ritual performance symbols are capable of generating meaning in excess of what any one symbol might be deemed to represent; they can constitute a symbolic language, in effect. In the Balinese and the Masonic contexts ritual allows practitioners to be able to think through human relationships occurring beyond the confines of the ritual itself; the ritual provides through symbols a reasoning for relationships and a blueprint for human conduct. Not every ritual practitioner or contemporary observer may be aware of this impact, but, following Bateson, there is every reason to think of there being a continuity between the internal and external world of the ritual and an extension of the internal values ritual inculcates into the external values ritualists then consciously or unconsciously display.[48]

The Masonic writer who has been most expansive on the significance of symbols to Masonic work is Albert Pike, the remarkable frontiersman, lawyer, and reluctant Civil War general. Although Pike cannot be said to speak for modern Masonry, his thinking is certainly extremely significant, if not central to it. He held that Masonry was about the fundamental desire to attain truth. While the quest for truth is in itself a strong Protestant theme, Pike insisted that the way to reach it was not through any specific, concrete philosophy or theology but through the multivalency of symbols. Because he knew that there were "thoughts and ideas which no language ever spoken by man has words to express," he urged his fellow Masons to use symbols to access the "profoundest thoughts" of mankind. Like Turner, who explored the idea transnationally in the 1950s, Pike knew that symbols were flexible and capable of containing layers of multiple meaning.[49] The Masonic use of the swastika and the cross, for example, spoke to a sacred symbolism that long predated Christ and to symbolic meanings that link to Native American traditions, alongside those of

Arabia, Egypt, and the Druids. Pike spoke of Masonic symbols concealing rather than disclosing profound truths, which had always been hidden "under symbols and often under a succession of allegories: where veil after veil had to be penetrated, before the true Light was reached, and the essential truth stood revealed."[50]

Mark C. Carnes presents nineteenth-century Masonry's emphasis on death and omission of overt worship of a loving Christ as a more manly version or alternative to liberal Protestantism, but in fact Masonry can more easily be seen as a nostalgic reversion to pantheism and a reversion to the symbolic ritual at the heart of magic and the premodern world.[51] The world Masons reconnected with through ritual was often pre-Christian (King Solomon's Israel, King Cyrus's Persia, or precontact Indian America), a world replete with symbols, operating within its own symbolic time (every lodge came together at "daybreak" and ended at "dusk" irrespective of the actual hour), and the reason they sought it out was, as Pike put it in one ritual, in order to relearn sacred truths that had "faded out from men's souls before the world grew old."[52] Such a reversion may have been an unarticulated critique of "feminized" and Christ-centered Victorian Protestantism or a means of resolving varieties of gendered conflict within the wider society, but it may also have been just what it purported to be: a retreat into the mystical and spiritual realm where conventional understandings of gender and faith did not apply. When practicing lodge ritual at least, Masons chose experiences that reverberated in terms of certain traditional Indian worldviews and practices, in the sense that they were attempting to relate to sacred truths through symbols. Symbolism is not of course the exclusive preserve of Native peoples, but it is at the heart of much Native spiritual practice. As Richard Erdoes puts it, "We Indians live in a world of symbols and images where the spiritual and commonplace are one."[53] As I said in chapter 3, there is much to suggest that Freemasonry's ritualistic core is pre-Christian. "Its religion is that general one of nature and primitive revelation," Pike's powerful Masonic mentor Albert G. Mackey said, "—handed down to us from some ancient and patriarchal priesthood—in which all men may agree and in which no men can differ. It inculcates the practice of virtue, but supplies no scheme of redemption from sin."[54] A more modern author puts it explicitly: "Masonry resembles the mystery religions and as such represents, not Christianity, but a return to paganism."[55] Significantly this has always been a contention of the Catholic Church in its diatribes against the fraternity, as for example rather forcibly in Pope Leo XIII's *Humanum Genus* of 1884.[56]

This discussion of ritual theory as applied to the performance of Masonic ritual by Indian and Euro-American Masons might be summarized with the simple assertion that Masonic ritual and ritual per se are potent for practitioners both consciously and unconsciously because they create and develop society while allowing a significant degree of individual and political flexibility. Ritual's spiritual core we can neither access nor assess, but it is evident from Masonic testimonies over time that for many Masonry's spiritual dimension and their own individual progression through its forest of symbols was at least as important as its social and political elements. Freemasonry is British in origin and was predominantly white and Anglo-Saxon as it developed on American soil, but its cultural forms and ritual shared a great deal with other cultures. Indeed the Masonic respect for ritual has as many correspondences with the slippery Confucian idea of *li* as it does with anything from the Euro-American heritage.[57]

Throughout this book I have referred to Freemasonry as spiritual as opposed to religious because although a ritual-based practice, it cannot be termed religious without considerable qualification. That said, Freemasonry fulfilled much of what defines a religion according to the foremost thinkers on the topic. The definition Geertz used in 1973, for example, fits. He wrote that religion supplies a worldview (admittedly in Freemasonry's case not necessarily an absolute worldview) whose ethos "1) supplied a system of symbols which acted to 2) establish powerful, persuasive and long-lasting moods and motivations in men by 3) formulating conceptions of a general order of existence and 4) clothing these conceptions with such an aura of factuality that 5) the moods and motivations seem uniquely realistic."[58] Further, Masonic practice shares the characteristic Durkheim said was common to all religions: a sense of the "sacred" and the "profane." Since Masonry's origins non-Masons have been routinely referred to by those within the fraternity as "the profane."[59] Perhaps Masonry should best be thought of as a religion of the common man, at least in the nineteenth century, for repeatedly Masons have echoed versions of the phrase Kipling has one of his First World War soldiers say: "So far as I've had any religion, it's been all the religion I've had."[60]

Yet Freemasonry has never been a received religion since its chief organizational agents have tended not to proclaim it as one. Toward the end of the nineteenth century some Masonic writers did describe Masonry as a religion, but the more consistent argument from Masons has been that their fraternity served as a "handmaiden" to established faiths, capable of encouraging its brethren to serve as exemplars of their own religion while never actually replacing it.[61] Evidence from Masonic publications suggests that they found within the lodge a way to express a spirituality more compelling than traditional Protestantism and outside of sectarian boundaries. Dumenil suggests that in fact Masons found theirs to be a "superior" religion, but she also argues that by the end of the nineteenth century this sense had declined.[62] Bullock provides evidence that in the postrevolutionary era Protestant clergymen were increasingly joining the fraternity without qualm, and in turn lodges were increasingly attending churches in groups.[63] Although Carnes cites Albert Pike in *Morals and Dogma* stating that "every Masonic Lodge is a temple of religion; and its teachings are instruction in religion," Pike is unlikely to have meant that Masonry was in and of itself a religion, but rather that its lessons spoke to religious themes and prompted a better understanding of whatever faith the fraternal member pursued.[64] Instead, as Pike explains elsewhere in the same text, Masonry should be thought of as transcendent of specific religions and as speaking to truths essential to all mankind. His description of Masonry is close to Toland's pantheism and closer to ideas about man communing with nature than to any received faith. "Masonry, when properly expounded," he explains, "is at once the interpretation of the great book of nature, the recital of physical and astronomical phenomena, the purest philosophy, and the place of deposit, where, as in a Treasury, are kept in safety all the great truths of the primitive revelation, that form the basis of all religions."[65] Even so, if one *were* to view Masonry as being in competition with other faiths, there is evidence that by the early twentieth century there were more Masonic lodges than churches in all of America's large cities, and many Masonic writers, especially at the turn of the century, were explicit about the fact that although Freemasonry may not have been a dogmatic religion, it was a "mystic quest" to reach union with the Divine nonetheless.[66] Thus it was an ancient tradition, linked, as Pike put it, to the "sacred traditions of all the primitive Nations," unmediated by any priesthood and untrammeled by the conventions of any specific creed.[67]

Spiritually Freemasonry is syncretic, drawing on many religious traditions. Morality has always rested at its core, wedded to a tolerance of spiritual diversity expressed through charity. This morality is cosmopolitan; it presupposes that the imperative to moral action is universal and should be universally applied by a tolerant (but simultaneously exclusive) brotherhood. Although Masonic spirituality is inclusive (Masons meet "on the level" as spiritual equals), it nonetheless requires belief in a single all-powerful God, an omniscient deity invoked as "the Great Architect." Through Masonic ritual all Masons of whatever faith can be united in a common spiritual language that urges them to amity with fellow Masons and to charity within their communities. As the Masonic writer William Preston styled it in 1772, "The distant Chinese, the wild Arab, or the American savage, will embrace a brother Briton; and he will know, that, besides the common ties of humanity, there is still a stronger obligation to engage him to kind and friendly actions."[68]

According to Dumenil, it was Masonry's very commitment to ritual that eventually consigned it to ongoing decline. Though participation was at its highest in the 1920s, this was also when service clubs such as Rotary International (founded in 1905), Lions International (founded in 1917), and Kiwanis International (founded in 1915) began to seriously compete. They placed much less emphasis on anything serious but provided the same opportunity for good fellowship and fine dining. Dumenil argues that it was Masonry's "inability to jettison its religious component [that] left the order unacceptably out of step in an increasingly secular world and led to a decline in popularity and prestige from which it never completely recovered."[69] Certainly ritual and all forms of performance have fundamentally changed in status since Freemasonry's heyday. According to Turner, "true theatre" at its height allows for an interpenetration of the world and the self; it can produce a sense of ecstatic harmony with the universe such that "the whole planet is felt to be in communitas."[70] Today, however, in a world supersaturated with signs and images, performance of all types, including ritual, has lost some of its specialness. The dominant society no longer venerates it as being uniquely transformative. As Herbert Blau puts it, "At the level of community, whatever the powers of performance once were, they no longer are."[71]

Yet particularly for Scottish Rite American Masons at the beginning of the twentieth century the sense of theatrical specialness involved in taking part in ritual was intense. Right from entering the lodge anteroom, the candidate and his companions entered a different realm, signaled by their donning the costume appropriate to their degree event, be that the clothing of an ancient Jewish priesthood, the heavy chain mail of medieval knights, or the buckskin, loincloth, and cloak of noble Indian patriarchs. Modern readers brave enough to tackle the lengthy records of Masonic activity in this period usually marvel that so many men were fascinated by material that today seems so impenetrably verbose and dull. But men were fascinated by it, spent hours memorizing it, and relished acting out its stories. Within the lodge American men shared with traditional Indian cultures the different understanding of repetition, language, and sanctioned movement ritual requires. This tolerance for repetition and the ability to take pleasure in sometimes tiny variants from an established ritual theme was repeatedly commented on by early anthropologists visiting Indian country. Alexander Goldenweiser called it "involution"; William Fenton explained the way Iroquois ceremony could morph over time and yet retain its intrinsic character by writing candidly in 1953, "Persons living in such cultures develop a tremendous capacity for boredom, an ability to take the long view, to enjoy the long cycle of songs with very slight alteration in the stanzas or the melody. The individual Indian cherishes the variant of his home locality and he accommodates to other variants only to the extent that they are related or can be related to his own. So what the individual says and does is deeply rooted in his people's past."[72]

It seems that Masonry's oral tradition functioned similarly to oral traditions in many American Indian and non-Indian cultures and that Masonic sign language developed for the same reason Plains Indian sign language had in the nineteenth century. Anderson's *Constitutions* as revised in 1738 make explicit reference to "the *oral traditions* [of Masons] which was darkened by the blending of nations" and refers to "the Masons Faculty and universal Practice of conversing without speaking, and of knowing each other by Signs and Tokens . . . which became necessary because of confusion of dialects."[73] Indian use of signs is associated with the necessity of finding a means of communication across tribal boundaries, particularly on the Plains after Indian peoples were forced to journey ever further west to escape non-Indian encroachment in the nineteenth century. The topic has not received recent sustained academic attention, but it was a fascination when the discipline of anthropology was beginning in the United States, and its foremost student was the army man and ethnologist Garrick Mallery.[74]

The Masonic Journey

According to W. Kirk MacNulty, a key aspect of Masonry's attraction for thinking and spiritual men, as reflected in the symbolism of its tracing boards used as training devices for each degree, was the opportunity it offered the individual Mason to undertake an interior journey under the spiritual umbrella provided by his fellow Masons. Within his brotherhood and guided by his peers, he could travel in a metaphysical sense toward deeper understanding of the very essence of life. In fact, MacNulty suggests, this may explain Masonry's symbolic prioritizing of death and its paraphernalia, a motif especially clear in the third degree. Following

Renaissance thinking Masons perceived of themselves as psychologically or spiritually "dead," having lost consciousness of the Divine, a loss referred to in the biblical Fall. Something in the Mason's journey from East to West, in his journey through successive degrees and their associated rituals, would allow him once again to experience this original link with the Divine.[75] Bringing the Divine Spark into consciousness and in so doing developing as a powerfully spiritually aware individual was, MacNulty suggests, a key attraction of Masonic ritual.[76] In a book devoted to the topic, *Freemasonry: A Journey through Ritual and Symbol*, MacNulty expands on these ideas. He argues that the Masonic lectures that accompanied the rituals and their symbols never attempted to explain them; they merely referred the initiate to a wealth of Renaissance literature he could study. The point of Masonic ritual was the interpretation of its associated symbolism for and the application of its principles to the individual Mason's own life. The emphasis on the sensory was linked to an Enlightenment faith in the senses' power to instruct and to a Lockean understanding that deep knowledge was available through impressions gleaned from the senses. At the fraternity's heart is a discipline MacNulty suggests "we would today identify with Psychology—or perhaps with contemporary academic research into the nature of consciousness."[77] In general terms the psyche is represented by the Temple of Solomon, a three-story structure within which at the highest echelons one can become conscious of the Divine. These three levels of awareness, MacNulty argues, are analogous to Jung's psychological model—the individual consciousness, the personal unconscious, and the collective unconscious—but this is not the only aspect of Freemasonry that can be connected to Jung. The idea of "Masonic time," Masonry's emphasis on a separate, mythic history, and the thread of thinking traceable in Freemasonic writing concerning an essential masculinity, concerning an archetype of righteous maleness that alters only superficially over time, all seem Jungian in inspiration. Jung died in 1961, but in many ways his work integrates several aspects of Masonic thinking since the 1700s. Jung, it is perhaps worth noting, as a young boy was certain that within himself he had another, eighteenth-century identity, that of an old man.[78]

Thus the first three degrees, that of Entered Apprentice, Fellowcraft, and Master Mason, take a Masonic male on a spiritual journey toward mastery and maturity psychologically, from the ground floor of his psyche, which is in touch with the material world, to the upper floors of his unconscious, a psychological space deemed to be "secret" in the sense that it is only with psychological maturity that one can gain insight into it. Although there are variations within different Masonic traditions, the furniture of any lodge will always contain a composite symbol known as the Three Great Lights, namely, a volume of sacred law, the square, and the compasses, all of which collectively represent the three upper levels of the individual's metaphysical structure. Also key to Masonic symbolism is an idea of complementarity and of an essential duality in all things (which, among other things, explains the checkered floors in Masonic spaces). Furthermore in his ritualistic experience the Mason is introduced to Jacob's ladder, which symbolically offers a pathway from East to West toward the Divine, with its three principal rungs: Faith, Hope, and Charity. There is a great deal more to the symbolic world of Freemasonry, but even this brief outline gives a sense of what Masonic labor involves and another answer as to why Masons have always prided themselves on their contributions to charity: it is a direct reflection of their moral worth. Charity is axiomatic if the work of Masonry involves gaining self-awareness and a reflexive sense of how one's actions reverberate within one's community. Such powerful psychological effort should not be carried out alone. Those

Masons who took the fraternity's edicts seriously and set about sculpting their inner self no doubt very much needed the community of fellow Masons within their lodge to help them keep their feet on the ground. When viewed through this lens Masonic ritual is therefore much more than a psychological release from rigid social roles, more than a Turnerian liminal or liminoid state within an ongoing social dialectic.[79] It is a highly personal, inner journey experienced alone but within the warm embrace of the fellowship of one's lodge. In this sense it is the perfect antidote to the vapidity and weightless shallowness said to characterize modern life. Masonic ritual offers the potential for any unnerving spiritual hollowness experienced in the contemporary world to be replaced with an intensity rooted in the male self, a power and a consciousness that across centuries is held to have been generated by a man's fellowship with his peers.

On Death and Resurrection: The Third Degree

Even though various Masonic traditions have further degrees (up to thirty-three in the Scottish Rite, for example), the third degree ritual is generally recognized as the most significant. It centers on the ritual reenactment of the death of the Principal Architect, the least senior of the three Grand Masters at the building of King Solomon's temple. His ritual death is supposed to have happened when the "work [on the temple] was nearly completed," and because of his death the "secrets of a Master Mason" were lost, since they could be communicated only when all three Grand Masters were present and participating.[80] Essentially, MacNulty suggests, this ritual involves the initiate in a process of "dying to oneself" so as to experience or truly recognize himself as a spiritual being. It is a "trial" he alone can choose to undertake but that he can complete only with the help of the Divine. If and when the initiate does experience the transformation prompted by the third degree, it will happen in the course of "the ordinary duties of [one's] station in life." Thus the Master Mason aspires to a level of consciousness where he can truly make use of the Mason's creative symbolic tools: the pencil (creativity), the skirrett (a tool that reins in the pencil, standing for understanding), and the compass (a tool of proportion). As MacNulty puts it, the purpose of Craft Masonry (the first three degrees) is to create this sort of psychologically mature individual, "one who stands in the light of the spirit, with his feet on the ground of the everyday world and recognizes, in fact, the single, integrated manifestation of Divine will through all the worlds."[81] Furthermore the bizarre-seeming imagery of Freemasonry (for example in the diagram on the Masonic apron George Washington gave to Gen. William S. Schuyler, a member of his staff, in about 1770) is actually often a sort of technical drawing showing how Truth (and perhaps Faith, Hope, and Charity) can provide Masons with access to the Divine, with a means to build the "temple" of the human interior. Thus the "secrets" that a Mason might be said to possess are in fact the secrets of his unconscious and whatever knowledge he may have of the Masonic labor of any fellow Mason.

For the best of recent scholarship, however, this psychological reading has been secondary to viewing Masonry in general and the central third degree in particular as articulating the values of early capitalism. The Hiramic legend is viewed as an idealized defense of the individual private property inherent in the artisan's skill and as representing an idealized version of capitalist production and market relations. Such an approach downplays the spiritual and performative aspects of the ritual at Masonry's core. It also fails to account for the ebb and flow of the popularity of the Masonic message. But it does highlight the contradictions that Masonry helped to articulate and thus assuage. Clawson argues that the fraternity "maintained that the moral community that had been banished from the workplace could be successfully reconstructed in civil society and effectively used to alleviate the worst failures of the new social system. It was precisely the contradictory character of its message that gave Freemasonry its appeal as it entered the nineteenth century."[82] For Clawson, the craft aspect of Freemasonry is more than just symbolic; it speaks to a tension in the working man's world, a male need to gain access to the world of the traditional artisan, if only through sociability and ritual. Certainly there is much to suggest that following times of roaring economic expansion reverence for the artisan gets revived. The recent past provides a ready example: 2008 saw the publication of Richard Sennet's *The Craftsman*, which held up skilled labor as a means of resisting corporate mediocrity. The book appeared amid more widespread valorizing of the local, the slow, and the small after a period of globalization, massification, and change at unprecedented speed in many aspects of life in the developed world.

To some extent the centrality Masonry accords to death can be traced to its European and revolutionary beginnings. There was, for example, a cult of death in France in the nineteenth century, held to be connected to all the death brought about during the Revolution, causing a "necromantic" tradition within French Republicanism.[83] Yet perhaps it is more accurate to say that the idea of "personal death" and bodily resurrection is medieval. Certainly bodily resurrection is one of the three core beliefs of rabbinic Judaism, and it is a tenet of the earliest Christian creeds. Even so, as Philippe Ariès explores, the medieval stress on personal death developed in the context of a pre-Christian attitude that death was familiar and near, an expected part of life, even an event about which people were often forewarned.[84] It is probably more appropriate to view the Masonic obsession with death in this pre-Christian context, as an indicator of Masonry's actual or invoked pre-Christian roots.

When thinking about death and its meanings it seems unreasonable to ignore Sigmund Freud. Certainly the third degree ritual brings to mind Freud's theories about how collective order gets constituted and maintained.[85] He argued that ritualistic killing of a father figure (in this case the "father" of Masonry and original custodian of its secret truths, Hiram Abiff) lay at the heart of primitive society and that the attempt by the group's sons to atone for the killing inculcated community in the form of religion. Thus social bonds are generated by the quest to atone for an original act of violence against a father figure who symbolically binds all men in his wake to the task of making reparation for his death, which is repeatedly commemorated through ritual. It is a method of society-making Juliet Flower MacCannell calls "the regime of the brother." MacCannell, perhaps rather depressingly for pro-Masonic scholarship, argues that the post-Enlightenment stress on fraternity as opposed to a paternal monarch has over time led to all sorts of ills, from colonialism to totalitarianism and the nuclear world. She argues that in the brother's regime only an illusion of community was created, a means whereby the ego's inherent aggression toward the Other could be masked.[86] Of course in Freud's formulation the ritual killing of and reparation to the father were similarly illusory, an imperfect tool. Religion and its accompanying ritual only ever offered compensation for repressed instinctual sexuality, helping to redirect such energies into work and society. Thus religion, and here for the sake of argument we must include Freemasonry, was in Freud's analysis built on guilt over an original parricide. As Freud puts it in *Totem and Taboo*, "Society was now based on complicity in the common crime; religion was based on the sense of guilt and the remorse attaching to it; while morality was based partly on the exigencies of this society and partly on the penance demanded by the sense of guilt."[87] This is not the place to rehearse the avalanche of criticism that exists on Freud and his reliance on the idea at the core of this theory, the Oedipus complex, but it is still worth bearing all this in mind as we begin to think seriously about Masonic ritual and its attraction over centuries.

At least until the twentieth century, when the rise of individualism recast how death was perceived, the bulk of archived commentary shows that for the average Mason Freemasonry's open and candid talk about ritual was reassuring, as was the knowledge that his Masonic brethren would ease his passage into the next world through ritual.[88] For example, an optional lecture on the Entered Apprentice degree spoke of the solace of approaching death secure in the knowledge that as a man one had led a virtuous Masonic life and could therefore meet one's maker unashamed: "And after you have passed through the little change that men call death, and the Kindly Master of all good workmen shall call you from labor to refreshment and rest for a little while, before setting you to labor anew in some happier world and wider field of endeavour, you will enter upon the great adventure with light and joyous spirit and meet the Master face to face—a workman who need not be ashamed—a labourer worthy of his hire—a gentleman, unafraid." Indeed the initiate was encouraged to see his life symbolically as a single stone added to the great temple of Masonic activity across the ages. "The temple of speculative Masonry," the same source points out, "is erected by piling precept upon precept, symbol upon symbol, instruction, explanation, admonition, example and historical facts like a series of perfect and polished stones of which each brother is expected to furnish his quota, emblematically carved, marked and numbered to denote his talent and ability for the work, until a moral structure is erected, a Temple not made with hands, eternal in the heavens."[89]

As part of such an ultimate history the individual Mason could face death safe in the knowledge that he was both ritualistically prepared and morally worthy.

And yet here again is a Masonic paradox. Claims to moral rectitude notwithstanding, Freemasonry has always been about having a good time, about conviviality, eating, drinking, and bonhomie. Masonic literature has never hidden the fact that the fraternity has always made food, wine, and merriment central to its activities. In fact, as Jacob notes, one of the first identifiably Masonic tracts was the French *Essay in Praise of Drunkenness*. Even though Masons liked to contextualize it as part of brotherly harmony and unity, they generally wanted affluence in all its guises.[90] An organization devoted to often lavish consumption was also able to embrace rhetoric (including Rousseau) that called for a return to nature and to simplicity. Luscious banquets have for generations been part of the reason for Freemasonry's inherent costliness, since each time a candidate graduated to another degree (bearing in mind that by the time we reach the nineteenth century multiple membership in Masonic organizations or analogous groups was common) he was required to donate to the lodge, furnish the appropriate wardrobe and jewelry, and celebrate the occasion by contributing to a fitting feast. In this sense Freemasonry can be viewed as a symptom of excess capital in European and then Euro-American cultures, and its conspicuous consumption as much as its ideas and anachronistic practices indicative of a new political and civic hegemony. While early Masons may have been concerned to demonstrate their differences from court culture, with its emphasis on rank, ostentation, and overt hierarchy, the version of hierarchy they perpetuated within lodge walls was always dependent on privilege and, to a lesser degree, wealth.[91] Within Freemasonry at least, attaining moral and spiritual heights was compatible with exclusivity and luxury.

Indian and Masonic Themes and Correspondences

We should never underestimate the emotional pull of Masonic rituals, the intensity of the loyalty they could inspire. Sometimes sociability is about a wider range of human needs than we are able to re-create.

——MARGARET JACOB, *Living the Enlightenment*

Almost by definition people see rituals in which they do not believe or share as meaningless and absurd, while accepting their own rituals as belonging to a completely different category of meaningful actions serving real functions.

——DAVID STEVENSON, *The First Freemasons*

By their performances shall ye know them.

——VICTOR TURNER, quoted in Richard Schechner and Willa Appel, *By Means of Performance*

This section's title is something of a misnomer, for the correspondences that could be said to exist between Native American and Masonic life are links and resonances also shared by many other cultures in many other contexts. Even so some correspondences do stand out. A reverence for the sun and sun symbolism, for example, which in the Masonic context may have Druidic antecedents, is also found across Native America. In fact when the first pan-Indian organization was formed in 1911, the Society of American Indians, the sun (along with the eagle) was chosen as the symbol most commonly respected by multiple Indian communities. The Seneca Iroquois author, museum man, anthropologist, and high-ranking Mason Arthur Parker pushed hard for the sun symbol to be adopted, telling the respected Indian artist in charge of the project, Angel DeCora, that it was "distinctly Indian" and "a universal object of attention and was used by all the Indian tribes from Point Barre to Patagonia, and was revered as much by the Sioux and Iroquois as it was by the Mexicans and Peruvians."[92]

Another shared correspondence concerns respect for number and direction. Much has been written about the reverence for certain numbers and directions within a number of Native American heritages and traditions, about how Indian community life and with it Indian identity are intimately linked to and derive directly from space and place. The two are not directly comparable, but it is worth noting that Freemasonry also places great general and ritual significance on numbers, direction, and orientation and on places and spatial configuration. Places might not be "alive" in the same sense as in a number of Native traditions, but sacred power is located spatially for Masons, as opposed to primarily temporally, as it is in key European and Euro-American traditions. The number thirty-three has specific ritualistic significance in Scottish Rite Masonry, so much so that the lodge in Peoria made sure its rooms were precisely thirty-three feet in width, height, and length. The postrevolutionary Royal Arch degree invested the numbers three, seven, and nine with mystical significance, three being the number of the Trinity and nine its square. Numbers also govern the movements of actors in Masonic ritual, and the movements of Masons within lodges are governed by a mathematical precision of sorts, in particular in relationship to east and west.

Another Masonic-Indian correspondence discussed previously is the veneration both sets of cultures share for language. Masons called the rituals of identification and initiation the "Mason Word," connecting their activity to the almost magical qualities ascribed to God's word in John's gospel and in the Apocrypha, the Wisdom of Solomon.[93] Similarly in many Indian traditions language has transformative spiritual power, as do symbol and thought itself. In the words of the Kiowa author N. Scott Momaday, in Indian oral traditions "language bears the burden of the sacred, the burden of belief."[94] On the same theme Rasmussen in 1931 described the use of nonordinary language or powerful "magic words" among the Netsilik, Copper, and Iglulik peoples. "Magic words," he wrote, "descend from father to son, but may also be bought for a good price from a shaman. As soon as one has given away magic words, magic prayers, or magic songs to another, they only work for the new owner, who must never speak them where others can hear them."[95] When a culture discerns power in language, its protection takes on particular significance. The keeping of secrets, particularly the keeping of certain ritualistic secrets, has always been a facet of tribal life. In the years when Indian religion was under greatest threat, when its very existence was deemed evidence of insurrection and of flagrant disregard for the country's obsession with Indian assimilation to WASP mores, secrecy was vital to the survival of both Indian medicine and Indian lifeways.

In Masonry keeping certain words and bonds secret is a sacred undertaking, and writing down Masonic rituals is deeply transgressive.[96] Strangely, however, even though members have always been required not to discuss with nonmembers their experience of the fraternity's practices, in truth a great deal about Freemasonry has been well-known for a very long time. Indeed one could say that one of Freemasonry's most remarkable capabilities is its ability to spawn a series of often lucrative published exposés. Printed (sham) revelations go back as far as *The Post Boy* (1723) and still find a market today, even though anyone seriously interested in finding out the basics of Blue Lodge Masonry has been able to for centuries.[97] Following the Morgan Affair scores of books and pamphlets appeared revealing the supposed evils of the fraternity, and ex-Masons even reenacted their initiation ceremonies for money before the public. A great number of Masonic monitors containing instructions and extracted nonsecret sections of ceremonies, lectures, and rituals have also been available, including the well-known *Freemason's Monitor* by Thomas Smith Webb (1797).[98]

Given that key aspects of Indian ritual are sacred and secret and that Native American spiritual practice is extremely diverse and, like any other body of spiritual practice, has developed considerably over time, it is foolhardy to attempt to isolate each specific instance where correspondences with Masonry exist. However, a look at some of the close study done on the predominant Native peoples of the Northeast, the Iroquois, does suggest either that the anthropologists involved tended to interpret Indian ritual in Masonic terms or that a number of true correspondences actually exist. In looking at the Iroquois we perhaps inevitably have to rely on the most diligent non-Indian student and recorder of Iroquois ritual in the twentieth century, William N. Fenton. He published *The Iroquois Eagle Dance* in 1953, a ceremony he described as "regimenting all [Iroquois] ceremonies" and as being similar to ceremonies practiced by the Shawnee and Cherokee as well as many other Native communities. Although Arthur Parker described the Eagle Dance as "secret," Fenton seems to have found out about its outline easily enough.[99] In his book he is explicit about the importance of the spoken word and about the spiritual power attributed to specific words spoken in specific contexts. We hear of ritualistic objects passed down ceremonially across generations, as Masonic ritualistic objects were; of gifts and presents and food being distributed by those leading the ritual, just as Masons would service their own initiations and pay for the feasts and paraphernalia that accompanied their own progression through successive levels of the fraternity. We also learn of ritual being used to cure various negative mental states; Fenton is present at an Eagle Dance he describes as "the third attempt to find a cure for a troubled mind." Interestingly Fenton's Iroquois ritualists are aware that the costumes their dancers wear are not "traditional" Seneca Iroquois design; they wear Plains Indian headdresses and what he terms "'play' Indian costumes." What matters is ritualistic performance rather than strict adherence to specific aspects of practice. Thus the Eagle Dance could vary from place to place, and these variations, Fenton notes, were respected by those who practiced it. The ritual is conducted for the benefit of one individual, and the other roles, and their respective seating arrangements, are prescribed. Fenton explains that the Eagle Dance Society, like every other organization in Iroquois society, had its own "administrative functionaries," and women rarely spoke within it, even though politically Iroquois women have always taken on key roles. Just as in Masonry, the function of the Eagle Dance ritualism is to form and solidify relationships. As Fenton puts it, in common with the whole cycle of Iroquois war dances, the ritual is used to cement friendships or to create fictitious kinship relationships. He suggests that it is also used to ceremonially bring together father and son or cross-cousins and thus lessen the chances of war. Indeed he notes that kinship maintenance lies at the heart of all Iroquois ceremonial and political relationships: "The principle of fictitious kinship underlies adoption; it is at work in the concept of ceremonial friends; it is projected onto the tribal level in the Confederacy; treaties confirmed by wampum belts make kindred of contracting parties; and father-son and uncle-nephew relationships unite tribes participating in the widespread Calumet Dance."[100]

Fenton notes that the number four (and sometimes ten) is held to be special, and he provides evidence that the origin myth for the Eagle Dance ceremony came from the sun.[101] Direction is respected, just as it is in Masonic traditions. This is also the case in the more well-known Ghost Dance, a rite connected with the spirits of the dead; in the Longhouse tradition, according to the anthropologist Frank Speck, women sit on the western side and men on the eastern.[102] One of a number of linked medicine societies, the Eagle Dance Society had male and female members, who suffered "similar dreams or ailments which a clairvoyant has diagnosed as Eagle sickness."[103]

In terms of searching out Masonic correspondences with the Eagle Dance, perhaps most interesting is the first of the two origin legends with which it is associated, that of the Good Hunter called Bloody Hand, who gets restored by a council of animals. It is a legend that corresponds strongly with the narrative attached to the third degree ritual for initiates as Master Masons.[104] Parker writes of the Eagle Dance, "It is believed that the society holds in its songs the most potent charms known. It is said that the dying, especially those afflicted with wasting diseases, and old people, have been completely restored by its ceremonies. This is because the Dew Eagle, to which the society is dedicated, is the reviver of wilting things. The Dew Eagle refreshed the scalp of the Good Hunter by plucking a feather from its breast and sprinkling the scalp with the dew from the lake in the hollow of its back."[105] In the Iroquois context at least, resonances with Masonry would have been easy for fraternal members to discern.

The larger truth is that the majority of things that attracted Indian Masons to the fraternity were the same things that attracted any man. For example, Masonry offered to extend kinship relationships; within a guiding organizational metaphor of the family ("mother" lodges, "sister" lodges, etc.) the fraternity made "brothers" out of strangers. This would have attracted any number of non-WASP communities, Indian included. A number of Indian traditions used family as a means of structuring broader sets of relationships, as Lewis Henry Morgan found when he encountered the Seneca Iroquois in the mid-nineteenth century. He wrote in *League of the Ho-de-no-sau-nee, or Iroquois* that the league was "designed to be but an elaboration of the Family Relationships. . . . The several nations of the Iroquois, united, constitute one Family, dwelling together in one Long House; and these ties of family relationship were carried throughout their civil and social system, from individuals to tribes, from tribes to nations, and from nations to the League itself, and bound them together in one common, indissoluble brotherhood."[106] Of course Morgan was determined to fit the Iroquois and all indigenous peoples into a schema, a "family of man" that stretched over millennia, with white Anglo-Saxons at the vanguard. He relegated contemporary Indians to the past and argued that they were remnants of a distant "savage" stage of human development.

Yet in another sense Masonry was not about expanding relationships at all, but about limiting them, or at the very least setting boundaries to forms of sociability. It allowed for gregariousness and a form of egalitarianism, but in a highly codified and unique setting that was generally good for business. This betrays its English roots. As Paul Langford puts it in *Englishness Identified*, his study of early English character in the period when the English were setting about the tricky task of ruling the world, "Sociability as non-interference was an intensely English concept. The English manner was described as setting a kind of ring around everyone, within which it was possible to feel at ease." English clubs were described at the time as examples of social materialism, as a vehicle whereby the taciturn and exclusive English could make contacts but at the same time politely remain on one level, alone. As one commentator explains, the reason the English were routinely rude to strangers was because "the first maxim should be to know nobody by whom they are not likely to profit."[107] All of this can be traced to the stress over status caused by the onset of English legal equality and freedom. Lacking inherent rank, the English required some method of differentiation and exclusivity; to paraphrase Lionel Trilling, snobbery was something they were obliged to invent with the advent of bourgeois democracy.[108]

Although the form of Masonry's kinship-making ability was highly specific, it was nonetheless valuable. After all, what there was of an American social safety net, especially in the years between the Civil War and the Second World War, was provided by the insurance schemes, retirement homes, hospitals, and orphanages of fraternal orders. What reciprocity there was in an industrializing world increasingly bereft of such quid quo pro was found in Masonry and other fraternal associations. Men put capital into their lodges, literally by paying for life, accident, and health insurance and socially by forging and maintaining bonds with their peers. As David Beito points out, fraternities "successfully created vast social and mutual aid networks among the poor [and] facilitated a kind of coinsurance to mitigate local crises such as natural disasters or epidemics." He adds, "By joining a lodge, an initiate adopted, at least implicitly, a set of values. Societies dedicated themselves to the advancement of mutualism, self-reliance, business training, thrift, leadership skills, self-government, self-control, and good moral character. These values reflected a fraternal consensus that cut across such seemingly intractable divisions as race, gender, and income."[109] The twentieth-century boom in Masonic and fraternal organizational membership occurred at the same time as a durable boom in union membership, suggesting that fraternalism was meeting a more general need in this era for collective identity and collective protection from the vagaries of an increasingly volatile labor market. In the long term, however, this was to prove something of an organizational weakness. As the insurance needs of the average American were met by private firms and by government in the 1920s and 1930s, one of Freemasonry's key attractions melted away. Even so Freemasonry has always played a definite role on American soil in what might be called the politics of respectability. Membership tended to bestow good character on those who achieved it and facilitated a degree of social mobility, since a Mason is required constitutionally to help any brother Mason find employment.

Another meaningful attraction of Freemasonry was its educational role as a form of subgovernment within large systems of power. Historians were describing American associations in this way as early as 1829. William Ellery Channing described them as "a sort of irregular government created within our constitutional government," and Arthur Schlesinger said that voluntary association provided the American people "with their greatest school of self-government."[110] Masonry has always had an educational or at least personal developmental dimension. One historian of early modern Britain described early lodges as "memory theatres," "vehicles for the dissemination of the new natural philosophy and its applications," where "models were ritually copied and a shared cultural knowledge was created."[111] Another described early eighteenth-century Masons as "actively concerned with mental improvement."[112] Paul Elliott and Stephen Daniels provide evidence that scientific lectures were delivered in early British lodges and that Freemasonry played a significant role in the American colonies in helping to spread scientific ideas.[113] Particularly during the first third of the twentieth century fraternal lodges were "schools for democracy," inculcating business mores and teaching aspiring men about leadership and the mechanics of fitting in socially in an organization. William Muraskin points out with reference to Prince Hall Masonry that the lodge was a venue where black men could learn new skills and gain a new sense of themselves: "Masonry as an institution has been concerned with . . . inspiring and training its membership in leadership roles. Through the fraternity, members have learned to perform many bourgeois social roles with which they have limited or no prior experience. By teaching these roles, and by promoting an arena for their enactment, Masonry has worked to bring leadership potential within its membership to practical fruition."[114]

Over time the virtues Freemasonry instilled and the value it bestowed upon members were increasingly displayed publicly. Masonic parades were multifaceted events, at points echoing aspects of the military parade, emphasizing nationalism, in another sense operating as a sort of folklore procession, local with a gala atmosphere because of the outlandishness and anachronism of certain Masonic outfits.[115] Outdoor parades allowed Masons to conjure a Masonic world, imaginatively spreading the Masonic hierarchy beyond the confines of the lodge. Just as Mardi Gras Indians perform carnival on the streets of New Orleans and in so doing imaginatively re-create and repossess Africa, Masonic parades publicly create a world dominated by Masons, their values, and their largely (but not exclusively) white, Anglo-Saxon, Protestant constituents. Roach explains how Mardi Gras Indians "publicly imagine a space, a continent, from which the white man and his culture have vanished or retreated to the peripheries."[116] Similarly the panoply of Masonic ceremonies, including in the nineteenth century the laying of foundation stones and staging of events to demonstrate an intimate Masonic connection as patriots with the interest of the state, all served to inscribe a reality and a history unique to the Masonic worldview. Yet, as in all parades, the Mardi Gras and Masonic public activity masked a fundamental unease, for there would be little point in publicly parading one reality complete with costumes if that reality were already securely self-evident without the benefit to the imagination provided by the public event.

The Attractions of
Freemasonry to Indians
and Others, Part Two

6

"Masons in Their Hearts": Masons and Indians

The supposed correspondences between Indian spiritual life and life within the Masonic lodge have long fascinated American Masons.[1] The idea of such a link goes back at least far as an 1880 report by the Bureau of American Ethnology and Dr. J. Mason Spainhour's record of excavating Native burial sites in North Carolina. Noting the spatial orientation of the upright bodies and the "altar" and paraphernalia he found there, he was convinced "beyond doubt that these three persons had been buried by Masons, and those too, that knew what they were doing."[2] A more recent example of the same theme is Robert G. Davis's discussion "Analogies between Masonry and Indian Secret Societies" published in 2001 in the small but fascinating pamphlet *A Shared Spirit: Freemasonry and the Native American Tradition*. Davis is quick to displace the long-standing idea that Native Americans were precontact "Masons," but like so many Masonic authors before him, he acknowledges that there are remarkable similarities between Masonic practice and much traditional Indian practice. Indian secret societies, Davis tells his fellow Masons, "paralleled our own fraternity to an amazing degree," and portions of Indian rites are strikingly similar to Masonic degrees even though "it can be said safely that [Indian peoples] knew nothing of the Hiramic legend or the temple built by Solomon."[3]

Davis goes on to point out a number of structural similarities, including the fact that some Indian societies share with fraternal societies the idea of membership in one society being a prerequisite for membership in another and the fact that a number of Indian traditions are taught by "degrees." He cites the Midewiwin society of the Chippewa and their neighbors, "a secret society of four or more degrees, into which one could be successively inducted by the expenditure of a greater and greater amount of property on the accompanying feasts." The Midewiwin, or Grand Medicine Society, had its origins in the eighteenth century and, according to both Henry Rowe Schoolcraft and Christopher Vecsey, was an intercultural phenomenon blending traditional and Christian elements.[4] Even though it perpetuated various older traditions, Midewiwin was probably a postcontact religion. Like Masonry, it included reverence for a Supreme Being and had various origin myths that were acted out at each meeting. Echoing key elements of Freemasonry, especially the all-important third degree, Vecsey notes, "Its members met at ornate, scheduled ceremonies which featured the symbolic slaying and revivification of initiates in specifically designed lodges, using prescribed paraphernalia such as sacred seashells, animal-skin medicine bags, drums and rattles. Emphasizing the connections between morality and afterlife, a portion of its structure tried to guarantee the attainment of eternal rewards after death. The Society was also characterized by its elaborate pictographic records and hierarchical priesthood."[5] According to Schoolcraft, like Freemasonry, Midewiwin inculcated "national pride" in its members; it focused the southwestern Ojibwes on values like truth and morality and helped to cohere group loyalties.[6] It seems that this sort of comparison of Midewiwin ritual and Freemasonry was especially popular around the time of the Civil War, with figures such as the Cherokee journalist, novelist, and anti-abolitionist John Rollin Ridge writing articles on the topic for the *Hesperian* journal.[7]

Davis notes other analogies between Masonic and Indian practice, including the use of fraternal oaths and penalties, the use of passed-down regalia, the passing down of orally recorded songs and ceremonies, the use of specifically oriented lodges and reception rooms, the use of catechisms and the delivery of lectures to initiates for degrees, a shared Masonic and Indian belief in a Supreme Being (or Chief Architect), and, most particularly, the shared belief in immortality and the shared ritualistic emphasis on resurrection notable in the Ghost Dance of the late nineteenth century. Davis finds other key Masonic themes in a variety of Indian groups. The Masonic emphasis on charity as a prerequisite for fraternal membership he finds in the Omaha Honhewachi society; the idea of brotherhood he equates with the more general traditional Indian idea of the essential kinship between all things, animate and inanimate. The Masonic reverence for sacred words and secrecy he links in particular to Iroquois ritualistic practice, discerning similarities between the Iroquois word for the Great Spirit as cited in Pretre de St. Sulpice's *Lexique de la Lange Iroquoise* and that used for the Great Architect by Masons. The respected Oklahoma Mason Jim Tresner also discusses the spiritual similarities between Indian and Masonic practice. He is quick to point out that Indian medicine men or shamans do not serve as religious intermediaries in the way that Protestant ministers might do.[8] Rather he compares them to those who fulfill the role of Senior Deacon in the Masonic lodge, facilitating "rebirth" and leading the initiate from darkness into light.

Most Masonic writings on Indians since the mid-nineteenth century have followed the same pattern, opening with a denial that Indians possessed innate Masonic knowledge prior to contact, then exploring at length a number of correspondences between various Indian and Masonic ritual practices, before finally concluding that Indian Masons do indeed have a special purchase on and understanding about Masonry at its ritualistic core. A good example is the regularly reissued *Indian Masonry*, originally published in 1907, by Robert C. Wright. In its way the book is pro-Indian, opening with a plea that non-Indians not judge all Indian peoples by those suffering few they may have met. Wright asks his readers, "Suppose a race came here able to overpower us. The brightest and best of our kind, if unable to join that race, would be irresistibly driven, little by little, farther and farther away, leaving behind renegades, criminals and toughs, the very offscourings of our civilization." He argues that the "white man" and the Indian are essentially the same, separated only by degrees of education. For Wright, Masonic impulses are universal and Indian kinship essentially similar to Masonic fraternalism. He wrote of "an interesting institution found among the Wyandottes and some other tribes—that of fellowship. Two young men agree to be friends forever, or more than brothers. Each tells the other the secrets of his life, advises him on important matters and defends him from wrong and violence and at his death is his chief mourner. Here are, in full reality, all the elements of a Masonic lodge. Those men were Freemasons in their hearts."[9]

Wright reminds his readers of the edict that Masonic brothers should regard "the whole human species as one family" since the fraternity "*unites men of every country*, sect and opinion and causes true friendship to exist among those who might otherwise have remained at a perpetual distance." Ignoring the diversity of Indian communities, he writes in social Darwinist and racialist terms, reiterating the centuries-old idea that "the Indian is a great actor" and registering amazement at the "startling likeness" of Indian signs to "ancient Masonic symbols." He writes of "the smoldering savagery within the white man's breast" and of the correspondences between Indian medicine, Christian scripture, and Masonry.[10] A particular focus is the shared notion of the "raising" of spiritual bodies up steps, as with the Masonic use of Jacob's ladder. He equates the Masonic belief in the West as the direction where a brother finds rest and the ultimate payment of wages with a Creek belief in the West as the direction the spirit travels toward to join its ancestors. He lists the directional reverence in terms of the orientation of communal buildings shared by Masons and Indians (presumably Iroquois) and devotes a chapter to the Masonic and Indian reverence for the number four and for the swastika as a spiritual symbol.

Wright reserves the most space for a discussion of the "Grand Medicine Lodge of the Ojibwa Indians," basing his description on Midé testimony given in the distant past (probably following treaties made after 1854 or 1867) to a Dr. Hoffman of the Bureau of Ethnology after the Ojibwes (Anishinaabes) moved to the Red Lake and White Earth Reservations. His source was probably Walter J. Hoffman's "The Mide'wiwin or 'Grand Medicine Society' of the Ojibwa," which appeared in the seventh annual report of the Bureau of Ethnology in 1891, edited by its founding director, John Wesley Powell. In Wright's comparison of Anishinaabe practice with Masonic practice the resonances and correspondences would have been familiar to any Mason: the use of initiation into successive ritualized degrees, with accompanying symbols and artifacts or teaching tools; emphasis on the shape, orientation, and dimensions of the lodge itself; the unintelligibility of the rituals to the uninitiated; the increasing cost of successive initiations; the use of ritualized language; and reverence for a "Great Spirit." The third Anishinaabe degree Wright presents is especially close to the Master Mason ceremony, with the initiate "falling forward apparently unconscious" only to be rejuvenated by his friends. Wright was under the impression that the Anishinaabe rituals detailed by Hoffman limited the roles available to women, even though available evidence points to the contrary.[11]

Wright devotes another chapter to Zuni fraternities, which, like the Masonic "reunions" of his era, continued for four days. But it is the Midé ethnology that most fascinates him, from their use of "sacred migis," so like Masonic jewels, to the similarity of Masonic roles with those of Midé shamans. He ends with a message of inclusion, even though throughout his discussion he failed to take on board the larger processes of assimilation, adaptation, and miscegenation that would have upset his depiction of Indians as homogeneous and innately savage "red men." Instead he reminds his readers that modern Masons under the veneer of civilization are themselves very close to savagery and, as such, very close to being Indian:

> The Redman in his simple way, with a fair chance, will display all the good qualities of faith, hope and charity, brotherly love and relief. There are, no doubt, among them those who know the inmost soul and the Grand Architect, far better than many a man of quick business brain, who swiftly hunts the almighty dollar upon shifting sands, in the teeming marts of this mind-straining country, but who has no time to take thought of nature, or nature's God, or the duty he owes to his fellow man. Shall we Masons, who tell the E.A. [Entered Apprentice] of the universality of Masonry, dare to say that the Indian is not a Mason?[12]

The best of human qualities and especially the deepest spiritual truths were, according to Wright, known to Masons and, among all of America's ethnic groups, also to a few select Indians. His was an essentially nostalgic notion of Indians as spiritual giants but also as developmental pygmies, trapped in a stage of evolution through which their non-Indian fraternal brothers had long passed. Wright was able to include Indians within his fraternity because of the very specific qualities of what Masons term "Masonic time," wherein time is transcendent and measured solely in terms of man's spiritual journey toward the Great Architect and brotherhood is the best means to achieve that end. For example, a man completing the Scotch Rite Fourth or Secret Master's Degree has reached the symbolic age of eighty-one, and the lodge is therefore lit with eighty-one candles.[13] The Masonic sense of time is reflected in its many symbols of mortality, including the coffin, the hourglass, and the scythe, and in its use of symbols of eternity (∞) and of resurrection, such as the pentagram and the pyramid. To Wright, Indians and others across history were able to access Masonic verities because they have always been available in Masonic time and a vast collective unconscious. As he puts it, "'Tis the brotherhood in man which makes us reach forth in a firm belief that there is something, an innermost personality, which outlives our present and carries it into another world. This thought is spread amongst all mankind and is inborn in the human mind. It is well proven that the mind of man is but a common substance, and thoughts and ideas of the same kind flow freely throughout the vast sea of mind, divided only seemingly by bodies which are like vessels holding but portions of that which is in fact joined as of the whole."[14]

The Pocahontas Syndrome: Emblematic Indians
in *Freemasonry and the American Indian*

One of the few publications that exclusively concerns itself with Native American Freemasonry is *Freemasonry and the American Indian* (1956), written by the prolific Missouri Masonic writer William R. Denslow.[15] At its heart is the idea that Masonry provides more than a conduit for intercultural exchange, the idea that repeatedly Masonic affiliation puts men in touch with a higher realm that causes them to prevent conflict across Indian–Euro-American divides. Perhaps predictably no similar Masonic text exists on interaction between black and Euro-American Masons, although leading black intellectuals in the emancipation era did make claims that Masonry on occasion caused white men to act outside of the imperatives of slavery and white supremacy.[16] In contrast, in Indian Masonic rescue stories the larger social, political, and colonial context of Indian and Euro-American interaction in war is elided and Masonry put forward as a way whereby good Indian Masons, or "proto-Masons" somehow capable of understanding a Masonic signal of distress, are able to save the lives of their non-Indian fraternal brothers. Like Pocahontas, the iconic supposed Indian protectress of a European male, time after time the Indian Mason is portrayed as having stepped outside of his own cultural context, as having seen the error of Indian violence and therefore saved the life of a European "brother."

Like the Pocahontas story, such stories of Masonic rescue are mythohistoric facts that speak more accurately to what Euro-Americans would prefer to be true rather than to anything conventionally verifiable. Just as there is no consensus among historians as to what actually happened between Pocahontas and Capt. John Smith when he was interned, we will probably never know whether the occasions when Indian Masons saved their Euro-American brothers ever actually happened.[17] These rescue stories circulate, echoing the message of the imposing 1837 statue *The Rescue* by Horatio Greenough, placed at the eastern front of the U.S. Capitol, as testimony to the rectitude of white ways. They suggest that through Masonry the best of the Indian race saw the inevitable superiority of white thinking and the appropriateness of ensuring white survival. Similarly Greenough's statue suggests that the rescue of whites and indeed the rescue of Indians from their own savagery is inevitable, even preordained.

For the same reason, older Masonic sources such as Mackey's *Encyclopedia of Freemasonry* cite a long list of Indian Masons who were also cultural mediators known to have either adopted non-Indian lifeways or saved fellow Masons in distress or who were recognized as political power brokers useful to non-Indians.[18] Aside from a number already mentioned, these include Joseph Brant's contemporary, the Seneca diplomat Red Jacket (Sagoyewatha, ca. 1750–1830), the revolutionary-era "Munsey" Delaware John Konkerpot (d. 1835), and the Ojibwe George Copway (Kah-ge-ga-gah-bowh, 1818–69), whom MacKay describes as "an ardent Freemason." A Methodist minister, Copway was also a historian, biographer, speech writer, and essayist who wrote one of the first American Indian autobiographies, *Life, History, and Travels of Kah-ge-ga-gah-bowh* (1847). It is possible he gained his exposure to Freemasonry just as he was writing his autobiography given that he received his degrees in Federal Lodge No. 1 in Washington DC sometime prior to 1848.[19] In his *Life* Copway describes the Ojibwe company who took degrees in the Grand Medicine Lodge, or Me-tac-we-gah-mig, and explicitly compares it to Freemasonry: "There were four grades in the institution; and as I have often thought, somewhat similar to the Masonic institution." Each element of the Ojibwe company Copway describes would have been familiar to fellow Masons, from the use of directional space to practices "done to deceive the ignorant," the teaching of the "science of medicine," instruction on morality, the importance of silence, and the significance of charity. Most significant, Copway describes the promise at the heart of the Ojibwe medicine group as being exactly that of third degree Masonic teaching: "If you are a good hunter, warrior, and a medicine man when you die, you will have no difficulty in getting to the far west in the spirit land."[20] Mackey also lists as Masons the Pottawatomi Shabbannee, credited with saving the early settlers of Chicago from the

Sauk leader Black Hawk; the Cherokee leaders John Ross (1790–1866) and his strong supporter Jesse Bushyhead (1804–44); the Creek principal chief Pleasant Porter (1840–1907), who is listed elsewhere as having attained the thirty-third degree;[21] the Chickasaw Gabe E. Parker (b. 1878), register of the U.S. Treasury in 1913–14 and superintendent of the Five Civilized Tribes; and the Pawnee James Murie and the Sioux Amos Onerod (Jingling Cloud).

Although Denslow was sure of the Masonic heritage of those he listed, he was aware that most of the Masonic Indian rescue stories he compiled had dubious roots. He noted that many concerned the western plains and happened between 1848 and 1855. Thus they may well have served to lend glamour to a crossing that was either uneventful, unsuccessful, or both. In fact such stories were so plentiful that Denslow quipped, "*If you had not* crossed the western plains without being assaulted by Indians, given a Masonic distress sign, and finally saved, you were an exception to the rule."[22] The most unlikely Masonic rescue stories of all concerned the fierce defender of Indian lands, the Shawnee leader Tecumseh (1768–1813). Perhaps the virulence of Tecumseh's hatred for non-Indian incursion into Indian lands and the power and efficacy of his attempts to protect his people from all things non-Indian made the myth of his Masonic brotherhood all the more attractive. It made the desire to see a higher Masonic force at work, to see an essential kinship operating above and alongside the sordid realities of ethnic annihilation and strategic warfare even more acute. Thus Denslow, aware of how far such tales were likely to be from the truth, still quotes senior mid-nineteenth-century Masons recalling Tecumseh's attention to his "Masonic obligations":

An officer, in a skirmish with a party of British and Indians, in the late war (1812), was severely wounded and unable to rise; two Indians rushed towards him to secure his scalp as their prey; one appeared to be a chief warrior, and was clothed in British uniform. The hatchet was uplifted to give the fatal blow—the thought passed his mind that some of the chiefs were Masons, and with this hope he gave a Masonic sign—it stayed the arm of the savage warrior—the hatchet fell harmless to the ground—the Indian sprang forward—caught him in his arms, and the endearing title of Brother fell from his lips. That Indian was Tecumseh.[23]

Denslow then adds to Mackey's outline of notable Indian Masons by providing details of Masonry's significance in a long list of Indian lives, men such as the "honorary" Creek Cherokee revolutionary war leader William Augustus Bowles (Estajoca, ca. 1764–1805), the Choctaw leader Peter P. Pitchlyn, the Cherokee supreme court judge David Carter, and Pushmataha (1764–1824), the Choctaw military and spiritual leader and diplomat. Masonic history in Indian Territory owed most to the Cherokee, and so Denslow devotes space to those noted men involved with its first lodge: John Ross and his nephew William P. Ross; David Carter, lodge treasurer; and G. W. Adair, John S. Vann, J. Foreman, and J. M. Lynch. He goes on to list noted Creek Masons, including the supreme judge George W. Stidham and the mixed-blood Creek Seminole Brig. Gen. Alexander McGillivray (Hippo ilk Mico, 1750–93). Consistently he avoids commenting on the forced removal of Indian communities these mid-nineteenth-century Indian Masons were much involved with, or that removal (or as Denslow terms it, "relocation") occurred in spite of the fact that some of these communities and their leadership had heavily assimilated American mores. Instead removal is presented as a sad inevitability and the factionalism that arose among Indian communities as a result of broken treaties due to "old wounds." Freemasonic principles and influence are put forward as Indian communities' "greatest healer." For Denslow, Masonry in Indian

Territory is somehow wholly separate from the suffering and death that resulted from forced migration imposed by American authorities. It is an unmitigated good epitomized by heartwarming stories of compassionate American Masonic soldiers sharing their rations with starving Indian families.[24]

Although published in 1956, Denslow's book teems with the sort of social evolutionary thinking that informs its two main anthropologist-archaeologist protagonists, the Seneca Iroquois Arthur Caswell Parker (1881–1955) and his fraternal brother and friend Alanson Buck Skinner (1886–1925). Alongside much discussion of what the author calls "the Red Man's mind" we learn, for example, that only the most intelligent Indians had the good sense to become Freemasons: "The more intelligent Indians came from a limited number of nations. First were the Iroquois of upper New York; another group was the Five Civilized Tribes that were moved bodily from the southeast United States to Oklahoma Territory. These Indians readily adapted themselves to Freemasonry and hundreds of them were initiated into the order in early years."[25]

Both Parker and Skinner were dedicated Freemasons, Skinner within the York Rite and Parker within the Scottish Rite, where he gained its highest degree, the thirty-third, conferred only by election by the body's Supreme Council. Both learned their intellectual orientation from F. W. Putnam of the American Museum of Natural History in New York and from the work of the social evolutionist (and play-Indian fraternalist) Lewis Henry Morgan (1818–81). Skinner wrote extensively on Indian spirituality and culture, with a particular focus on the Menominee of Wisconsin, and worked for the American Museum of Natural History and later for the Museum of the American Indian, Heye Foundation, New York. Not a Native himself, he was nonetheless adopted by the Menominee, married a Wyandot woman, and was given a Wyandot Deer Clan name. Parker, by comparison, was of at least one quarter Seneca Iroquois extraction and claimed a long line of illustrious Iroquois ancestors. These included, four generations back, the Seneca prophet Handsome Lake (1735–1815); his half-brother, the leader Cornplanter; a paternal great-grand-mother descended directly from Jigonseh, the "Peace Queen" of the Neuter Nation, who was instrumental in the founding of the great Iroquois League around 1525; and Old Smoke, or Gaieng-watoh, who led the Seneca at the Battle of Wyoming, Pennsylvania, in 1778. Arthur Parker was at pains throughout his life both to connect himself to this noble lineage in Iroquois history and to connect the Iroquois and all Indians to the best of modern American society, Masons included.[26] It is from Parker that much of the printed Masonic assertions that Red Jacket was an Entered Apprentice Mason stem. Parker also claimed that his grandfather, the Mason Nicholson H. Parker, was a grandnephew of Red Jacket. The family was particularly proud of a large oval, silver medal (which Masonic sources claim as Masonic) that belonged to Red Jacket and passed down the family tree to Ely S. Parker, also Red Jacket's grandnephew.[27] This 1792 Peace Medal was hand-engraved by the silversmith Joseph Richardson of Philadelphia and was given to Red Jacket by American Freemasonry's preeminent figure, George Washington. Red Jacket's skill as an orator would no doubt have impressed Masons of the time, and there is much about his stance that complements aspects of Freemasonry. His reported speeches were habitually prefaced "Brother" (although this was a convention of the time), he consistently advocated Iroquois neutrality between the United States and British Canada, and he made eloquent pleas that religious tolerance be extended to his people.

Parker's contribution to the Masonic lore about an inherent Indian Freemasonry was considerable. He lent his imprint as an eminent authority on the Iroquois to all of the old Masonic Indian suppositions, and he was careful to couch as much as was appropriate of what he said publicly in language with specific resonance for Masons. In Denslow's book, for example, he is quoted describing the use by Indian secret societies of sacred and jealously guarded "lost" words delivered only within the lodge in a low voice. His objective was to advance the idea that Indian peoples had always been like patriotic Masons, fraternally minded, morally upstanding, in mystical and philosophical communion with nature; significantly he insisted that those who were involved in ritual and fraternal activities were likely to "constitute a dynamic influence" in their communities.[28] Although Denslow and Parker never met, they corresponded extensively, and Parker had oversight of Denslow's work prior to publication. He was delighted that Denslow was foregrounding Masonic Indian life and shining a spotlight on modern Indian success stories, writing to the author, "We just don't know our Indians, thinking of them as they were in 1492 and not in terms of three centuries of acculturation."[29]

Exemplary Masonic Indians: Arthur Caswell Parker and Ely S. Parker
In many ways Arthur Parker (1881–1955) spent his life attempting to emulate the version of Indianness and Masonic virtue he felt was epitomized by his great-uncle Ely S. Parker (1828–95). A lifelong and illustrious Mason, Ely was "raised" in 1847 at Batavia Lodge No. 88, then founded Miner's Lodge No. 273 in Galena, Illinois, and served as its first Master from 1858 to 1860; he then became the first Master of Akron Lodge No. 527 in 1863. He was named Grand Orator of the Grand Lodge of Illinois in 1861, had Ely Parker Lodge No. 1002 named after him, became a high priest in Royal Arch Masonry, and was also a revered Knight Templar, giving his name to Ely S. Parker Council No. 60. For Arthur Parker, Ely's life story mapped a mixture of patriotism, worldly success, inherited status, and talent justly rewarded that he ardently but mistakenly hoped would also characterize his own life.

Remarkably for the time, Ely was able to achieve high rank both within his own Seneca Iroquois society and within American society more generally. In 1852, at only twenty-three, he inherited the grand sachem title Do-ne-ho-ga-wa, Keeper of the Western Door of the Iroquois Confederacy. He used his excellence as an interpreter, scribe, and orator to fight for Tonawanda Seneca land, facilitated Lewis Henry Morgan's anthropological researches, and supervised the civil engineering at Galena. Befriended by Ulysses S. Grant, he had a good war, was commissioned in 1863, and became Grant's military secretary. His commission came about through Gen. J. E. Smith, whom he had earlier raised as a Master Mason in the Galena lodge. Ely can be seen in many representations of Grant at Appomattox, including in Mathew Brady's photographs. After the war, in 1869, Grant made him the first Indian commissioner of Indian Affairs. Perhaps surprisingly, once in office he behaved just as any paternalistic white official might have, advancing Grant's "peace policy," withholding Indian rations when he saw fit, and working to end the treaty-making system. His career ended in ignominy when he was subjected to a highly political investigation for fraud by the House Committee on Appropriations, but he always remained proud that he had avoided the United States having to fight expensive Indian wars and that he had moved tribes closer to autonomy and "civilization." Sadly he ended his days surviving on handouts and favors from old friends from his military days.

Like Arthur, Ely saw Masonry as a unique sanctuary within American society where racial prejudice against Indians did not impinge (although neither figure had any truck with the idea of black Americans having an equal place within Masonry or within society outside of it). He also saw Masonry as the final resting place for Indian forms of kinship and ritual and Masons themselves as the future custodians of memories about Indians and their terminal decline.

Ely Parker's is one of the strongest testimonies we have of Masonry's ability to rescue Indians from modern racism, in contrast to the long list of Masonic stories about Masonic Indians rescuing Euro-American Masons from Indian savagery in war. He told fellow Masons at a banquet marking the triennial meeting of the Grand Chapter and Encampment of the United States in Chicago in 1859:

> Where shall I go when the last of my race shall have gone forever? Where shall I find home and sympathy when our last council fire is extinguished? I said, I will knock at the door of MASONRY, and see if the white race will recognize me, as they had my ancestors, when we were strong and the white men weak. I knocked at the door of the *Blue Lodge*, and found brotherhood around its altar. I knelt before the Great Light in the Chapter, and found companionship beneath the Royal Arch. I entered the Encampment, and found valiant Sir Knights willing to shield me there without regard to race or nation. I went farther. I knelt at the cross of my Savior, and found Christian brotherhood, the crowning charity of the Masonic tie.
>
> I feel assured that when my glass is run out and I shall follow the footsteps of my departed race, Masonic sympathies will cluster round my coffin and drop in my grave the evergreen acacia, sweet emblem of better meeting. If my race shall disappear from this continent, I shall have the consoling hope that our memory will not perish. If the deeds of my ancestors shall not live in story, their memories remain in the names of your great lakes and rivers, your towns and cities to call up memories otherwise forgotten.[30]

Ely was speaking in the "Indian" idiom most available to him at the time in Euro-American discourse, a rhetoric of Native doom. Maureen Konkle points out that this was almost inescapable for educated Indians addressing Europeans publicly after 1840 in light of the weight of the hegemonic consensus of the time that the Indian racial group was destined to disappear. She argues that for Ely to be accepted and heard at all he had to accept the demise of his racial group as a given even though the stellar social and educational performance of his own thriving family over time belied the whole premise of a "vanishing Indian race."[31] Such an approach is problematic, but it at least allows assimilated Indian figures like Ely Parker to be considered in historical analyses rather than, as has tended to happen in the past, be dismissed as benighted and somehow "unIndian." As the historian Arif Dirlik reminds us, if we hold to the idea that indigenous or colonized peoples are most authentic when they are least engaged with all things European, we deny their experience in time.[32] We write as white their active responses to what were at points insurmountable challenges to the expression of indigenous identity.

While the quote from Ely cited above is relatively well known, what he did and said immediately afterward is not. According to Masonic sources, he shared with his fraternal brothers the Masonic Red Jacket medal and in so doing made a link across time with his Masonic brethren, presenting a tangible Masonic thread that ran from Washington in 1792 down through generations of his family to his fellow Masons in 1859. He presented a symbolic artifact that spoke to an abiding peace between American Masons and Indians and which in that sense suggested another history entirely from that of the contemporary rhetoric about disappearing Indians. The *Freemason's Monthly Magazine* described the occasion in 1863:

> Few eyes could withhold their tears as he poured forth in words like these the utterance of a full heart. Silence for a time prevailed after he sat down, when he arose and said:—"I have in my possession a

memento which I highly prize; I wear it near my heart. It came from my ancestors to me as their successor in office. It was a present from Washington to my grandfather, Red Jacket, when your nation was in its infancy. You will be glad to see and handle it, and I should do no wrong to give you the opportunity." As he spoke thus he removed the wampum from his neck, and drew from his bosom a large massive medal, in oval form, some seven inches by five, and it passed from hand to hand along the tables. On one side of this medal were engraved, in full length, the figures of two chiefs—Red Jacket, in costume presenting the pipe of peace, and Washington, with right hand extended as in the act of receiving it. On the other side were the Masonic emblems, with the date, 1792, if our memory is correct.[33]

Ely Parker did not in fact receive the Masonic burial he had hoped for, but in publicizing a Masonic Indian heritage across generations linked intimately to Washington he kept up a Masonic tradition, in which Indian individuals could be fully Indian (rather than "melted," somehow homogenized Americans) and fully patriotic within a powerful American fraternity.[34] In doing so he kept open a door through which subsequent Indian generations could gain access to American Masonry.

Arthur Parker was, if anything, an even more ardent Mason than his great-uncle. As a New York Seneca Iroquois museum man, anthropologist, and writer, he was able to put a great deal of effort into publicizing the links between Indians and Freemasons as part of his larger abiding project of tying assimilated Indians to the best in American life. Masons put themselves forward as representative Americans, and Parker very much wanted Indians to seem so too. An elitist and a racist, he exemplified many of the proclivities and biases of his class and his time.[35] Once, for example, he reassured fellow Masons that as an Indian he shared with them an exclusively white vision of the true American character by printing a personal story that strengthened the ties between Indians and Masons via anti-black racism. "A short time ago," he wrote, "a black Indian with a huge Masonic buttin [*sic*] rushed into my office and gave me what he thought was a grip [handshake], wanted to borrow five dollars and get my recommendation. His grip I knew not, neither did he get my recommendation or my five dollars. I told him what race he belonged to and that a police officer awaited him at the foot of the stairs. Oddly enough to avoid being thought of as a black he called himself 'White Elk,' but he was really a buck of another color, and one with which the Red man does not mix."[36] Parker wanted his ethnic group to be associated not with the group then suffering Jim Crow segregation in the South and racist aggression in the North, but instead with the ruling classes, of which a sizable number were Masons or at the very least social fraternal men of some sort.

Fraternities generally were attractive to him because of the sense of belonging they provided, the badges of inclusion they bestowed that meant so much both among the Iroquois and in middle-class America. As he put it in one of his articles, secret fraternities were all about allowing men with common aims to gather "where they may promote their principles and engage in their ceremonies unmolested by those who have not been found worthy and well qualified."[37] Belonging was important to him because he was a liminal figure on many fronts. A capable Indian intellectual at a time when, to paraphrase Frederick Hoxie, Indians were asked as a group to remain on the periphery of American society and to be ruled by outsiders who promised to guide them toward "civilization," he ran up against many stumbling blocks to his ambition. He came from a long line of Seneca who had assimilated, but in the early twentieth century the term had been redefined so that in essence it meant Indian acceptance of the fact that they could not participate in American life as equals.[38] This was more than frustrating for an immensely hard-working Seneca of exceptional heritage who approached the world with a sense of inherited entitlement. An added difficulty was the fact that intellectually Parker remained wedded to the anthropologist Lewis Henry Morgan's racist classificatory scheme, even though it left only limited space for his own identity as an Indian intellectual and condemned his "race" to the evolutionary past. Eventually his life experience as a stalwart worker for the first national cross-tribal indigenous reform group, the Society of American Indians (1911–21), convinced him painfully that as a homogeneous, unified political entity his "race" did not in fact exist. In a very real sense his multiple fraternal memberships were compensation for the lack of social context available to him elsewhere. Perhaps ironically in the Society of American Indians one of the fellow members he had most trouble with was also a Mason, the surgeon, author, and editor of the Indian magazine *Wassaja*, Carlos Montezuma (1867–1923).

Parker enjoyed multiple fraternal memberships, but the one to which he devoted the bulk of his fraternal energies was the Ancient and Accepted Order of Freemasons. He joined Sylvan Lodge No. 303 in Sinclairville, New York, in 1907 at age twenty-six, took another eleven years to achieve the second, Fellowcraft degree, and thereafter maintained an extensive range of fraternal relationships alongside membership in both York and Scottish Rite Freemasonry and associations with the Knights Templar, the Royal Order of Scotland, the Sons of the American Revolution, very possibly the Ku Klux Klan, and late in life the Philalethes Society. His greatest fraternal achievement was undoubtedly attaining the thirty-third degree, that of Sovereign Grand Inspector General of the Ancient and Accepted Scottish Rite, in 1924, when he was forty-three, the year Indians throughout the

United States were awarded full citizenship. As we have already learned, Masonic status does not necessarily correspond to the number of the degree awarded. Rather the third degree, that of Master Mason, is generally considered the most significant because its lessons speak to spiritual maturity, death, and the afterlife. It is, in Masonic language, "sublime," with a symbolism that speaks to the progressive development of a man's soul and its potential for ultimate resurrection. Nonetheless the thirty-third degree was awarded by election, and organizationally it was the supreme accolade Parker could have received as a Mason from his brothers worldwide.[39] It gave him a place at the administrative head of the Ancient and Accepted Scottish Rite. According to Mackey, "The peculiar duty of [Sovereign Grand Inspector Generals'] mission is to teach and enlighten the brethren; to preserve charity, union and fraternal love among them; to maintain regularity in the works of each degree, and to take care that it is preserved by others; to cause the dogmas, doctrines, institutes, constitutions, statutes and regulations of the Order to be reverently regarded, and to preserve and defend them on every occasion and finally, everywhere to occupy themselves in works of peace and mercy."[40] The role made the recipient an active member of the Scottish Rite Supreme Council and the highest ranking officer of the Rite within his jurisdiction. Certainly the award meant a very great deal to Parker. In personal correspondence he wrote of the honor being "almost overwhelming," adding, "If I pass the probationary period and am eventually brought to the Great East of the H.E. to be crowned a S.G.I.G. [Sovereign Grand Inspector General], honorary, I shall feel that I have received the highest honor that men and Masons can give—namely, the testimony of the greatest and truest fraternity the world has ever known. . . . I cannot express myself now, for I am filled with conflicting emotions. I am mighty happy and capable of doing all the undignified things that jubilant persons are, and yet the weight of honor awes me into discretion."[41]

Part of Parker's attraction to his fellow Masons was the fact that he was a booster both for Masonry in general and for Indian Masonry in particular. Each of the articles he wrote for Masonic publications added to the mythology about Indians as custodians of ancient, mystical Masonic truths. In "American Indian Freemasonry" in 1919, for example, he suggests that Indians in a generic sense drew lessons and symbolism from the "Temple of Nature" and preached "unwritten gospels" that emphasized exactly the values cherished by Masons: "Fortitude, Loyalty, Patriotism, Tolerance, Fraternity, and Gratitude." Indians too, he explains, placed exceptional value upon secrecy, since their societies were in "possession of ritualistic words that belonged exclusively to the cult or fraternity" and were "jealously guarded." The Seneca, he knew from personal experience, had an "inherent Freemasonry" and possessed "the thread of the legend of Osiris," the ancient Egyptian legend of death and resurrection with direct links to the Third Degree ritual. A booster for the museum movement as well, Parker even suggests that Masonry should set up its own museum of archaeology and history since "every relic that is found on the sites where once lived the primitive peoples of the world is a lost letter, syllable or word."[42]

The old chestnut of whether Indian peoples possessed some form of proto-Masonic knowledge or understanding was the issue to which he most consistently returned. In 1920, in "Freemasonry Among the American Indians," he says what his fellow Masons so wanted to hear, that ancient Indians knew "extra-limital [*sic*] masonry, as if some uninstructed groups of mankind saw through a glass darkly,—and craved more light." Indians of yore had "the ability to construct an organization similar under the circumstances of forest and plains life to the Freemasonry of the white man." It was a bond that explained why so many contemporary Indians were Masons. "Today there are numerous Indians who are Free and Accepted Masons," he told his brothers. "One can scarcely travel in Oklahoma, Nebraska, Kansas or the Dakotas without meeting Indians who belong to the ancient fraternity. Many of the most influential Indians of the Dakotas and especially of Oklahoma have full knowledge of the mysteries of Masonry and have sought further light in the concordant orders." Like so many Masonic authors before him and since, Parker invoked the Menominee of Wisconsin and their fraternal/medicine societies, which had "several degrees culminating in the resurrection of the candidate who represents a slain hero." From his own experience he provided details of the Iroquois ritual that echoed, he claimed, the rites of Osiris: the Little Water Medicine Society ritual of the Iroquois Ancient Guards of Mystic Potence, or Ne-Ho-noh-chee-noh-ga-Nee-ga-hee-ga-aa. Parker held that it represented evidence of an ancient universal Masonry known to Indians and still practiced by them. The term *mystic* of course was especially resonant in the Masonic context since a "mystic tie" was the source of the kindness that bound fraternal brothers together.

The Little Water Medicine Society

A lot of what has been written about the Little Water Medicine Society in one way or another links to Arthur Parker. He was able to tie it so often to Freemasonry because sometime after being adopted into the Seneca Bear Clan in 1903 he became a member, as his great-uncle Ely had before him, taking on the title Deputy at Large of the Guards of Mystic Potence, or Little Water Society. He claimed membership in two other Seneca fraternities, the Society of Mystic Animals and the Company of Whirlwinds, which he wrote about in two anthropological discussions of Seneca secret societies in 1908 and 1909.[43] According to Fenton, who toward the end of his life controversially published a book on the Little Water Medicine Society based on fieldwork he carried out from 1934 to 1959, it was Arthur Parker himself who named the ritual society that periodically celebrates the cure of fellow members by Little Water medicine, the Society of Mystic Animals.[44]

Much of what is on record about the Little Water Medicine Society corresponds directly to Masonic practice, and in particular to the third degree ritual and the murder and resurrection of Hiram Abiff. At the core of the Society is the founding legend, shared, according to Fenton, by a number of northern Iroquoian peoples, the legend of the Good Hunter, or "Bloody Hand." The Good Hunter is good because he shows respect to other beings and in his hunting behavior maintains reciprocity and balance between species. He is scalped and left to die in the woods, in several versions is unaware that he is dead, but is in every case eventually resuscitated by medicine animals. They do so by making powdered medicine from meat cut from the thighs or hearts of living animals who had been released, healed themselves, and survived. Thereafter the cure is celebrated by those who have received the great good medicine or who have dreamed about its rites and paraphernalia. The all-night ceremony used to renew the power of the medicine as described by Fenton has the same overall structure as a Masonic lodge meeting, with a conducting officer, servants, the collection of individual contributions, the laying out of ritual paraphernalia, the drinking of berry water at intermissions, and the holding of a terminal feast. According to Fenton, the Society has its roots in bundles used for healing fractures and gunshot wounds by Seneca war parties during the eighteenth century. He cites Arthur Parker's report that Seneca fighting with the British mourned losing their bundle at the Battle of Oriskany in 1777 (where Joseph Brant had a key role) and notes that Parker implied that the celebration of the Society's rites was primarily a male honor. The Society's ritual songs required excellent memory skills, and the task of being custodian of the medicine, given that the ability to make more of it was lost, was considered an awesome responsibility.[45]

What are we to make of all this? There is little supporting evidence that the Little Water Medicine Society was mostly celebrated by males, especially in light of the primary social, lineal, and political position women traditionally enjoy in Iroquois society. Also it is less the case that Little Medicine ritual follows Masonic ritual patterns and rather that both ritual forms correspond in outline to a great deal of ritual as practiced the world over. In retrospect it seems almost harsh that Fenton received so much opprobrium for publishing Little Water Medicine Society details in 2002 when Parker had already revealed the Society's origin legend and basic details in his Masonic writings almost one hundred years earlier. In old age Fenton, a lifelong Boasian, still held to a salvage ethnographer's rationale. He knew the ritual specifics he wrote about were sacred to Seneca believers but asserted, "The materials in two boxes of my field notes cry out for release, explanation and synthesis."[46] Perhaps it is closer to the truth to argue that the Society and its ritual served multiple purposes then and now. We will never know whether its resonance with Masonic ritual is linked to the history of Indian involvement in Freemasonry, if there is indeed what Masons might call a "proto-Masonic understanding" within Seneca ritual history, or if the third degree ritual so revered by Masons has roots subsequent to the original Seneca ritual practice. But we can be sure that as far as Parker was concerned, Little Water ritual served a useful purpose, linking powerful, mostly white Freemasons to a beleaguered and suffering indigenous minority woefully in need of the sort of tolerant brotherhood Masonry espoused.

Parker was most explicit about the connection between the

Little Water ritual and the third degree ritual in 1950, in an article about his great-uncle titled "Ely S. Parker—Man and Mason." As we know, the Master Mason ritual mimed the murder by three Fellowcraft Masons of Hiram Abiff, the principal architect of King Solomon's temple. They murdered him to obtain the secrets (the Mason Word) and therefore the traveling and working privileges of a Master Mason. In a three-section ritual the third degree has the Fellowcraft initiate reenact Abiff's murder, only to be eventually raised up or symbolically resurrected "by the strong grip, or lion's paw, of the tribe of Judah" and given "the grand Masonic word" in a ritualized intimate physical embrace known as the five points of fellowship.[47] The description of the Little Water ceremony that Parker provided in 1950 made the correspondences with the Master Mason degree fairly clear. Just like the Masonic ritual, the Little Water ceremony took place in a "lodge" with "two altars, one east and one west": "It had three sections, and it was devoted to a ceremony taught by the hero who had resisted the blandish [sic] of three ruffians who demanded the secret of his power. He refused to divulge this or betray his trust and so was slain. When his forest friends, symbolized by various animals, found him, they sacrificed the vital sparks of their own bodies, while an aide collected them in an acorn cup, the contents of which were poured down the throat of the prostrate hero. He was then raised to his feet and to life by the powerful clasp of the Bear's claw." Keen to let fellow Masons know that the ritual had "exercised a profound influence on the Seneca people," he noted, "The writer has seen educated and well-to-do Indians from city homes return for the ceremony of this society, and several Freemasons, Indian and white, have been admitted."[48]

If we follow Clawson's analysis of the Master Mason ritual, Parker was doing powerful symbolic work by tying Indian ritual to the key Masonic ritual. As explained previously, Clawson's class-based analysis sees the ritual as "an idealized defense of individual private property," presenting "an idealized version of capitalist production and market relations."[49] Parker was testifying to his assimilated status by linking himself to a ritual that idealized individual private property. After all, the Dawes Act of 1887 only a few generations earlier had attempted to pulverize communal Indian landholding and force surviving Indian communities to adopt individual ownership as a new and mostly alien way of life. Inserting Seneca ritual into Masonic thinking about the most revered Masonic degree made the Seneca part of Masonry's innermost core. "Indianizing" the third degree was not inappropriate in Masonic terms, since its liminal rituals in Turner's sense spoke to the same antimodern impulse in nineteenth-century men as did Indian stereotypes. Both the stereotyped Indian and the faithful artisan of the third degree existed imaginatively in opposition to the world that modern men perpetuated, and they were made all the more attractive because this was so.

All his life Parker held to the notion that Indians have always possessed "a pre–Grand Lodge Masonic philosophy in a generative form." In 1947, at age sixty-six, he gave a speech to a lodge in Vermont entitled "The Age-Old Appeal of Universal Freemasonry," in which he expressed a deep-set wish that throughout America's brutal history of fighting over Indian land all concerned had "recognized the essential 'Brotherhood of Man.'" Some better understanding might have been reached had America acknowledged that the "deeper meaning of Freemasonry" was "ageless as well as ancient" and known to American Indian peoples. By this stage Parker had polished his arguments supporting the idea that Indians had always been Masons in all but name. Like Masons, they too recognized a "force in the universe that is beyond man"; Indian pantheism was in itself, he argued, a form of fraternalism.[50]

Before leaving Parker, it is appropriate to reference another well-known Iroquois whose Masonic history echoed Parker's own, the Tuscarora leader and founder of the Indian rights group the Indian Defense League of America, Clinton Rickard (1882–1971). Parker and Rickard kept up frequent correspondence, and like Parker, Rickard took the spiritual dimension of Freemasonry very seriously. Along with a number of other noted early twentieth-century Indian leaders, such as Henry Roe Cloud, Charles Eastman, and Carlos Montezuma, he saw his Masonic membership as yet another way he might educate the non-Indian community and as a means of garnering support for the fight for Indian rights. Rickard "inherited" a leaning toward Freemasonry from three friends of his father's and first found solace in Ransomville Lodge No. 551, Ransomville, New York, in November 1913, after losing all his possessions to flooding and almost his whole family to illness, including his wife and four-year-old son. He went on to complete all the available Masonic degrees up to the thirty-second and Shrine, to give lectures about Indian rights to Masonic groups throughout the region, and to get help from his fellow Masons in drafting pro-Indian resolutions to Congress. Rickard told his biographer, Barbara Graymont, that his fraternal identity had been of service when he was arrested, although innocent, by the Canadian government. Certainly lodge work remained close to his heart all his life. Aside from his own lodge and other fraternal commitments, he was an honorary member and color bearer of the Ely Parker Lodge of Buffalo, New York, and for more than forty years attended each of its initiations.[51]

The Mystic Chords of Memory Binding
Freemasons and the Colonized Other

One of the persistent delusions of mankind is that some sections of the human race are morally better or worse than others. . . . A rather curious form of this admiration for groups to which the admirer does not belong is the belief in the superior virtue of the oppressed: subject nations, the poor, women, and children. The eighteenth century, while conquering America from the Indians[,] . . . loved to sentimentalize about the "noble savage." . . . [Admiration] begins only when the oppressors come to have a bad conscience, and this only happens when their power is no longer secure.

—BERTRAND RUSSELL, "The Superior Virtue of the Oppressed," *Unpopular Essays*

The historical sense involves a perception, not only of the pastness of the past, but of its presence. . . . This historical sense, which is a sense of the timeless as well as the temporal and of the timeless and the temporal together, is what makes a writer traditional.

—T. S. ELIOT, "Tradition and the Individual Talent"

In this section I attempt to go deeper into the myth of a timeless bond of knowledge shared by Freemasons and colonized Others across the world. To do so I invoke Michael Kammen's magisterial study of how collective memory works in America, *Mystic Chords of Memory*, and the original poignant phrase itself, used by Abraham Lincoln on the occasion of his first inauguration, in 1861.[52] Lincoln evoked the idea of national bonds of affection and coined the phrase "mystic chords of memory" for the same reason Masons posited a shared myth of fraternity and understanding between themselves and the colonized Others they encountered: to appeal to, as Lincoln put it, "the better angels of our nature," to forge, rhetorically at least, unity across a fundamental divide. However, as Kammen points out, for Lincoln in this instance, as so often in American history, such an appeal to a unifying, shared past failed to assuage passionately held differences.[53] Kammen explores the ways not only memory but also collective amnesia have served American national interests over time, depoliticizing the past as a means of minimizing conflict.

In the instance of the American Masonic myth of a shared past with Native Americans, the emphasis has been on the invention of tradition for the same purposes. It is an instance of what Foucault once termed "popular memory," a small but significant building block making up the imagined political community of the American nation-state.[54] Its purpose is at once fraternal (to compliment Freemasons) and political (to make the nation appear more natural, older, and more historically inevitable than it might otherwise seem). The myth that Anglo-Saxon colonial centers share Masonic rituals, teachings, passwords, and even handshakes with colonized Others worked to salve any conscience colonizers might have felt about their activities and to suggest that they were at the vanguard of a historical movement that was preordained, since their arrival was somehow already known to those they came to dispossess. For Masons, in particular those of the late nineteenth century, fellow Indian ritualists were appropriate companions and potential guides in the quest to reconnect with primitive truths that had "faded out from men's souls before the world grew old," as the twenty-eighth degree of the Scottish Rite puts it.[55] In the mythic, regularly conjured world of ritual "Masonic time," Indian cultures coexisted with versions of ancient Greek, Roman, Egyptian, and Islamic cultures. In these separate worlds, brought into being in dark, private lodge rooms, Masonic rectitude was confirmed and a legacy of moral and personal truth was passed on from exotic and imaginary Others who were the supposed custodians of what modern Americans had perhaps irrevocably lost.

The idea that the noble savage was a welcoming brother to potential settlers has a pedigree that stretches back in Western thinking at least to Greek antiquity, and it played a key role in European propaganda that sought to attract Europeans to the New World. Given that they were men positioning themselves as quintessential Americans, Freemasons may well have consciously or unconsciously sought to align themselves with the sinlessness of a prelapsarian past, to position themselves, as R. W. B. Lewis once put it in terms of the nineteenth century, as "American Adams." In this sense Masons were cherry-picking the best of both an American and a European past, reconstituting themselves as the white male heroes of world history. The American Adam, as Lewis explained, was *more than* Indian and *more than* European; he was "a radically new personality, the hero of the new adventure: an individual emancipated from history, happily bereft of ancestry, untouched and undefiled by the usual inheritances of family and race; an individual standing alone, self-reliant and self-propelling, ready to confront whatever awaited him with the aid of his own unique and inherent resources . . . Adam before the Fall."[56]

There is also a long history of Euro-American men being mistaken for or passing as Indians and thereby gaining access to Indian spiritual secrets. As Joshua David Bellin points out in a discussion of the antebellum painter George Catlin, some version or other of the theme is traceable in several of the formative texts in the American literary canon, including James Fenimore Cooper's *The Last of the Mohicans* (1826) and *The Prairie* (1827), Robert Montgomery Bird's *Nick of the Woods* (1837), Nathaniel Hawthorne's *The Scarlet Letter* (1850) as well as his unpublished "elixir of life" manuscripts, and Herman Melville's *The Confidence Man* (1857). Catlin reveled in what he supposed was his elevation among the Mandan to the status of spiritual master, echoing Freemasonry in his description of how he attained his Mandan "degree" and with it knowledge of great mystery: "I took the degree (not of Doctor of Laws, nor Bachelor of Arts) of Master of Arts—of mysteries—of magic and of hocus pocus. I was recognized . . . as a great *medicine white man*; and since that time, have been regularly installed *medicine* or mystery, which is the most honourable degree that could be conferred upon me here; and I now hold a place amongst the most eminent and envied personages, the doctors and conjurati of the titled community."[57]

Catlin's tone has a strong tinge of ridicule, of nervous laughter at induction into the spiritual life of another culture, a behavior that recurs often in captivity narratives and in early ethnology and American literature. However, the quintessential literary depiction of intracultural exchange in this regard is not American but British: Rudyard Kipling's (1865–1936) "The Man Who Would Be King," a story that uses Freemasonry as the bridge between cultures and across class. Here Kipling very ably both expresses and parodies the abiding Masonic shibboleth closely tied to the colonizing process in both the British and the American context: the idea that ancient Masonic truths can somehow transcend barriers of culture, colonial status, and class. Admittedly Kipling was to be more explicit about Native American knowledge of Masonry later, in the tale "Brother Square Toes," for example, where he refers to Seneca Indian "proto-Masonry," that is, a Masonic knowledge held by indigenes that is older than Freemasonry itself. A character remarks, "I saw my chief's war-bonnets sinking together down and down. Then they made the sign which no Indian makes outside of the Medicine Lodges, a sweep of the right hand just clear of the dust and an inbend of the left knee at the same time, and those proud eagle feathers almost touched his bottom."[58] But it is in "The Man Who Would Be King" that Kipling most fully explores Masonic identity and the complexities of colonialism and a real or imagined global brotherhood. It is to this story as a conceptual roadmap to the phenomenon of global brotherhood that we now turn.

Kipling and the Fantasy of Global Brotherhood

"The Man Who Would Be King" is a comic but also profound short story that ranks among Kipling's best writing. Masonic to its core, it powerfully encapsulates a fundamental Masonic desire for the fraternity's virtues and knowledge to be *already known* to the precolonized Other at the point of contact with Europeans or Euro-Americans. The story was first published in late 1888 in Kipling's collection *The Phantom Rickshaw*, just three years after Kipling was raised as a Mason (by dispensation since he was underage) at Hope and Perseverance Lodge No. 782 E.C. (English Constitution) in Lahore, India, where he was born. Just how much the cosmopolitanism and Masonic racial inclusivity Kipling experienced in this lodge impressed the young author is clear from his poem "The Mother Lodge":

> We 'and't good regalia,
> An' our Lodge was old an' bare,
> But we knew the Ancient Landmarks,
> An' we kep' 'em to a hair;
> An' lookin on it backwards
> It often strikes me thus,
> There ain't such things as infidels,
> Excep', per'aps, it's us.
>
> Outside—"Sergeant! Sir! Salute! Salaam!"
> Inside—"Brother," an' it doesn't do no 'arm.

Kipling especially loved the conviviality of Masonic banquets and the exposure Masonry offered him to new worlds and new cultures. Although his period of active Masonic involvement lasted only a few years (he reached the level of Master Mason), he retained various connections to Masonic organizations throughout his life, and several of his well-known narratives, such as *Kim* (1900), have clear Masonic underpinnings.[59]

"The Man Who Would Be King" concerns two Masons who are tramps but who ultimately become kings, both in status and on a deeper level, in terms of a genuine inner, regal quality they display through personal sacrifice. The pair, Peachey Carnahan and Daniel Dravot, put themselves under a "Contrack" not dissimilar from various eighteenth-century Masonic "charges," and by a series of comic turns find themselves anointed kings of the fictional land of Kafiristan. Their story echoes the notorious exploits of Sir James Brooke, the English soldier lauded for "pacifying" Borneo who was eventually recognized in 1841 as the rajah of Sarawak. Key to the whole narrative is the fact the Kafiristanis practice a form of Freemasonry. After meeting one tribesman who uses the Fellowcraft grip or handshake and knows the "Mason Word," Peachey exclaims, "It's a miracle! The Chiefs and the priests can work a Fellow Craft Lodge in a way that's very like ours, and they've cut the marks on the rocks, but they don't know the Third Degree, and they've come to find out. It's God's Truth! I've known these long years the Afghans knew up to the Fellow Craft Degree, but this is a miracle. A God and a Grand-Master of the Craft am I, and a Lodge in the Third Degree I will open, and we'll raise the head priests and the Chiefs of the villages." Dan and Peachey thus usurp Masonic, religious, and sovereign authority; equally important, as heroes they upset the dominant nineteenth-century oppressive force Kipling called "the God of Things as They Are." The pair's future plays out a parody of aspects of the Bible, from Creation to the leadership of the early Hebrew kings, the uniting of the tribes of Israel, and the final crucifixion of Peachey and his eventual quasi-resurrection. As Paul Fussell Jr. pointed out back in 1958, however, his resurrection may well be primarily Masonic and pre-Christian.[60] By amazing coincidence Dan discovers a Masonic Master's mark cut into a stone that matches his own apron, and the discovery allows him such total power in Kafiristan that he fantasizes he can present its people to Queen Victoria. In prophetic anticipation of his own eventual beheading, he swears to them at one point, "I'll make a damned fine Nation of you, or I'll die in the making!"

Kipling was aware of how susceptible Masonry is to parody, but through Dan and Peachey he nonetheless suggests that Masons should be seen as the real kings of empire. After all, as Fussell explains, Peachey as the servant of his lord, Dan, suffers crucifixion for his fidelity to the idea of the king in man.[61]

In chapter 3 I explored the republican impetus at the heart of Masonry, but as Kipling's story shows, the involvement of elites, and especially the aristocracy and royalty, has also been a key aspect of the fraternity's growth. Since 1721 English Grand Masters have tended to be either noblemen or princes, and Anderson's *The Constitutions* (1723) made much of kings as far back as Noah, Moses, and Solomon, who were held to have been Masons who had used the fraternity to found nations and dynasties. The message at the heart of Freemasonry was thus that the true qualities of kingliness were also Masonic virtues.

Indeed it is only the inner qualities of the true Mason, Kipling's story suggests, that can save empire builders like Peachey from overreaching themselves, losing their moral compass and attempting to people the world in their own image. Consider the ironic pathos Kipling gives to Peachey's wild plans for the Kafiristanis: "'I won't make a Nation,' says he. 'I'll make an Empire! These men aren't niggers; they're English! Look at their eyes—look at their mouths. Look at the way they stand up. They sit on chairs in their own houses. They're the Lost Tribes or something like it, and they've grown to be English. . . . Two million people— two hundred and fifty thousand fighting men—and all English! They want only rifles and a little drilling.'" Peachey exemplifies the fantasy that Masons were the custodians of a spiritually sanctioned right to rule across the globe, a right somehow preordained within the ancient customs and practices of the very people they sought to colonize. Indeed so providential was the Euro-American Masonic right to rule that colonized peoples were thought to be *waiting for* the arrival of Masons, waiting to recognize a lost word or sign of their true community.

Kipling's vision of a proto-Masonry binding Europeans and colonized indigenes across time and space, uniting them in their shared knowledge of abiding and sacred truths, can usefully be viewed as a form of what Mary Louise Pratt terms "anti-conquest," one of those "strategies of representation whereby European bourgeois subjects seek to secure their innocence in the same moment as they assert European hegemony."[62] Masons using Freemasonry and its myths to assuage various qualms about racial, cultural, class, or gender divides is a theme that recurs throughout this book. It stems from a truth Pratt also touches on: the fact that reciprocity in some form or other has always been part of capitalism's ideology of itself. The myth of a shared past between Masons and indigenes bound representatives of Euro-America to noncapitalist Native societies within which reciprocity really did serve as the basis for social interaction. As Pratt points out, this was important to Masons across time because it legitimized their actions, since the idea of an exchange freely entered into is one of the most important stories capitalism tells about itself. The myth of reciprocity, of a shared exchange on a mythic or any other level, retained and sustained a larger myth, that of colonial innocence.[63] It is worth remembering that the lodge, after all, was an emotional space and that the relationships between Masonic brothers were familial, as were the relationships between individual lodges across the globe. Neighboring lodges were referred to as "sister" lodges, the lodges they stemmed from as "mother" lodges, and the authority of the lodge and of the Grand Lodge was thought of as being "paternal." If the home was a morally pristine separate sphere for women, then the lodge was an analogous place where all the virtues associated with domesticity could be cultivated and performed by males.

Making Indian Brothers

As Michael Rogin reminds us, postrevolutionary Americans had a complex and at points ambiguous relationship with their "mother country," Great Britain. Alongside the desire for freedom from Britain's imperial reach came a less often acknowledged but nevertheless real material and psychological need for succor in a foreign land. As a result, he argues, Americans made liberty into a maternal figure. In an age of slavery and progressive Indian displacement and ethnocide, Americans became, imaginatively at least, "sons of liberty." This process of "making family" out of Others who did not share Euro-American aims and who were in fact suffering under various yokes of oppression deliberately placed on them by Euro-Americans has a history that becomes more obvious in the eighteenth century. One of its early exponents is Tocqueville, who in his travel essays and in *Democracy in America* (1840) writes consistently of Indians in familial terms in relation to Americans: both are "children" of a larger "mother," Nature. As Rogin explains, "American rhetoric filled the white-Indian tie with intimate symbolic meaning. Indians were, every treaty talk insisted, our 'friends and brothers.'"[64] Admittedly this was a reflection of Enlightenment rhetoric, but it was also a political fraternalizing, a convenient sleight of hand that justified Euro-American access to Indians and their land. Tocqueville knew that this brothering would ultimately prove fatal for Indians and that the younger brother would supplant his older brother. He described how, in the vastness of the American landscape, Euro-Americans took Indians "by the hand in brotherly fashion [*fraternellement*]" to "lead them away to die far from the lands of their fathers."[65]

Laura Janara has explored the envy at the heart of this invented familialism on the part of Euro-Americans and suggests that the displacement of the older by the younger "brother" made Indians not into "others" at all, but into primitive versions of Europeans' more civilized selves. She claims that Tocqueville's work signals a warning, since "U.S. appeals to intimacy or familial closeness in relations with other peoples may involve drives—of postcolonial anxiety and democratic envy—to dominate and expropriate."[66]

If we leave "illegitimate" Prince Hall Masonry to one side, the numbers of non–Anglo-Saxon Protestants who shared in Masonry's vision of universal brotherhood were small and confined to elites. Nevertheless, in rhetoric and in a proscribed sense in practice, Freemasonry perpetuated the ideal of global fraternity long after it had been supplanted by racialized thinking in dominant American and British ideology. What is interesting is how contradictory Masonry was. American Indian brothers were given status within certain lodges as personifications of a mythologized Masonic past, with special access and understanding of ritual, but simultaneously in society more generally Indian peoples were thought of as childlike and even infantile. This characterization was necessary in order to justify colonial policy in the seventeenth and eighteenth centuries and government policy in the nineteenth and twentieth that separated Indians from their land and resources. There is evidence that British Masons in India allowed indigenous membership on the understanding that Indian Masons were "younger brothers" to their more civilized white brethren, from whom they were permitted to learn within the lodge.[67] Yet in North America there is also repeated evidence over time that Native (but not black) individuals found the Masonic environment uniquely liberal and inclusive. All this suggests that the process of settlement by colonial powers is complex and internally inconsistent when the social and the political are taken together and that no one approach (such as Cannadine's *Ornamentalism* or Said's *Orientalism*) can adequately explain its variety or the capacity for cognitive dissonance some of its primary agents possessed. Masons, who were also colonial agents, were able to uphold positions of racial exclusiveness and superiority in political life, but within the lodge they were quite happy to hold compensatory and wholly contrary views. Such contradictory impulses and the ability to be at ease with seemingly mutually exclusive outlooks at once was a unique American, Indian, and Masonic capability.

Native American Freemasons

7

The Revolutionary Era

> It is crucial for us to remember that the American revolution was not truly a war to throw off the yoke of colonization as is popularly imagined, but rather a family squabble among the colonizers to determine who would be in charge of the colonization of North America, who would control the land and the lives of the inhabitants. America never became postcolonial. The indigenous inhabitants of North America can stand anywhere on the continent and look in every direction at a home usurped and colonized by strangers who, from the very beginning, laid claim not merely to the land and resources but to the very definition of the Natives.
>
> —LOUIS OWENS, "As If an Indian Were Really an Indian: Native American Voices and Postcolonial Theory"

The Revolution created a painful crisis in American Freemasonry, but its internal contradictions proved to be its saving grace. On one level the "royal art" had no place in a new republic; it clearly had British roots and belonged to an imagined "family" of brotherhood that mirrored the British Empire's span of the globe. Yet Masonry proved able to dexterously fudge the issue, and in time it mirrored the new union organizationally, taking on its own state and regional form of independence. During the war it was able to offer its usual mix of psychological balm in the midst of a troubled world. Membership taught polite manners and brought uprooted men together in bonhomie, and as has been shown, it was thought that it offered the chance of leniency from a Mason on the other side of the battle if a man were taken prisoner. After the conflict the fraternity emerged stronger than before because it aligned itself with the values of the new nation, which saw itself as a seedbed for a "natural aristocracy." The term is complex and paradoxical, and its use at this juncture testifies to just how unstable and in flux the transition was for European Americans as they forged a path beyond the aristocratic world of the past toward a more liberal, democratic world in the future. Freemasonry's significance in this era and its growth as a crucible for leadership reflect Rogers M. Smith's idea that there were "multiple traditions" in America that were by no means simple, binary, or unilinear in their development.[1] Freemasonry's role as sanctuary for a new form of aristocracy also undercuts the Tocquevillian narrative of the United States as being shaped by unusually free and egalitarian ideas and conditions from its inception.

In a period characterized by spiritual as well as political surge and conflict, Masonry's deist and nonsectarian underpinnings made it perfect for the times. So much has been written on the Christian underpinnings of early America that it is easy to forget that the nation's founding document actually relegated religion of all sorts to a secondary role. As Jon Butler reminds us, "The religious world invoked in the Declaration was a deist's world, at best: at worst, the Declaration was simply indifferent to religious concerns and issues. The god who appears in the Declaration is the god of nature rather than the God of Christian spiritual revelation, as when Jefferson wrote of 'the laws of nature and nature's God.' In other allusive appearances this god emerged as 'the Supreme Judge of the world,' to whom American would appeal 'for the rectitude of our intentions,' and as 'Divine Providence,' on whom they would rely for protection."[2]

The clergy were aware that potentially America could find itself spiritually adrift, and so they felt moved to speak against prominent individuals such as Franklin, Jefferson, Madison, and Washington, whose support for Enlightenment thinking seemed dangerously close to support for secularism. Protestant clergy in particular settled on deism as a good focus for attack, claiming that it was no religion at all, merely the veneration of reason and nature. Thomas Paine's *Age of Reason* (1794) was denounced, religious and nationalist paranoia whipped up over a group linked to Freemasons known as the Bavarian Illuminati, and the red-haired deist Jefferson reviled from the pulpit as an agent of the Devil in the midst of his 1800 bid for the presidency.[3] At the same time evangelical Christians put themselves forward as being on the side of individualism and republicanism.[4]

Such attacks did little to prevent Masonry's deist attributes and selective inclusiveness proving of specific diplomatic and personal value to a long list of Indian leaders. The first Indian Freemason is thought to have been the Mohawk Joseph Brant, whose mentor was the dominant northeastern colonist Sir William Johnson. Other revolutionary-era Indian Masons include the Seneca orator Red Jacket, the Shawnee prophet Tecumseh, and the mixed-blood leader of the Muskogee, Alexander McGillivray (1740–93). Yet another Indian Mason is the fascinating Eleazer Williams (ca. 1787–1858), a Wisconsin minister who claimed he was Louis XVII of France, the "lost" dauphin and rightful heir to the French throne. The Muscogee leader William Augustus Bowles was also a Mason but not Indian by blood. Raised as a Mason in the Bahamas in 1786, Bowles entered the Prince of Wales Lodge No. 259 in London in 1790, where he was introduced as "a Chief of the Creek Nation, whose love of Masonry has induced him to wish it may be introduced into the interior part of America, whereby the cause of humanity and brotherly love will go hand in hand with the native courage of the Indians, and by the union lead them on to the highest title that can be conferred on man." Bowles was there with a number of Native friends, including the Cherokee Going Snake and the Creek Tuskeniah, an associate of Tecumseh, all of whom were in England seeking support for an uprising in Santo Domingo led by two other Freemasons who would ultimately spearhead the Haitian Revolution, Jean Jacques Dessalines and Toussaint L'Ouverture.[5]

Performing "Indianness" at the Boston Tea Party

The Boston Tea Party was a specific occasion when Masonry and "Indianness" came together. According to Bullock, the dumping of tea into Boston Harbor may well have been facilitated by the local Masonic lodge, which scheduled a meeting as an alibi for their members involved in the incident. For their part, St. Andrew's Lodge has long claimed that the trigger event for the Revolution was planned in their hall, the Green Dragon Tavern.[6] Several prominent Masons at the time were actively agitating to free the thirteen colonies from British rule, and the Masonic hall was where a number of revolutionary groups met. The St. Andrew's Lodge Master was a member of the North End Caucus, and the Senior Grand Warden, Paul Revere, along with three other St. Andrew's Masons, were members of the Sons of Liberty.

The Masonic element in the events surrounding the Boston Tea Party places new emphasis on the fact that those involved in dumping the tea did so dressed up as "Mohawks." It is thought that they donned the appropriate robes (which allowed them an extra layer of symbolism rather than truly obscured their identities) in the Masonic hall. If so, it may be that in "becoming Indian" in order to carry out an act of violent (and expensive) patriotism, those involved were invoking a symbolism that went beyond the equation of Indians with a quintessentially American identity. They also cloaked themselves in an outfit respected by the Masonic community, outfits that may even have been worn in ritual by Masons. (After all, rooms with "Indian" robes can still be seen in the Masonic Hall in Guthrie, Oklahoma, and its ground floor has a themed recreational "Indian Room" complete with a "good luck" swastika and pan-Indian-style decoration.) We cannot know for certain, but perhaps it was a short step from performing as Indians in Masonic rituals to performing as patriotic Indians at liberty to dump tea in Boston Harbor.

The question remains as to what extent the patriots were inspired to perform this symbolic strike for a more participative democracy by exposure to actual Indian leaders, a stratum whose general presence, example, and involvement in colonial statecraft has begun to be documented.[7] We have no written evidence that actual Indians had any involvement with the St. Andrew's Lodge, but the idea of Indian liberty and eloquence both rhetorically and in terms of Masonic performance could well have been influential. The combination of Masonry, playing Indian, and the revolutionary impulse exists, although evidence of direct Native involvement does not. Yet as Philip Deloria insists, this does not mean it should be wholly discounted, given that across a long history of Indian play "native people have been present at the margins, insinuating their way into Euro-American discourse, often attempting to nudge notions of Indianness in directions they found useful."[8]

The adoption of Indian disguise by rebellious early Americans may have been an importation of the conditions of carnival in Bakhtin's sense, a replication of the equalizing, collective mayhem and general disregard for the social order that characterized certain holidays in Europe.[9] However, it may also have been a different sort of performative tradition, an extension of Masonic ritual performance and a spillover of the freedom to reinvent personal identity that has always characterized fraternal ritual life. "Indianness," however understood, may have empowered the extension of certain Masonic precepts such as justice and morality into the real world, beyond the confines of the lodge and onto the wider national and political stage.

Joseph Brant

Just three years after the Boston Tea Party we find the first record of the initiation of an American Indian to Freemasonry, the Mohawk Joseph Brant, or Thayendanegea (1743–1807). Brant was a key political figure of the late eighteenth century in the Six Nations of the Iroquois, a group of nations whose military, political, and cultural power at that time was pivotal. In one sense it is not surprising that the first recorded Mason should be Iroquois, given how elaborate Iroquois ritual protocols had become by this stage. The symbolism and elaboration involved may well have made Masonic ritual comprehensible to Iroquois representatives, and Iroquois ritual in turn comprehensible to Euro-American Masons. Dean Snow has explained that the Iroquois Confederacy was ritual-laden because real power always remained at the village rather than the national level and almost never meaningfully operated at the level of the five (later six) constituent Iroquois nations. "In the absence of substance," Snow writes, "the Iroquois created a labyrinth of forms, to the delight of later generations of anthropologists, not least of whom was Lewis Henry Morgan." The Iroquois Confederacy, it is worth noting, emerged in the seventeenth century as the political vehicle of the Iroquois League, which had formed in the fifteenth or early sixteenth century as a means of fostering peace among five of the Iroquoian-speaking nations of modern New York. The Confederacy used belts of tabular wampum as its symbolic currency. Both the League and the Confederacy fractured during the American Revolution, but later separate Leagues formed in New York and Ontario. The structure of the first League was based on a significantly older, matriclan system and funerary (condolence) ritual, designed to obviate the need for revenge killing and hostility.[10]

Brant's Freemasonry was very obviously a symptom of the British Empire's influence on his life. His exhaustive and admiring biographer, Isabel Thompson Kelsay, dubbed him "a man of two worlds," but in truth he operated within multiple overlapping contexts.[11] Freemasonry was just one of his fluencies; he was also a representative of his people, the Mohawk, a member of the larger cross-tribal Iroquois Confederacy, and a loyalist to the interests of Great Britain. His is a fascinating story of "middle ground" diplomacy, of personal drama (among other things Brant stabbed his own son to death after his son made a drunken assault), and of war fought to defend Iroquois interests through defense of the interests of England as a colonial power. Born in Akron, Ohio, in 1743, he impressed the powerful political figure and later Freemason Sir William Johnson, then the English superintendent of Indian Affairs. Johnson sent Brant to Moore's Indian Charity School in Lebanon, Connecticut (which later received its charter as Dartmouth College) in 1761, where he came under the care of the elder Dr. Wheelock. There he received what was considered at the time to be an excellent education, learned English, and adopted Anglicanism. Interestingly the school was also to prove a turning point in the life of another Indian, the handsome and respected leader Louis Annance. Annance became a noted Protestant in his own St. Francis Indian community in the area around Moosehead Lake in Piscataquis County, Maine, and was a member of North Star Masonic Lodge No. 8 in Lancaster, New Hampshire.

There is evidence that Brant formed a special friendship with a Lt. Augustine Prevost, initiated at Sir William Johnson's lodge, St. Patrick's, in 1767. According to an 1863 Masonic source, Brant's affinity to Prevost and to local Masonry was symptomatic of a general shared fraternalism at play between Indian and European cultures at the time: "These wild noblemen of the forest had themselves their own mystic organizations, some of whose features and ceremonies were so akin to the Royal Art that they have been denominated Indian Freemasonry. They, at times, admitted their white friends into these associations with initiatory rites, and gave them Indian names. There was also a kindred custom among them of selecting some bosom friend, whom they afterward, on all occasions regarded as their counterpart, and whose joys and sorrows became a part of their own."[12]

At the outbreak of the Revolution Brant sailed for England with Guy Johnson, Sir William Johnson's nephew, and in around 1776 was initiated as a Freemason at Hiram's Cliftonian Lodge No. 417 at the Falcon Tavern, Princess Street, Leicester Fields, in London.[13] As has often been pointed out, his visits to England were as a foreigner of high rank; he ate dinner with the Prince of Wales, had his portrait painted by the celebrated painter George Romney, and spoke with James Boswell. It was even reported that George III presented Brant with his Fellowcraft apron.[14] According to Brant's earliest biographer, William L. Stone, Brant refused to kiss the hand of King George III when introduced because he saw himself as "King of the Mohawks" and therefore as being of equal rank. He did, however, in courtly fashion offer to kiss the hand of the queen.[15] For all its Masonic warmth, the visit served a primarily diplomatic purpose, tying Brant to the Crown and ensuring his people's support in the ensuing hostilities overseas.

Because Brant believed that a British victory would mean the return of Mohawk lands to his people, he remained a staunch

Loyalist and played a key role in bringing Iroquois might to bear in fighting on the British side during the American War of Independence. Known as "Monster Brant" because of the brutality with which he and his men fought, he played an especially significant role in the battles at The Cedars (1776), Oriskany (1777), Cherry Valley (1778), and Minisink (1779). Afterward he received a commission as an officer in the British Army and with it a pension and a land grant along the Grand River in Upper Canada.[16] He became a member of Lodge No. 10 in Hamilton, Ontario, and went on to found one of the earliest Masonic lodges in Upper Canada, Lodge No. 11 at Brant's Town. It is thought that he served as its Worshipful Master at least until 1801.[17]

We can only surmise to what extent Brant's Freemasonry affected his success as a diplomat and cultural broker. All the records of the exchanges of the time are addressed to "Brethren," and many of the key players, including the governor of Upper Canada Colonel Simcoe, with whom Brant became very close, were Masons. Indeed Simcoe was introduced to Brant through a letter from the noted Mason the Duke of Northumberland in 1791, which made much of the kind of virtues a Mason would appreciate and which closed, "Your affectionate Friend and Brother, NORTHUMBERLAND."[18]

Brant is particularly well-known in Masonic literature for saving fellow Masons in distress from cruel fates at the hands of Indian fighters. Such stories should perhaps be seen alongside numerous other reports of Brant's just dealings in war (including saving babies), which were in part a response to the opprobrium engendered in London and the Americas over the injustice of using what were deemed mercenary and barbaric Indian fighters to defend British interests.[19] The best known Brant Masonic rescue story involves a Capt. John McKinstry, who was wounded and captured at the Battle of The Cedars, near Montreal, on May 20,

1776. The Masonic historian Wallace McLeod tells us, "He was about to be burned at the stake, when he gave a Masonic sign of distress. Brant at once had him released, and he was in due course paroled and sent home. It is said that, from that time on, the two men remained close friends."[20] Other combatants Brant is thought to have saved (some temporarily) in the course of the war include Lt. Jonathan Maynard, Sergeant Parker, Maj. John Wood, and Lt. Thomas Boyd.

As McLeod points out rather disarmingly, it is difficult to confirm the details of these episodes, but they make a good story.[21] Yet Masonic authors of the time took such tales very seriously; some, such as the prominent Masonic writer John Fellows, took special exception to Indian Masons using the elitism of Masonry to save some and not others. He wrote of one rescue, "While this transaction reflects honor upon this officer as a *Mason*, it at the same time leaves an indelible stain upon his character as a *man*, which equally attaches to his *King* and government. What! Employ savages as auxiliaries in war, and then stand by and look coolly on, while they amuse themselves in . . . scalping their prisoners, unless the latter can give the talismanic signal, and pronounce the Shibboleth of Masonry?"[22] Others, such as the Masonic author Wilmer Edgar Bresee, are symptomatic of a long line of Masonic writers who praised Brant as an exemplary Mason and savior across ethnic and military divides. Bresee closes his discussion of Brant by wishfully contemplating how "the course of history would have been had Brant listened to the pleas of his old friend and neighbor and Masonic Brother [General Herkimer] to remain neutral in the great conflict that was just then beginning."[23] We know only that Brant and the Brant family held Freemasonry to be significant. Brant's son John (Ahyouwaighs, 1794–1832) also become a Mason and continued a specifically British form of rank and culture within Mohawk life in Canada.

Sir William Johnson: Irish Mason and Iroquois Sachem

Brant's patron, Sir William Johnson (Warraghiyageh, ca. 1715–74), provides us with another fascinating example of the significance of ritual performance and of Freemasonry in colonial and indigenous life in the colonial era. Rather like that other famous Mason of the nineteenth century, Albert Pike, Johnson was a man of gargantuan appetites. A huge drinker, he was also rumored to be the father of seven hundred children by both Indian and white mothers. A natural leader and a lover of the outdoors, he inspired great loyalty. Colonel of the Six Nations in 1744, commissioner of New York for Indian Affairs in 1746, he was superintendent of Indian Affairs for the colony of New York from 1755 until his death in 1774. A figure of unsurpassed regional power in the years prior to the Revolution, he dominated a private empire of 170,000 acres in Upper New York and excelled as the preeminent political and military figure on the frontier. He did so as a result of his keen understanding of the power and significance of ritual and ceremony to both Indian and British American life. A master of strategic adaptation, Johnson transformed himself from colonized Irish Catholic to Protestant colonial soldier and spiritually and politically dominant sachem within the Iroquois Confederacy. His is a story beautifully rendered recently by the Irish writer Fintan O'Toole, who shows in sinuous detail how Johnson negotiated at the interstices of various circles of power. Late eighteenth-century Iroquois were accomplished consumers by this stage, engulfed by a scale of trading of which previous Iroquois generations had no comprehension. They swapped their own manufactures for European commodities and enthusiastically sold pelts at what seemed from the Indian perspective to be an exceptionally profitable rate of exchange. Johnson was at the heart of this from 1740 onward, as trade gradually became unseated from its context of ritual exchange with symbolic and diplomatic meaning and took on a more purely economic emphasis.

What smoothed Johnson's path to power was his understanding of the persisting importance of reciprocity and ritual in Iroquois society, an understanding transferred from his Irish background. He had grown up in an Irish landscape where myth was deeply embedded and where a ritualized relationship to stones, trees, and water was important.[24] His homeland was two miles from Tara, the most sacred space in pre-Christian Ireland, linked to the divine race the Tuatha de Danaan. It is an area sometimes referred to as the Irish Stonehenge, with its remarkable megalithic passage tomb (Duma na nGiall), dating back to around 3000 BCE. Johnson's people also celebrated a ritual at a holy spring on a special day for Masons, St. John's Day, June 24, a survival of the ancient animist religion that had been incorporated into early Christianity in Ireland. "It marked the summer solstice," O'Toole explains, "with an interwoven homage to the sun and the dark, to the underworld from which the spring emerged and the bright water that flowed free for a moment before returning to its Stygian origins."[25]

Thus Johnson grew up in an environment that was as powerfully alive in terms of the life of the spirit as the Iroquois world of the eighteenth century in which he later found himself. His world growing up encompassed Protestant rationalism, Catholicism, and an older layer of pre-Christian ritual and myth, just as Iroquois society encompassed Christianity and its own layers of spiritual history honoring the Great Spirit and relationships with various forces and entities. As O'Toole explains, "The Iroquois view of the world as one in which parallel realities co-existed and sometimes met, in which the power of the dead must be taken seriously, and in which all things were alive with spirits, was not nearly as alien to this white European Christian as might be supposed."[26] Johnson's grounding in pre-Christian ways helped him to succeed in Iroquois life and to usurp traditional ceremonial roles, effectively re-creating mythic forms that had become archaic. He used scalps in traditional ways; he undertook long ritual journeys, for example in 1756, when he traveled to and from Onondaga, where he performed the condolence and requickening ceremonies to mark the death of Red Head; and he made special use of his knowledge of the particular significance of clan mothers to Iroquois political life.

Like many skilled mediators, Johnson was both useful (he was described by the Mohawk sachem Hendrick as "a Tree that grew for our use") and manipulative, using his cultural awareness repeatedly to enhance his prestige. (Hendrick also said of him, "His knowledge of our affairs made us think him one of us.")[27] Johnson was eloquent in English and learned the Mohawk language, but it was his background that allowed him to understand the performative dimension of power in the Iroquois context. His actions went far beyond the respect of protocol; they were the ritual actions of a preeminent sachem. When combined with providing for "his" Indian people (for example, when he brought to Onondaga a small herd of oxen and eighteen horses laden with presents), his authority in terms of directly influencing Indian politics was almost indisputable.[28] Johnson took the time to grasp the performative complexities of Iroquois ritual and thus to mark himself as a worthy leader in Indian terms. As O'Toole explains, "A ritual sachem of the Onondaga council—as opposed to the village headmen who conducted day-to-day business—was above all a performer, a man who could embody and give voice to the old forms. Johnson had become a formidable actor and rhetorician, and by refurbishing and demonstrating mastery of the forms, he was demonstrating chieftainship."[29] As one of his early biographers put it, Johnson, with his tall limbs and "poetic" features, was able to paint himself and dance with the Mohawk such that "he was at one with his fellow dancers, one flesh, one heart, one brain."[30]

It is important not to be misled by O'Toole's emphasis and to think that Johnson's "Indian" spirituality was exclusively strategic. Rather it should be seen as part of a long history of non-Indian adoption of Indian ways and of non-Indian acceptance of the power and significance of Indian spiritual relationships to the seen and unseen world. The point was once made by Vine Deloria Jr., who quoted an *Atlantic Monthly* article from 1886 in which the author admitted, "It cannot be denied that the whites, who consort much with the ruder tribes of Indians imbibe, to a considerable degree, their veneration of medicine. The old trappers and voyageurs are, almost without exception, observers of omens and dreamers of dreams. They claim that medicine is a faculty which can in some degree be cultivated, and aspire to its possession as eagerly as do the Indians."[31]

Johnson deepened and consolidated his kinship ties to the Iroquois by having the luck to take as his consort relatively late in life another prestigious and skilled cultural mediator, Joseph Brant's sister Molly, whose Mohawk name was Degonwadonti, often translated as Several against One. His marriage further facilitated his encroachment into the political territory of the traditionally dominant Iroquois clan mothers, allowing him to be admitted to village and confederacy councils that had previously been closed to him. In so thoroughly tying himself to Indian concerns Johnson linked his own power to the significance or otherwise of Indians to the interests of the British Crown, but on a personal level his objectives were to advance his personal family name, gain wealth, and re-create abroad key aspects of the cultural context he had left behind in Ireland.

Freemasonry and its ritual allowed him to combine all of these factors. He was first encouraged to join a lodge by Irish soldiers in the British Army in the late 1750s. It is thought that he was then raised as a Mason in Union Lodge No. 1 in Albany, New York, in 1766 and formed his own St. Patrick's Lodge at Johnstown the same year, with himself as Master. O'Toole explains that the fraternity attracted Johnson because it had been popular with the crypto-Jacobite Catholic gentry of Johnson's youth in County Meath in Ireland, because it provided a focus for extensive feasting at the local inn, and because it allowed him to celebrate St. John's Day ritual activity just as he had done in his early life. Most important, however, was that it allowed for common social ground for both Indians and whites: "It combined the ritual practices that had become so much part of his Indian life with a European form of clannish conviviality. The lodge meetings, indeed, seem to have been Johnson's way of recreating in a white, largely Irish setting the combination of prescriptive protocol and enthusiastic feasting that he had discovered at Indian councils."[32] In practicing Masonry the Johnson family and the Brants were joining a club that included many of the key military and diplomatic players of the time: the influential missionary to the Six Nations, the Reverend Samuel Kirkland, whose persuasive powers were appreciated by Washington, and Gen. John Sullivan, whose expedition along the Susquehanna still reverberates today because of its acute brutality against Indian peoples.

No detailed material exists that might help us analyze how significant Masonic ritual was in the creation and perpetuation by Johnson, Brant, and others of the idea of Iroquois "mystique" identified by Dorothy Jones in her book *License for Empire*. Certainly the idea of an Iroquois empire was useful to the Iroquois seeking preeminence over the tribes of the Old Northwest, to the British, and later to the Americans. To what extent such a diplomatic tool was solidified and ritualistically developed within Masonry is impossible to quantify, but it is clear that the link is there, a point of intersection through ritual that served to allow one empire to interact with and for its own purposes to promote another.

It seems likely that Masonry prospered in Johnson's intercultural fiefdom because he found it useful as a means of bringing key individuals together across cultural boundaries. After all, colonial politics revolved around patronage and face-to-face contact oiled with the kind of eloquence that was Johnson's forte. Freemasonry's mix of ritual, selection, and brotherhood could be understood and related to on an early American frontier that was a minefield of competing interests, some of which had much more in common with Indian lifeways than with the mores of the still formative American nation-state. In fact in the years surrounding the 1760s the Johnson estates (near present-day Schenectady) were a gathering ground for a number of kin-based societies buffeted by new economic realities and by colonial expansion. A significant number of Highland Scots, for example, rented land from Johnson, some veterans from Highland regiments, others direct immigrants from Scotland. Like most others on the frontier they acted in their own interests, yet Highlanders had much in common with the Indians in Johnson's orbit. They too were a tribal set of peoples, who venerated their homeland and their ancestors. They too were considered by the English to be barbarians, and their respect for clan, kin, and aspects of communalism deemed alien.[33] All of the people on Johnson's land needed a means whereby they could peacefully perpetuate and selectively develop their cultural heritage. The ritual-based fraternalism of Freemasonry was a way elites could do just that, part of a wider sensibility Johnson fostered from Europe that tied disparate folk together in a hierarchical set of reciprocal relationships.

Tellingly it was to his Masonic community that William Johnson left the care of his eight children with his third wife, Molly Brant. He nominated five Masons as his children's guardians, "in full confidence that . . . they will strictly and as *Brothers* inviolably observe and Execute this my last charge to them." His Masonic brothers brought him peace of mind as he approached death; he noted, "[My] strong dependence on, and expectation of [them] unburthens my mind, allays my cares, and makes a change less alarming."[34] After his death Six Nations sachems performed a condolence ceremony, ritualistically burying Johnson and simultaneously resurrecting him by recognizing his successor, his nephew and son-in-law, Guy Johnson.

William Johnson's funeral, in the words of the anthropologist William Fenton, must have been "the spectacle of the decade." More than two thousand people attended, including Indian representatives who, according to contemporary sources, "all behaved with the greatest decorum and exhibited the most lively marks of real sorrow." Johnson, or Warraghiyageh, was an adopted Mohawk of the senior moiety of the Confederacy, so conducting his death ritual fell to the junior moiety and a speaker named Conoghquieson. Fenton felt able to infer the ritual content of the event from records left by Guy Johnson:

> Three words (with three strings); covering the body (double belt); covering the grave (belt of six rows); and remarks to the mourner: relief that the fires would continue to burn at Johnson Hall and at Onondaga (belt of seven rows). With a second belt of similar dimensions, the speaker swept the fireplace clean. A bunch of strings requested that Guy attend when their ceremonies were performed and advise the young men in the manner of Sir William.
>
> Knowing that the mourner was loaded with grief, they metaphorically cleansed his body and washed his insides with clear water, that he might again tend to business. Both sides were obscured by clouds, which the speaker dispelled, after which he restored the sun to its proper course (two strings).

Johnson's funeral was an event of the utmost diplomatic and social significance. As Fenton put it, "One cannot imagine

[Iroquois] reverence for the dead and the importance they attach to proper ceremonies. In short, they cherish the dead and attain their best in ritual."[35]

Masonic tradition continued in Iroquois territory, with Joseph Brant's children maintaining the family's fraternal links and Sir William Johnson's son John taking up the bonds of ritual brotherhood. Although said to be not very bright, John went on to serve as provincial Masonic Grand Master in New York in 1767 and as provincial Grand Master of Quebec in 1788. Brant's and Johnson's influence helped to keep Upper Canada Masonic, with Freemason's Hall, Niagara, a cultural hub for the region and the place where Indian politics was carried out. The whole of the eighteenth century was revolutionary for Native America, not just the years 1775–83, but at the high point of forced change, internecine politics, and destruction we find that a link solidified between Indian peoples and Freemasonry that would only grow as Indian peoples continued to negotiate change over succeeding generations.

Native American Freemasons

8

The "Settlement" of the West
and the Civil War Era

> Americans of all ages, all stations in life, and all types of disposition
> are forever forming associations. There are not only commercial and
> industrial associations in which all take part, but others of a thou-
> sand different types—religious, moral, serious, futile, very general
> and very limited, immensely large and very minute. . . . Nothing,
> in my view, deserves more attention than the intellectual and moral
> associations in America.
>
> —ALEXIS DE TOCQUEVILLE, *Democracy in America*

Tocqueville's advice to pay attention to American associational
life creates its own complexities when it comes to relations between Indians and non-Indians in the West. Perhaps unfashion-
ably, examining Indian-Masonic fraternal relationships tends to
paint a picture of, if not rosy cooperation, then at least genuine
and mutually enabling interaction. Reading Masonic records we
get a positive picture of interethnic brotherhood providing a basis for growth in the West. This, if it did apply, applied of course
only to Indian elite males; the larger truths of Indian dispposses-
sion, displacement, oppression, and acute discrimination in this
period still stand. It is essential to recognize that despite the picture of cross-racial cooperation painted by Masonic sources the

West is a place of successive conquest in the way Patricia Limerick and her successors have explained. Masonic histories should be seen, like all western histories, in the way Limerick has suggested, as part of "an ongoing competition for legitimacy—for the right to claim for oneself and sometimes for one's group the status of legitimate beneficiary of western resources."[1] Although we may find repeated testimony of positive interaction between Indian and non-Indian Masons, we must always remember that fraternal bonds in the main proved no barrier to the general narrative of Native displacement and atrocity in the nineteenth century. The fact that the primary architect of removal, Andrew Jackson, president from 1829 to 1937, was an important Mason goes some way toward illustrating the point, Jackson having been the first president to have previously served as Masonic Grand Master of his home state. That said, John Marshall, who enshrined what's been called "tribal quasi-sovereignty" as chief justice of the Supreme Court beginning in 1801, was also a Mason, specifically a past Grand Master of Virginia.[2]

Masonic sources point us toward a significant and often forgotten history of positive Indian-Masonic exchange and of Indian co-optation of Masonic forms and structures. Yet Masonry cannot be viewed exclusively as simply an acculturative force, since its structure and ethos were used by groups such as the Cherokee Keetoowah Society as a means of asserting and perpetuating Cherokee traditional values. Rather it would seem that Freemasonry was a vehicle for individual Indian men to achieve whatever their aims were at the time. Just as it did for Masons across the United States, the fraternity provided a context within which individual and group aims could be expressed, and it was at points both part of the wider society and discrete from it. Another important caveat should also be noted, however. While Indian Masonry in the mid-nineteenth-century West was significant, its place is difficult to pin down and it should not occlude the role of other, more inclusive political movements or that of Cherokee women, whose efforts ensuring that Cherokee culture persisted were fundamental.

Today it remains important to contemporary Masons, especially Oklahoma Masons, to stress that the links between Indians and Masonry in the West were deep-seated and positive. A wealth of anecdotal evidence testifies to Masonic signs having been used by Indians for generations as a means of finding common ground with settlers and as a way of gaining food and forging kinship. The contemporary senior Mason Robert Davis describes how the teacher Edmond Doyle, past Grand Master of the Oklahoma Grand Council, shared "Masonic intercourse" with an elderly Choctaw in 1876 using Masonic signs and symbolism. This was said to be a form of Choctaw "Horse Masonry" that included handshakes, words, symbols, and legends that were passed down from father to son. Davis also refers to the "full-blood" Cherokee group known as the Night Hawks, who shared the Masonic reverence for secrecy, exclusivity, and oaths, and he credits Masons such as Doyle, the missionary Joseph S. Murrow, the minister Robert W. Hill, and the key Masonic figure Albert Pike with "building a lasting bridge of communication and trust between the white and red men of the territory." He claims that "the fraternity of Freemasonry made the settlement to the new territory [i.e., the forced migration of tribes from the Southeast to what is now Oklahoma] one which enabled the Indian male culture to develop successfully within the framework of the competing, and expanding, Caucasian society." Davis argues that both Indians and Freemasonry arrived at the same time in what was then known as Indian Territory, and he credits Freemasonry with being the key ingredient that brought "law and order, civic pride, sound growth and successful integration of the white and red citizens."[3]

Leaving aside the fact that Indians did not in fact gain universal citizenship until 1924, Davis's point can still be too quickly dismissed as wishful thinking. After all, the mix of traders, ministers, and army officers that came to the Territory contained many Masons, as did the leadership of the Indian peoples displaced, most of whom had been raised in lodges in Washington or in Fort Smith, Arkansas. The list of significant Indian Masons in the first half of the nineteenth century includes the Cherokee leaders John Ross and his nephew William Potter Ross, the Cherokee politician David Carter, the Choctaw warrior Pushmataha, the Choctaw leader Peter Pitchlyn, the Seminole warrior John Jumper, and the Creek leader Yahola. Oklahoma is unique; nowhere else saw Indian membership in Freemasonry on such a scale, with much of the early Masonic lodges in Indian Territory predominantly Indian in membership. Leadership of the first organized Indian lodge, Cherokee Lodge No. 21, opened under petition from the Grand Lodge of Arkansas in 1848, was entirely Indian. William P. Ross, who had achieved the Master Mason degree in Washington DC the same year he was there signing a treaty, was its first secretary and one of its early masters. According to federal lodge records, Ross's Masonry provided senior white officials with a means on at least one occasion to overcome internal Cherokee factionalism: "He (Ross) and other headmen of the Cherokee nation were at the capital to arrange a treaty made necessary by the late enforced removal of the tribe from Georgia to the Indian Territory. These headmen were arrayed in two hostile factions, and the negotiations were at a standstill. But at one of the meetings of the Federal lodge, the rival leaders, all Freemasons, were brought together by the exertions of Worshipful Master S. Yorke Atlee and other members, and the treaty was then successfully concluded."[4]

For contemporary Masons such as Jim Tresner, the very fact that Ross was permitted to preside over a Masonic lodge at that time is evidence of the fraternity's inclusiveness and power to heal cross-cultural divides. But it is perhaps more appropriate to see Ross's Masonic membership as part of his general openness to assimilation and as being in keeping with his willingness to extend his strategic relationships in the non-Indian world. As a Mason Ross was duplicating the fraternal behavior of those non-Indians he saw as his peers; Freemasonry was simply one more innovation among a litany of new traditions during a tumultuous time in Indian Country. He served alongside David Carter as Treasurer and other Indian members who were Cherokee Supreme Court judges or who printed the Cherokee Nation newspaper, the *Cherokee Advocate*. Another five lodges were organized serving Choctaw and then Creek Masons before the wholesale fraternal disruption brought on by the onset of the Civil War.[5]

Davis's pride about how intertwined Masonic and Indian history has been in the West mirrors that of other Masonic writers in the past. J. Fred Latham wrote in 1957, "The history of the Indian Territory, and indeed that of Freemasonry in the present state of Oklahoma, is so closely interwoven with that of the Five Civilized Tribes it would be difficult—almost impossible—and entirely undesirable to attempt to separate them."[6] Others, to their credit, had little patience with Indian stereotypes or anti-Indian prejudice within Masonry itself. H. L. Haywood wrote in 1953 about the Wyandots, who organized the first lodge in Kansas but who, preposterously, were denied the honor of being No. 1 lodge because they were Indian and had to settle for becoming No. 3. He also wrote with disdain of the lurid Indian stereotyping of the 1880s and of the "abandoned imbecility" with which it got perpetuated even though "as a matter of fact, both hard and cold, the Indians who settled Indian Territory were superior mentally, morally, and religiously to many of the whites who settled in their midst."

Haywood was proud to list the Cherokees in Tahlaquah, Oklahoma, who received the first charter from Arkansas, the Choctaws who started Doaksville Lodge in 1852, and the Creeks who founded Mus-co-gee Lodge in 1855. These early lodges served, he explained, like the lodges of the revolutionary era, as schools, churches, relief agencies, and post offices: "And the Indian brethren, especially the powerful and wealthy Choctaws, were at the forefront in all possible social and humane endeavours."[7]

As I explored in chapter 6, there is a long-held wish within Masonic circles that in the American context Freemasonry be seen to have fulfilled its ideal of creating universal brotherhood. Too often, as in Tresner's remarks referred to earlier, the ugly, brutal, sometimes genocidal realities of non-Indian settlement on Indian lands and Indian displacement east to west have been downplayed in favor of the myth of an enlightened Masonic middle ground. Even so, almost all the key Indian figures in Indian Territory in the years surrounding the Civil War were Masons, both those who signed treaties deemed to be to the detriment of their own peoples and those who did not.

Indian Masons, it seems, used the fraternity as a social resource, as a place or set of places where they might garner support for their respective causes, which by necessity shifted over time. Along with their Christian churches, their lodges provided another avenue of cultural exchange and another means whereby the perpetuation of things Indian could be negotiated. The lodge environment can be seen as largely acculturative since Freemasonry was primarily a non-Indian organization, but a number of lodges were also very much Indian spaces in the sense that they were either dominated by Indians or spaces that could be used for Indian aims, however varied. According to the Seneca anthropologist Arthur Parker, writing in the early 1920s, when it came to "civilizing the Indian" on the frontier, although it has largely gone unrecorded, "the strongest contacts were through the lodges." Officers on frontier posts were Masons, as were government officials and some missionaries. In this sense it would be surprising if Indian leaders were *not* Masons. Aside from the work done within the lodges, frontier Masons were the ones organizing the building of schools and hospitals and in some cases the provision of relief. And of course, as Parker notes, Masons in Indian Territory carried out a great deal of unorganized charitable work.[8]

Masonry provided a common organizational and ritualistic experience for a number of Indian and non-Indian elites, but fraternal bonds did not prevent brutal Indian dispossession even though Masonic writers have claimed that such bonds ameliorated it. Fraternal empathy did not cause Andrew Jackson to waver from a determination to view Indians in the East as precisely what they were not: helpless children best removed from their own homelands for their own good, people who "cannot live in contact with a civilized community and prosper."[9] While contemporary Masons such as Patrick Minges join older Masons such as J. Fred Latham in claiming that officers charged with carrying out removal showed Masonic "compassion," this was at best within a tiny parameter. The fraternal kindnesses shown by Masons such as Gen. Winfield Scott during removal (for example, by acquiescing to requests to delay made by Indian fraternal brothers such as John Ross) in no sense outweighed the atrocities that occurred during the process they oversaw or counterbalanced actions such as Winfield's authorization of the execution of the Cherokee leader Tsali and his sons, who resisted removal.[10]

Albert Pike: Defender of Indian Territory

One man who connects a number of the Indian Masonic figures of the mid-nineteenth-century West is the grandfather of Scottish Rite Freemasonry, the Boston-born lawyer, poet, and prolific esoteric writer Albert Pike (1809–91). Remarkably intelligent, but also much carped at during his lifetime for being arrogant and conceited, he was a truly Byronic figure with immense appetites who served as Confederate commissioner for Indian Affairs and military commander during the Civil War. His Civil War exploits interrupted his writing the book for which he is best known, the magisterial, unreferenced Herculean effort that is the 861-page distillation of the philosophies of the Gnostics, Hebrews, Alexandrians, Druids, and Essenes and exploration of the ancient mysteries of Egypt, Persia, Greece, and India, *Morals and Dogma* (1871), a thirty-two-lecture accompaniment to Pike's revision of the work and rituals of the first thirty Masonic degrees under the jurisdiction of the Scottish Rite's Supreme Council. "A sort of man who when found, you make a note on," as one contemporary newspaper reporter described him, Pike was utterly unforgettable both in his time and across the mists of history.[11] Habitually dressed as if it were still the revolutionary era, imposingly large (he weighed around three hundred pounds toward the end of his life), with a magnificent mane of glossy hair, a huge beard, and moustache, he was often seen obsessively smoking an exotic meerschaum pipe. He was also a noted gourmand. Some of the tamer stories that survive describe him regularly setting off into the woods accompanied by wagonloads of prostitutes to set up camp to engage in prolonged sessions of indulgence in rich food, merriment, and liquor. A poet, prodigy, adventurer, and politician, Pike was the preeminent fraternal figure of his era. He also, however inadequately, tried to advance and protect Indian interests.

American Masonry has honored no other man more since Washington. Pike even has a complete room dedicated to him in that exceptional building, the House of the Temple of the Supreme Council in Washington DC. There he is described as "lawyer, linguist, teacher, scholar, frontiersman, editor, journalist, nation-ally-known poet, internationally-known philosopher, a mind of almost unimaginable intellectual scope, a man of unlimited compassion—Illustrious Brother Albert Pike, Grand Commander of the Mother Jurisdiction from 1859 to 1891." The room contains a miniature version of the life-size statue of Pike that remains, despite recent protests because of Pike's supposed links to the Ku Klux Klan, on Indiana Avenue Northwest in Washington, between the Municipal Center and the Department of Labor building. The larger statue was paid for by the Supreme Council. Here, clutching *Morals and Dogma*, Pike is the only Confederate officer honored among Washington's outdoor Civil War statuary.

Although his life history can be read in other ways, it is hard to disagree with the many Masons and others who see Pike as an early champion of Indian peoples and advocate of their rights.[12] This is in keeping with his presentation as the quintessential white frontier hero by his foremost biographer, Walter Lee Brown. Admittedly it is a characterization Pike himself would have richly appreciated. He grew up fully imbued with the romance of the West and frustrated intellectually and socially in the North. He fell in love with the idea of the frontier as a place where he would no longer be hidebound by convention and resolutely set off to find it. Just as D. H. Lawrence, another eloquent sensualist, would in the 1920s, in the 1820s Pike ended up in Taos, New Mexico, before he finally settled permanently in Arkansas in 1832. His extensive and daring travels on foot brought him considerable contact with Indian peoples, and he learned some Indian languages and customs. Yet his concern for and interaction with Indians was practical as well as social. Around 1852 he set about pursuing a land claim against the government on behalf of the Creek and managed to get a recommendation that they be paid for 8,849,940 acres. His success led to a commission to do the same for the Choctaw and Chickasaw. Pike was underemployed at the time he took on these cases, but pursuing them successfully was still a remarkable achievement given the paucity of occasions when significant Indian legal redress was achieved on any level in the nineteenth century. After much effort on his part, in 1856 the U.S. Senate awarded $800,000 to the Choctaws and Chickasaws, and Pike received $10,000 as a partial fee. The next year the Creeks were awarded $800,000 and Pike received $120,000 in gold. More Indian awards and subsequent payouts to Pike totaled $190,000 from Indian claims. Just what he did with what was at the time a staggering amount of money is unknown, but only five years after the payout it is thought that he was poor again. Given Pike's propensity to live in the moment (he once chartered a steamboat in which to party uproariously), it has been suggested that it was quickly spent on entertainment and rich living.

Pike's good standing in Indian Country led to his being appointed Confederate commissioner of Indian Affairs in 1861, charged with the task of tying the Indians of the West to the Confederacy and with raising Indian battalions and regiments. Pike was not the only Confederate negotiating with the Indians of western Arkansas, but he was central to key developments. Circumstances were on his side; Union forces looked weak from an Indian perspective because Indian Territory had been left without a federal garrison and the Union was too fearful to send the money owed in overdue annuities promised by treaty. Eventually Pike was able to complete treaties of alliance between the Confederate government and the Creek, Choctaw, Chickasaw, Seminole, Osage, Seneca, Quapaw, and Shawnee. Valuing Cherokee neutrality and aware that his people were owed $5 million under treaty, the old, diminutive, Scots Irish Cherokee leader John Ross (Guwisguwi, 1790–1866) held out against Pike but was finally forced to sign a treaty on October 7, 1861. Both Ross, who in appearance looked every bit the landed, conventional conser-

vative businessman he was, and the young leader of the Cherokee faction that opposed him, Stand Watie, who cultivated what
is thought of as a more stereotypically "Indian" appearance, were
Masons. Aside from being Masons, Pike, Ross, and most of the
Indian Masons referred to here were also slave owners, like most
of their social peers. Theda Perdue's work has explored how Cherokee slave owning was qualitatively different from how it was
practiced elsewhere in the South, but it remains the case that the
Cherokee national government was mainly slave owning. Of the
twelve signers of the 1827 Cherokee Constitution, eleven owned
22 percent of all the slaves of the Cherokee nation.[13]

Predictably, just how significant specific Masonic connections
were to the Confederate power play in Indian Country is hard to
ascertain. Certainly for some contemporary scholars, such as Patrick Minges, the fact that Pike raised men such as the Choctaw
leader Peter Pitchlyn, the Cherokee leader and in 1864 Confederate congressional delegate Elias C. Boudinot (1835–90), and the
national secretary of the Chickasaw Nation Holmes Colbert, to
the Scottish Rite thirty-third degree in 1860 is extremely telling.[14]
Minges concludes, "Pike's Masonic connections were a critical factor in consolidating support among the Five Nations for the Confederate States of America."[15] Ross became a Mason in Jasper, Tennessee, in 1827, and although his Master Mason certificate is with
his papers in the Gilcrease Institute, one of his main biographers
does not suppose him to have been active within his lodge.[16] Even
so, much of the leadership involved in the politics of the Confederacy in Indian Country (including Joseph and David Vann and
John Ridge) all shared a ritual and fraternal history and with it
access to a discrete Masonic vocabulary and symbolic worldview.

Ross's objective was to maintain Cherokee and Indian unity
in a politically impossible situation, and a number of Masonic
writers both at the time and since have been supportive of such

Indian attempts to remain neutral during the Civil War. As William Denslow puts it, "Freemasonry teaches loyalty to established government. The only government to which the Indian owed allegiance was his own."[17] The fraternal bonds that bound key Indian figures such as Ross, the Seminole leader John Jumper, Peter Pitchlyn (Choctaw), and Opothle Yahola (Creek) are seen as a key means whereby Indian communities negotiated the war. Pitchlyn in particular is described at length in Denslow's work as having used his Masonic links to assure Washington of Choctaw neutrality or allegiance to the Union. Even so, Pitchlyn was ultimately unable to prevent Choctaw involvement in the notorious battle at Pea Ridge in 1862, when at least one dead Union soldier was scalped, a public relations disaster for which Pike had to accept responsibility. Although the scalping may in fact have been committed by white Texans, Pike soon after resigned his commission.[18]

Pike had an eventful war, but he tried to put the defense of Indian Territory and Indian interests first. It would not in the end be possible for the Confederacy to deliver on the treaties he struck, but it is to his credit that they were significantly more favorable to Indian peoples than the status quo. In fact had Pike's recommendations been consistently applied by any U.S. government, Indian life in the United States would have been much improved, for they were framed so as to secure and maintain positive relationships into the future. Pike's ideas awarded Indian nations a degree of respect, sovereign autonomy, and political inclusion that in some respects still awaits Indian peoples today. For example, he tried to respect the desires expressed by fellow Masons and Indian leaders at a council in June 1861, where John Ross, John Jumper, Peter Pitchlyn, and Opothle Yahola spoke for the formation of a separate "Indian confederation," an idea similar to that put forward by the non-Native Creek leader and Freemason Augustus

Bowles a century before. Pike's 1862 proposals to Jefferson Davis urged complete separation of Indian Territory from all military connection to Arkansas and asked that the officer in charge of Indian Country not be subject to orders from elsewhere. He asked for strict preservation of Indian supplies and monies and for Indian troops to be well quartered and clothed, with the same pay and allowances as Confederate troops. The Cherokee Confederate treaty promised not to treat without the full constitutional authority of the nation, taking away the possibility of a minor leader betraying the wider interests of the tribe. The Cherokee also had the right to approve the Indian agents assigned to them and were awarded their own delegate to the Confederate Congress, and there was to be a general amnesty for all Cherokee accused of crimes in the South. Just as important, Cherokee men were not to enter into conflict unless their own lands were invaded, and only a minimum of Confederate troops were to be stationed on Cherokee soil. An 1862 Confederate Act preserved Indian customs on Indian land, privileged Indian applicants for government Indian roles, and gave Indian courts exclusive jurisdiction on a par with any other district court system. Ultimately the Confederacy could not deliver on its promises, but through annuities and financial allotments it nonetheless made available considerable sums to the Creeks, Choctaws, Chickasaws, Seminoles, and Cherokees.[19]

Pike was rewarded for securing the allegiance of the tribes with his appointment in 1861 as brigadier general of the Provisional Army of the Department of Indian Territory, with his headquarters at Fort Davis in the Cherokee Nation. The man who called for his appointment was also a Mason, Secretary of State for the Confederacy Robert Toombs. As Confederate commissioner to the Indian Nations Pike had an appropriation from the Confederate Congress of $100,000 for use through the Confederate

Bureau of Indian Affairs. He had the Indian Mason Stand Watie organize the Second Cherokee Mounted Rifles; another battalion was headed by yet another Mason, the Seminole war leader and committed Baptist John Jumper (1820–96), mentioned earlier; and a General Cooper led the Choctaws. In what was to be a brutal period in Indian Territory for Native peoples, Pike's Confederate Indian agent was the young missionary Joseph Samuel Murrow, who later went on to serve as the state of Oklahoma's Masonic Grand Master and then for many years as its Grand Secretary. Pike was never able to get his Indian troops adequately quartered or armed or properly backed by Confederate troops even though his letters stressed the need: "It is important that our Indians should have our troops by their side, that they may not conclude that they are fighting for us only and not for themselves."[20]

In the end Pike resigned in protest against his (much younger) district commander, Gen. Thomas C. Hindman, who had ordered him to send his troops to Arkansas in May 1862. Pike felt they should not be asked to serve outside of Indian Territory. He made matters worse by publishing his views on Hindman's abilities as a commander and by protesting further at how Hindman's predecessor had taken provisions, equipment, and money from Pike's command for use elsewhere. All of this got him arrested in November 1862, but the charges were soon dropped.[21] Pike's concern throughout was that he have sole command in Indian Territory so as to retain the respect of its Indian inhabitants. He wanted to "save the Confederacy this fine Indian country," and to do that he believed he "must be free, and have the means to carry out [his] plans."[22] There is evidence that as early as the beginning of 1864 he was anxious to safeguard Indian interests, specifically because he was convinced that the Confederacy was doomed. Therefore, with Peter Pitchlyn, he made plans to reestablish normal relations between the Choctaw and the U.S. government.[23]

To Mark C. Carnes Pike epitomizes the frustrated Victorian male who can find no usable way to express his understanding of manhood. Like Horatio Alger Jr., whose inspirational stories were replete with fraternal motifs, Carnes sees Pike as one of the "marginal men" of the time who "retreated from the routine patterns of work and family and immersed themselves in romantic literature, history or mystical religions."[24] Carnes describes Pike as something of a failure, or at least someone unable to reconcile the gender bifurcations of his time. So how should he be seen? Pike was undoubtedly challenged by the gendered change afoot when he lived, and like a number of prominent men of his time he had a complex marriage. But the traditions he invoked and the world he wished to inhabit transcended his era and his gender. He sought the recovery of a lost ethos, a return to the kind of harmonious spiritual equilibrium he saw in "primitive" traditions the world over. Fraternalism for Pike was a means whereby man could regain an awareness of his own dualistic nature and achieve the harmony and internal equilibrium that mankind had quested after throughout the ages: "[Only then could men comprehend how] to reverence ourselves as immortal souls, and to have respect and charity for others, who are even such as we, partakers with us of the Divine Nature, lighted by a ray of the Divine Intelligence, struggling, like us, toward the light; capable, like us, of progress upward toward perfection, and deserving to be loved and pitied." Pike's "HOLY EMPIRE of true Masonic brotherhood" was a spiritual Nirvana, a world he wished to conjure through fraternal ritual that was universal in outlook and inclusive in a way he felt far surpassed the politics of gender in his era.[25]

The idea of making women or blacks equal in this quest was, for Pike, unthinkable. Rather he sought to bring about a utopia based on the acquired wisdom of certain previous generations who had left clues to spiritual completeness in Masonry's shift-ing symbolism and ancient mysteries. He reached a point where his Masonic work began, he said, "to shape itself to [his] intellec-tual vision into something imposing and majestic, solemnly mys-terious and grand": "It seemed to me like the pyramids in their grandeur and loneliness, in whose yet undiscovered chambers may be hidden, for the enlightenment of the coming generations, the sacred books of the Egyptians, so long lost to the world; like the Sphinx, half buried in the sands. In its symbolism which, and its spirit of brotherhood, are its essence, Freemasonry is more than any of the world's living religions. So I came to see that symbol-ism is its soul."[26]

Pike's devotion to Scottish Rite Masonry's spiritual journey did in the end take over his life. From 1880 to 1883 he actually lived in the Supreme Council rooms in Washington, before ending his days in a residence known as the House of the Temple. His ambi-tion and achievements, materially and spiritually, cannot be judged solely in terms of the gender politics of his age. Rather Pike de-serves to be seen as an important figure in terms of the popular spiritual and ritual leadership of his time and as someone whose fraternal commitment led him to do his utmost for the Indian communities he knew and respected.

The Keetoowah Society

If Masonry could be said to have provided one of a number of frameworks surrounding how war was conducted in Indian Ter-ritory and how an assimilationist impetus was advanced, it was also used by Indian Masons as a ready organizational influence when it came to preserving the "Keetoowah spirit," the Cherokee "old ways" that prioritized freedom and communalism. Formed in the late 1850s, the Keetoowah Society was the fourth wave of Cherokee revitalization in the nineteenth century, embodying resistance to southern slavery, to individualism, and to the racialized inequality these enshrined. In the midst of a war that brought death, havoc, schism, and much suffering to Indian Country, Freemasonic organizational influences were an important part of the syncretic mix that Cherokee peoples drew upon to preserve what was most important and most threatened within their community. In one sense Keetoowah secret society fraternalism was used to counteract its opposite. According to Robert Wright in *Indian Masonry*, the Kïtúhwá secret society was organized by an adopted Cherokee citizen and missionary's son, John B. Jones, ostensibly to cultivate national feeling among Cherokee full-bloods in opposition to the innovations being sought by mixed-bloods. "Its real purpose, however," he explains, "was to counteract the influence of the 'Blue Lodge' and other secret secession organizations among the wealthier slave-holding classes, made up chiefly of mixed bloods and whites." Known as "Pin Indians" because they wore a pin to identify each other, the group "gave good service to the Union cause throughout the war" and thereafter "distinguished itself by its determined opposition to every scheme looking to the curtailment or destruction of Cherokee national self-government."[27] Cherokee Blue Lodge or Masonic pro-slavery influences later formed the Knights of the Golden Circle, led by Stand Watie and other Cherokee elites such as Elias Boudinot and John Rollin Ridge.

Thus Keetoowah marked the onset of a political realignment in Cherokee national politics, with conservative, largely nonelite full-bloods who were often northern Baptists ranged in opposition to elite, mixed-blood leaders, often southern Baptist or Methodist in affiliation, espousing the rhetoric of progress. Although Keetoowah triumphed, it was the Keetoowah group's ideology of exclusion and inclusion that ultimately proved most problematic. Keetoowah was inclusive in that it was open to all Cherokees but exclusive in the sense that Cherokee society was by this stage highly diverse, with many non-Indians intimately linked to Cherokee communities. One of John Ross's key objectives throughout the Civil War had been to secure unity not only within his own people but among all Indians. As leader of the Keetoowah he struck a new treaty with the United States on July 19, 1866, abolishing slavery within the Cherokee nation but controversially also conceding eight hundred thousand acres in Kansas. This was a severe loss, but at least Cherokee leadership remained, as Ross saw it, in Cherokee hands. Keetoowah had Cherokee "old ways" at its core, used Baptist and African and Indian church mechanisms, but also used the familiar organizational structure of Freemasonry, with its emphasis on secrecy, its ways of contextualizing lodge work and ritual, and its signs and tokens for recognition of members as a vehicle for achieving its aims. These, to paraphrase William McLoughlin, were to abolish slavery and to narrow the gap between wealthy "progressive" slave owners, with their large plantations, and the non-slaveholding farmers who had only one horse and a plough.[28] Keetoowah was syncretic Cherokee revitalization, but in its emphasis on initiation, lodges, districts, ritual, and fraternal unity it owed much to Freemasonry as an organizational platform.

Thus the Civil War era in Indian Territory reveals how Freemasonry was put to multiple uses by Indian and non-Indian alike. Perhaps most notably, as Butler points out, it provides yet further evidence of the appeal of secret and magical beliefs to middle- and upper-class men in the period, since up to one hundred thousand men joined American Masonic lodges between 1790 and 1840.[29] Overall the war served to enlarge and deepen Masonry's prestige. For Piatigorsky, this was in part because during the conflict Masons tried to operate as a "third force," unsullied by the divisions rending North and South and serving to bring the warring factions together.

Perhaps the greatest positive portrayal of Masonic higher ground during the war years stemmed from the repeated stories about Masonic funerals. Here one combatant (usually an officer) would allow his fellow Mason fighting on the other side a Masonic burial, transcending the present conflict and showing Masonic brotherhood to be a timeless inner bond joining men across all boundaries. As one Confederate officer put it, "As a Mason, I know it to be my duty to accord Masonic burial to the remains of a Brother Mason, without taking into account the nature of his relationship in the outer world."[30] Yet Masons were also seen as the establishment (such as at Port Washington in 1862) and as promoting the draft, inspiring resentment that in time involved Masons in the greatest riot in American history, on July 13, 1863, in New York.

During Reconstruction Indian Country was in disarray and most of the antebellum lodges lost their charters. Indian lands had served as the theater of war, and the treaties struck when hostilities ended left Indian peoples painfully open to exploitation by the railroads and opportunists from the East. Even so Indian Masonry eventually regrouped and new lodges were formed. When Doaksville Lodge No. 279 was chartered in 1871 all of its officers were Choctaw, and many of the luminaries of Caddo Lodge No. 311, chartered in 1873, were Indian also. A Grand Lodge of Indian Territory was formed in 1874 with the Scots Irish Indian George W. Stidham as its Grand Treasurer, but it took until 1896 for a man of Indian extraction to reach the status of Grand Master (Silas Armstrong, Frisco Lodge No. 24). Possibly because of the number of northern sympathizers it had contained, Cherokee Lodge No. 21 was never to have its charter from the Grand Lodge of Arkansas reinstated, but in 1877 Cherokee Lodge No. 10 was granted a charter by the Grand Lodge of Indian Territory, and it persists today.[31] As the twentieth century dawned, Chero-kee Freemasonry was able to retain some of its profile through the vaudeville and film humorist Will Rogers (1879–1935). Rogers was a proud Mason and in life and outlook exemplified some of the fraternity's most positive attributes.[32] One such was its commit-ted antisectarianism. He did not think any one religion was *the* religion, but admired how peaceful and happy "spiritualists" were when they died. "After all," Rogers said, "all there is to living is to go away satisfied." After his tragic death, a year subsequent to his being voted the most popular male actor in Hollywood, Masons and the American public alike mourned the loss of the Cherokee philosopher who had "never met a man [he] didn't like."[33] Raised a Master Mason in Claremore Lodge No. 53, A.F. & A.M. (An-tient Free and Accepted Masons), Claremore, Indian Territory, on March 13, 1906, Rogers had charm and unfailing good sense, especially when it came to Washington, which he called "the na-tional joke factory." He was deeply missed by Masons and the American public alike. As President Franklin D. Roosevelt said, he was "an outstanding American."[34]

Native American Freemasons

The Nineteenth and Twentieth Centuries

9

[Babbitt's] clubs and associations were food comfortable to his spirit. Of a decent man in Zenith it was required that he should belong to one, preferably two or three, of the numerous "lodges" and prosperity-boosting lunch-clubs; to the Rotarians, the Kiwanis, or the Boosters; to the Odd Fellows, Moose, Masons, Red Men, Woodmen, Owls, Eagles, Maccabees, Knights of Pythias, and other secret orders characterized by a high degree of heartiness, sound morals, and reverence for the Constitution. There were four reasons for joining these orders: It was the thing to do. It was good for business, since lodge members frequently became customers. It gave Americans unable to become Geheimräte or Commednatori such unctuous honorifics as High Worthy Recording Scribe and Grand Hoogow to add to the commonplace distinctions of Colonel, Judge, and Professor. And it permitted the swaddled American husband to stay away from home for one evening a week. The lodge was his piazza, his pavement café. He could shoot pool and talk man-talk and be obscene and valiant. Babbitt was what he called a "joiner" for all these reasons.

— Sinclair Lewis, *Babbitt*

The Indian Masonry of the nineteenth century and beyond was, in the words of the acclaimed Acoma Pueblo poet Simon J. Ortiz, evidence of "the creative ability of Indian people to gather in many forms of the socio-political colonizing force which beset them and to make these forms meaningful in their own terms."[1] Masonic Indians may or may not have joined Masonic lodges in the twentieth century for the same reasons as Babbitt did, but in joining they accessed a unique forum for educating non-Indians about Indians and for putting forward Indian values and viewpoints. In making an Indian identity synonymous with Masonic values, they maintained a special bond and subverted prevailing notions of Indian character and potential.

Perhaps we should not be surprised that Freemasonry has at points awarded Indians a starring role within its evolving ritual, since Masonry has from its very beginnings invoked a transcendent, all-encompassing sense of history that matches much of the myth that has been generated about Indian peoples. Both Masonry and mythologized Indians were said to be "timeless" and "ancient," and both stereotyped "Indianness" and Masonry were, it seemed, best realized through theatricality and performance. As Piatigorsky puts it pithily, "For Freemasons, from the time of their official historical foundation in 1717 onwards, the combination of historicism and theatricality has always had a special meaning and significance." In essence, he suggests, Masons have always been playing the part of their predecessors, working (operative) Masons. It is in ritual theater that the all-important Master Mason initiation establishes a connection between the individual Freemason and the biblical past as well as the past of all mankind.[2] Much extremely valuable work has explored how Indian identity in the white mind has tended to be atemporal, to operate outside of history, with Indians themselves only rarely comprehended as being coeval with living, modern Americans.[3] Bizarrely it has been because Indians and Masons share invented conceptual space in this sense that Indians have been accorded a privileged place within the fraternity. By making Indians part of

Masonic ritual, Masons gave their Indian brothers a role that was atemporal, since it existed within an infinitely repeatable enactment. As ritual actors Indians were powerful protagonists within a perception of reality specific to the fraternity and operating specifically within "Masonic time."[4]

Being Indian, Being a Man: Playing Indian within Fraternalism

"Indianness" has a long history in fraternal ritual, with direct links to how manhood (and by corollary boyhood) has been thought about over time in the American context. After the Civil War oath-based brotherhoods blossomed, providing new contexts for how manhood was viewed and enacted. Perhaps ironically this upsurge in ritualistic activity, which included a considerable degree of "playing Indian," coincided with a period of acute conflict between Indians and non-Indians. As a famous contemporary writer put it, the nineteenth century was America's Century of Dishonor.[5] The Civil War had slowed western migration, but its conclusion left the West thoroughly militarized and spurred even greater settler thirst for Indian land. The Great Santee Sioux Uprising of 1862 in Minnesota, the Five Civilized Tribes' treaties with the Confederacy, and the support given to the Confederacy by the Comanches and Kiowas were all the justification federal powers needed for further removal of Indian communities and reduction of Indian territories. In comparison to the noble warriors acted out in fraternal lodges, most actual Indians were suffering deeply. In the wake of the war the Bureau of Indian Affairs, which had been part of the War Department until it was transferred to the Department of the Interior in 1849, gained considerable power over Indian life, administering federal programs and acting as a trustee for Indian resources. There were notorious massacres of Indian communities by U.S. troops, notably at Sand Creek, Colorado, in 1864 and at Wounded Knee, South Dakota, in 1890, but in truth these were acute versions of a larger ongoing American war against Indian tribalism, Indian spirituality, and Indian values. In particular a repulsive form of educational and psychological warfare was ongoing against Indian children in brutal Indian boarding and day schools, augmented by child placement and adoption to non-Indian families. The primary piece of Indian legislation of the era, the General Allotment, or Dawes Act of 1887, was designed to foster rapid Indian assimilation to Euro-American ways, but in fact it simply broke up the remaining Indian lands that were held in common. What it did assimilate with dispatch was around two-thirds of the Indian land base into non-Indian hands. Many communities were forced onto economically unviable reservations, subject to repressive bureaucracy and unable to practice traditional modes of economic, social, and religious life. The American historian and eventual Pulitzer Prize winner Frederick Jackson Turner famously announced in 1893 that the frontier had "closed"; the idea then further solidified that Indians had somehow "vanished." Most Americans ignored the actual problems of Native peoples attempting against giant odds to survive and prosper within a dominant culture that relegated them to the periphery. Instead the national focus remained on invented Indians and a romanticized notion of frontier conflict that owed much more to Wild West shows, to dime novels, and in time to the movies than it did to the oppressive realities of contemporary Indian life.

At the same time as this obsession with romanticized versions of Indianness what E. Anthony Rotundo calls "passionate manhood" in mainstream American life came into its own. "Men began to look at the 'primitive' sources of manhood with new regard," Rotundo explains, "the martial virtues attracted admiration; and competitive impulses were transformed into male virtues."[6] As the nineteenth century progressed the older, communal form of manhood was eclipsed by a new, self-made version rooted in a new economics and politics that was based on the free play of individual interests. This shift from the community to the person made male identity more fluid, and it made the imaginative all-male hierarchies of the lodge especially attractive. It was an attraction also bound up with contemporary notions about what was special about boyhood. Boys in the mid-nineteenth century were talked about in the same way Indians were, as wild, primitive, savage, even as a race unto themselves. Boys' favorite game involved imaginatively becoming Indian; this allowed them to take on a persona deemed even more free and aggressively expressive than that of the cowboy. As boys grew into youths they organized themselves into groups, making new families using their imagination. Often these groups gave them a better education than what was then available in American colleges. As Rotundo points out, "Secret societies, lodges and fraternities grew up like weeds throughout the nineteenth century."[7] Ironically male fraternal spaces were often just as windowless and isolated as was much of middle-class domestic life, yet this was exactly what nineteenth-century boys and men sought to escape. Within the female domestic sphere, life for American men smacked of surveillance and of all the repression involved in the upkeep of good manners. Henry David Thoreau wrote pithily of just how uncomfortable domestic space was for the American male: "His house is a prison, in which he finds himself oppressed and confined, not sheltered and protected. He walks as if he sustained the roof; he carries his arms as if the walls would fall in and crush him, and his feet remember the cellar beneath. His muscles are never relaxed. It is rare that he overcomes the house, and learns to sit at home in it."[8]

In comparison the fraternal lodge offered a very pliable and comfortable all-male alternative and a version of family life without the social requirements that accompanied time spent with wives and mothers. According to Carnes, this "effacement" of actual family in favor of an all-male imagined fraternal family was key to fraternalism's attraction and explains why by the turn of the century one-eighth to one-quarter of all adult American males were fraternal members, with the proportion among the middle-class segment even higher.[9] It seems that having made women the guardians of moral virtue and general rectitude within the family, men were desperately keen to escape the very refinement and behavioral restraint they so often praised in their female counterparts. The relaxed but imaginatively highly charged atmosphere of the lodge was much more congenial than the home. As one gentleman quoted by Rotundo put it, in the lodge a man might "put his mind so to speak in a shooting jacket and slippers."[10]

Male "passion" could therefore be unleashed within the lodge, and American men could behave as they imagined "primitive" peoples did. This new identification with the supposed ways of primitive peoples was accompanied by a desire to seek out danger and wilderness, a desire that came imaginatively to the fore in fraternal ritual. As Rotundo explains, "The new rituals, which lay at the heart of fraternal activity and appeal, drew proudly and self-consciously on the customs of 'savage' peoples. The noted jurist Roscoe Pound said that Masonic rites had their origins in the 'development of societies out of the primitive men's house.' Men who saw themselves as the pinnacle of civilization were zealous to play the parts of those they considered part of the primitive past."[11] One example of overt Masonic identification with Indian ritualism as a demonstration of masculine fortitude and strength was the Indian Blood Brother Initiation, as described by the Mason Bliss Kelly, state news editor of the *Daily Oklahoman*.[12] Kelly recalled a secret meeting held in 1922 between a large number of Indian men and the commissioner of public health for the State of Oklahoma, John W. Duke, "a devoted Mason." As described, the ritual corresponded heavily with Masonic practice, with initiates, elections to membership, an emphasis on spiritual journeying, lectures on right living, an altar, a lodge Master, and the whole event ending with the class being "instructed in the signs of recognition, several of which were approximately the same as Masonic signs and grips. The sign of distress was the same, but the words were not understood." To be recognized as Blood Brothers the initiates had "to prove that they could endure long periods of strain without breaking" by having a thong passed under the muscle of the left breast and then dragging an attached stone around an enclosure in burning heat without stopping or drinking.[13]

Such an emphasis on an übermasculine primitivism was both a response to what was felt to be an excess of civilization in the wake of increasing urbanization, bureaucratization, and regimented work patterns and a response to women's increasing penetration of the public sphere. It is difficult not to see the proudly "masculine" and "primitive" roles played out in fraternal ritual from at least the mid-1850s onward as examples of the clichéd but often accurate psychological axiom that what is lost in reality gets restored and re-created in fantasy. The firm patriarchy and rigid gender roles acted out within the confines of the lodge assuaged the anxiety and neurosis-inducing lack of clarity pressing in upon its walls. As Carnes argues, emotionally Masonic rituals provided young men with benevolent and loving surrogate father figures, men capable of easing their transition into the increasingly complex realm of manhood.[14]

Within the fraternal lodge men could perform compensatory symbolic roles as artisans (the predominant representation of manliness of prior times), patriarchs, and very often as "primitive" Others. They could also be compensated psychologically for any lack of progress as workers in American bureaucracy since within the lodge members were rewarded with ever-higher levels of initiation and graduation to new levels of understanding. Here at least upward mobility was available to all who showed sufficient dedication. As perhaps all truly great social institutions do, Masonry thus resolved contradictions in a satisfying manner. It put forward a vision of society in which the cutthroat individualism of the age disappeared and in its place stood a collective, ritualized solidarity where all the social actors knew their place. White men were at its apex, and on occasion real and imaginary Indians shared with them an illustrious brotherly history across time.

Thus the turn of the century became what W. S. Harwood in 1897 called "the Golden Age of Fraternity." Reporting estimates that were conservative in comparison to his peers', he claimed there were five million fraternal members out of a total adult male population of nineteen million in 1896. These included some 810,000 Odd Fellows, 750,000 Freemasons, 475,000 Knights of Pythias, and 165,000 Red Men, alongside millions more who were part of the Grand Army of the Republic, the Knights of Labor, the Grange, or members of mutual insurance societies. Because many had multiple memberships, Harwood estimated that every fifth or eighth man belonged to one of America's seventy thousand fraternal lodges. The average lodge member spent a substantial sum, perhaps $200 on initiation fees and $50 annually on dues.[15] Another key explanation for this explosive growth in fraternal numbers was the activities of entrepreneurs (men such as Joseph Cullen Root, founder of the Modern Woodmen of America, and James J. Davis of the Loyal Order of the Moose) who saw a profit to be made in signing men up to groups that offered sociability, as well as the kinds of entertainment that prefigured the next century and that offered opportunities to pay into insurance and financial protection schemes. Yet at heart, and as we have already begun to explore, men's attraction to fraternalism in the postbellum world had much deeper roots.

The main choices for prospective Masons at the turn of the century were traditional Freemasonry ("Craft" or "Blue Lodge" Masonry), York Rite Masonry, Scottish Rite Masonry, or membership in the Ancient Arabic Order of Nobles of the Mystic Shrine, known as the Shriners. The York Rite reached its high point in the Gilded Age, but by the 1920s the Scottish Rite reigned supreme. Of course many chose to belong to all four of the main fraternal options at once and were thus able to take on multiple personas in their leisure time. Within the Scottish Rite a man could become an esoteric guru of sorts, a custodian of sacred knowledge passed on from ancient times; as a Blue Lodge Mason he was an architect—of himself and of his knowledge of self; as a Masonic Knight Templar he was a holy warrior; and within the risible Ancient Arabic Order of Nobles of the Mystic Shrine he could truly relax, play the buffoon, and engage in horseplay. In every case, however, the lodge was a place of escape. In its physical design, in its reverence for long-supplanted language, hierarchies, and possibilities, and in the fantastical worlds its theaters conjured up, the twentieth-century lodge was the antithesis of the Victorian parlor. Within it a man gained psychological certainty, be it through vanquishing explicit evil, reestablishing laws and morals, or ritually taking on the attributes of the greatest kings in history.

Yet when we look closely at Freemasonry and the groups associated with it as they peak in the late nineteenth century and beyond, it is hard to concur without reservation with the formidable commentators of the past who have urged us to see fraternalism as an outward-looking phenomenon, a key part of the bedrock of voluntarism underpinning American democracy. Following his visit in the 1830s to the United States, Tocqueville argued that in such an egalitarian society voluntarism was fundamental to its democratic success. Likewise for Arthur Schlesinger in 1949 voluntary associations were "microcosms of democracy" and "bulwarks of conservatism," while for Oscar and Mary Handlin in 1961 they were nothing less than "an essential factor in the development of American liberty."[16] Tocqueville's idea that American democracy is rooted in civic voluntarism was recently reinforced by Verba, Schlozman, and Brady in *Voice and Equality* and in a high-profile fashion by Robert Putnam in his book *Bowling Alone*. Freemasonry no doubt has been essential to the voluntarism at the heart of American democracy, but it is a form of voluntarism that is inward-looking, concerned with satisfying the personal and collective desires of its members rather than with democratic politics in the wider sense. In the Victorian era at least fraternalism's core activity was not to provide insurance schemes for its members or charity for society at large, and certainly not to discuss politics, which was forbidden by organizational decree. Rather its primary activity was ritual, and with it the chance for men to act out heroic and thrilling identities in fantastic costumes. The lodge offered a glorious sanctuary and a precious spiritual, social, and gendered escape from reality.

Here we are reminded of Matthew Arnold's injunction that culture is "above all, an inward operation. . . . Culture . . . places human perfection in an *internal* condition."[17] Masonic ritual was enjoyed by many men in many circumstances, but it was intended to create an environment where a man could appreciate himself and his potential contribution to society as an individual. To an extent in practice this shifted as the twentieth century developed and Masonic ritual took on a more mass-oriented, group atmosphere. At the same time American society more generally began a process of differentiation, in which the mass was deemed lowbrow and the highbrow became sacralized and its dissemination professionalized.[18]

It was Freemasonry's very inwardness and its commitment to the repeated creation of another, ritualized and highly sensory world that led to its losing ground beginning in the 1920s to the much less ritualistic or spiritually serious service clubs, such as Rotary, Kiwanis, and Lions. Ritual was minimized, secrecy largely ignored, and laughter and jollity almost enforced in these clubs. Selectivity in Masonic membership also increased, so that it became confined to those from specific professional categories. The new service clubs put the emphasis on the social rather than the sacred and responded to the newly developing need for leisure in a rapidly urbanizing world as opposed to the dwindling need for religious asylum. This turn-of-the-century transformation may have been linked to the fact that American Masonry had accentuated and intensified its theatricality and orality in the mid-nineteenth century. As Carnes notes, it underwent a transformation from 1840 to 1860 such that British Masons felt moved to denounce the revised American rituals as "too long, too complicated, and too theatrical."[19] Carnes suggests that the excessive length of rituals left little time for men to actually associate, but this flies in the face of perhaps fraternity's longest-held raison d'être. Furthermore the performance of such long, intricate, and solemn rites would have necessitated much liaison and conviviality prior to and subsequent to the actual performances themselves. Instead, following Russell Lynes, we can perhaps view the Masonic ritual of the late nineteenth century as evidence of an emerging American middlebrow culture, where men came together on their own terms, in their own theaters, to perform their own rituals without the sanction or otherwise of the wider theater culture.[20]

Masonic Theater and the Indian Role

As the Ancient and Accepted Scottish Rite adopted the full theatrical trappings of the popular entertainment stage at the turn of the century, it caused something of a building boom in terms of Masonic real estate as existing lodges remodeled their temples and new lodges were erected. There was an associated growth in the number and type of suppliers of Masonic costumes and paraphernalia. Men attracted to Masonry's new approach found that their women supported their newfound interest, helping to raise funds and organize events.[21] An influx thrilled to dramatic new forms of initiation experience that incorporated state-of-the-art scenery, lighting, and stage effects. In fact so successful was the way the Scottish Rite dramatized the twenty-nine initiation rituals that led its dedicated members through a historical and religious journey that it eclipsed its rival, the York Rite.[22] In comparison York had only ten degrees, but it did allow its members to wear military uniforms and to march together to demonstrate fraternal solidarity, and this was a decided attraction. Yet it was theater that allowed the Scottish Rite, which had been an elite mystical branch of the craft in the Gilded Age, to become the latest thing in the age of movies and popular drama. Its membership leaped from around forty thousand in 1900 to six hundred thousand by 1930.

A key part of the success of the Scottish Rite was due to the exhaustive work of Sovereign Grand Commander of the Southern Jurisdiction Albert Pike. He spent over a decade revising its works and producing a fully scripted two-volume dramatization of the fraternity's twenty-nine degrees, a sister volume to the revision produced in 1867 by Charles McClenachan. Both sets of rituals take place largely in the Middle East, and always the heroic Mason at the center reiterates a great moral truth. Interestingly while Pike's flowery and largely impenetrable books invoke nature as the great teacher and refer to almost every arcane and ancient form of religion (in particular Kabbalah, Druidic spirituality, and ancient Greece and Rome) they make few explicit references to America's most obvious ancient systems of belief, those connected with Native American communities. Rather the emphasis was on American males as the just and all-seeing inheritors of all spiritual worth across time. Masons' prosperity was put forward as a sign of their rectitude and indicative of the fact that they were the summation of the good that had evolved over eons. A short paragraph from Pike's 1871 *Moral and Dogma: The Council of Kadosh* gives a sense of this and may be taken as representative of the rest of its more than nine hundred pages:

> Masonry, when properly expounded, is at once the interpretation of the great book of nature, the recital of physical and astronomical phenomenon, the purest philosophy, and the place of deposit, where, as in a Treasury, are kept in safety all the great truths of the primitive revelation, that form the basis of all religions. In the modern Degrees three things are to be recognised: The image of primeval times, the tableau of the efficient causes of the Universe, and the book in which are written the morality of all peoples, and the code by which they must govern themselves if they would be prosperous.[23]

As Scottish Rite Masonry became more ritualistically elaborate it expressed its rituals in ever more immediate and visually stimulating forms. Much of the information we have on just how theatrical Masonic activity became at this juncture we owe to C. Lance Brockman, academic and curator of the Weisman Art Museum of the University of Minnesota, who secured grants from the National Endowment for the Humanities to mount symposia and an exhibition and edit the collection *Theatre of the Fraternity, 1896–1929*. As this hitherto largely hidden aesthetic history is unearthed it helps us to see even more clearly just how important performing these alternative versions of the past was to nineteenth- and twentieth-century men and just how involved they were in acting out the variety of roles involved. It also reveals how in the early decades of the twentieth century Masonic initiation occurred for the first time on a mass scale, enjoyed unprecedented social prominence, and luxuriated in a performative richness that was entirely new. Of course how dazzled the individual Mason became by his initiation experience was dependent on the extent of the resources of his local lodge, but we know that by 1910, if not earlier, most Scottish Rite initiations were group affairs conducted on fully equipped stages. According to Brockman, the change from a participatory to a presentational space, from lodge to theater, happened first in 1884.[24]

The Scottish variety of Freemasonry has roots in the United States going back to 1761. Its degrees progressively taught initiates about the struggle between "good and evil, insight and ignorance" by requiring that they pay close attention to speech, allegory, and symbol.[25] The shift to theater that began in the 1880s altered the emphasis of ritual activity such that these moral and mystical messages became visually explicit and men were able to become part of truly spectacular displays, wearing magnificent costumes and stage makeup. Within this staged world modern American males were able to act out manly virtues and male morality. At a time of unprecedented social upheaval and change, within the lodge at least, their status as part of a "timeless" hierarchy was assured. Having completed Craft or Blue Lodge Masonry's three degrees before joining Scottish Rite, they could put themselves forward for steady advancement up to a thirty-second degree and time and time again be part of rituals that made them feel rooted in a world history full of famous figures, from King Solomon onward. All of this happened first in the newer cities, especially in the West, and it was helped by record levels of innovation. At the time the theater was beginning to enjoy a newfound social acceptability, and theatrical paraphernalia such as costumes, scenery, and lighting were much more available than before. Lighting was perhaps the most significant innovation, as electricity allowed ritual to reach new heights in emotional and dramatic impact.

Whereas before a candidate was initiated singly in a small group and required to memorize and recite ritual language and enact ritual activity, by the 1920s the process and experience had become much more impressive, but also potentially passive, with sometimes thousands of men being inducted simultaneously. The new Mason found himself largely an observer of giant theatrical initiation events, and as a result older Masons complained that the outward representation of the event began to hold central place rather than the inner, spiritual journey required of the individual degree candidate. Furthermore it was feared that the shift from participating to spectating lessened the sense of community that ritual was designed to inculcate. In one sense, however, this increasing theatricality should not come as a surprise. From Masonry's earliest records the lodge room had always been constructed so as to conjure a sense of otherworldliness, and light and darkness had always been used to reflect the inner journey toward knowledge that each successive ritual was designed to foster. Lodge rooms were guarded by a Masonic officer known as the Tyler, who carried a sword. Architecturally they were designed to allow for secrecy and prevent eavesdropping. Even their decoration was designed to make it easy for brothers to forget the outside world and imagine themselves lost in the majesty of a Masonic version of the past.

During the acting-out of rituals, or "floorwork," of the first three degrees of Blue Lodge or Craft Masonry, the lodge room became Solomon's temple and as such usually had a pair of pillars at its western end. Blue Lodge Masonry also usually had brothers facing each other across a central altar, presided over by a religious book, usually the Bible, lit by candles known as the "lesser lights." Because Scottish Rite degrees were designed for Masons who had successfully completed the first three Blue Lodge degrees they were that much more elaborate, both in terms of the stories they depicted and the symbolic inner journey they intended to set the candidate upon. As William D. Moore explains, drawing on Charles T. McClenachan's *The Book of Ancient and Accepted Scottish Rite of Freemasonry* (1867), "Draperies of various colors and patterns were required, as were columns, candlesticks, altars of many shapes, and thrones of differing designs. While the lodge room represented Solomon's temple in the first three degrees, the Scottish Rite membership used ceremonial props and furnishings to transform the ritual space into various romantic locations, including a cavern, a secret vault beneath Solomon's temple, a bridge, the throne room of a Persian king, the road to Jerusalem, the summit of a mountain, a military encampment in the desert, and the court of Saladin."[26]

Masonic buildings in Chicago, New York, and Philadelphia had multiple such lodge rooms beginning in the 1870s, some in American Colonial style, others emphasizing the more traditional theme of Solomon's temple. The new stage machinery, exquisitely painted backdrops, lighting, props, and formidable proscenium stages all made it much easier to stimulate members into suspending disbelief and acting out newer and more satisfying scenarios. Key rituals such as the Hiram legend for Freemasonry, the Damon and Pythias fable for the Knights of Pythias, and the David and Goliath story for the Independent Order of Odd Fellows all lent themselves to particularly spectacular performance.

New tools added to the experience: magic lanterns and photographic slides replaced the tracing boards that had been used to explain the inner journey of the Mason and to special effects devices such as rain, wind, and thunder machines and the stereopticon could simulate movement and create illusion. One favorite stage effect revealed a secret word; another was an early version of the *Star Wars* light saber, an electrified sword that shot out sparks and made a noise like thunder. Yet another hit was the use of an English invention called Pepper's Ghost. It used lighting, glass, and a skeleton to show the degree initiate what he would look like when he was dead so as to help him see the true significance of the moral lessons he was learning.[27] Perhaps understandably leading Masons often denied that they were in essence creating top-notch theater in their lodges, but the introduction of such theatrical techniques and new mass initiation had a powerful, snowball effect.

As ritual life gained more texture and visual complexity, money flowed into lodge coffers, allowing Masons to reinvest in ever more lodges and brighter, better theater spaces. The Chicago stage, for example, was a colossal thirty-five feet wide by twenty-five feet deep and was "furnished with new scenery and properties and all the paraphernalia for displaying panoramic scenes, with a handsome illustrated drop curtain and rich drapery in front."[28] Scottish Rite Supreme Councils put few limitations on overall lodge design, and in this period new Masonic lodge buildings gained giant proportions, as many Americans know who drive past such buildings every day. The Fort Wayne, Indiana, "cathedral" was compared to a stadium, and the Los Angeles lodge was made of steel, brick, terra cotta, and marble and was 120 feet wide and 155 feet deep. The Detroit cathedral, completed in 1926, could seat almost 1,700 men; that in St. Louis in 1924 sat 2,950.[29]

One of the most impressive American lodges was built across four blocks in 1900 for $3 million in Guthrie, Oklahoma, on what had once been the state's Capitol Square. To give a sense of perspective, at the time one could buy a substantial house for $300,000. This is a special building, not least because it was built right in the heart of Indian Territory and because the foundations of Free-masonry in the state of Oklahoma are Indian. As the director of the current Oklahoma Masonic Degree Team, Terry Adams, explains, "Indians in Freemasonry go back to before our arrival in Indian Territory. Many of the principal Chiefs were Freemasons, most of them receiving their degrees in Washington DC or Fort Smith, Arkansas. The early lodges were practically 'all-Indian' in membership, with a scattering of military men and post merchants."[30] Guthrie was the fourth Masonic temple to adopt theater staging, and it did so with such gusto that some Southern Jurisdiction brothers suspected it of being "sacrilegious." The *Kansas City Star* went into rhapsodies about its beauty when it opened, in particular praising the "$10,000 of robes, vestments and paraphernalia, magnificent scenery for a stage 50 feet wide and 25 feet in depth," before quoting one commentator who proudly declared, "There is not a modern device known to stage equipment that cannot be found here. There are not to exceed half a dozen theatres in the country that have the electrical apparatus owned by this temple."[31] Guthrie in many ways consummated the change to theater initiation, for it made the shift in such a grand manner that the Supreme Council could not ignore it; neither, it appeared, were they minded to rule against it.

The extravagance and lavishness of the exterior of such buildings was matched by a luxuriousness and richness of interior design. There is ample evidence to support Clawson's claim that it is not enough to see nineteenth-century fraternalism simply in terms of its relationship to the religious and spiritual life of the United States; we should also see it "as a form of participatory theatre and a systematically marketed entertainment genre," that is, as one of a number of outlets that competed for the leisure dollar of the moneyed American male.[32] Thus the reason Masonic ritual was subject to such continual revision was not primarily in response to the changing spiritual needs of lodge members, but to adjust the main marketing tools to ensure that they fulfilled the primary aim of attracting ever more members. Other recent work tends to back up this emphasis on fraternalism in the early twentieth century as a self-perpetuating business and to point to there being a thriving market catering to male consumerism behind the grandiose fraternal interaction and ritual.

While there has been something of a scholarly consensus until recently that women were the primary consumers of the pre-Depression era, there is now greater awareness that in fact white men in the 1890–1930 period were an extremely large and important consuming constituency. In particular men were spending a great deal—in 1890 two and a half times as much as women—on clothing, including fraternal theatrical wear. According to the *Cyclopedia of Fraternities*, 40 percent of all males over twenty were members of at least one fraternal society in 1896; this suggests significant late Victorian male consumption in comparison with that of women.[33] Although annual dues and initiation fees were not insignificant, it was the ritual paraphernalia along with the accompanying meals and drinks to toast each other's performance that were most expensive.[34] At a minimum the Red Men fraternal group (from 1834) needed bows and arrows, knives, tomahawks, ropes, tents, shepherds' robes, sandals, and gongs; Freemasons and other groups needed top hats, jewels, bespoke seating, lambskin aprons, special glittering swords, drill corps uniforms, and embroidered banners.

The shift to the performance of ritual in theater settings within Scottish Rite Masonry occurred at the same time as American theater itself underwent a primary change. Instead of a theater experience that was decidedly social—where the audience was sovereign, and drinking, gaming, and rowdiness were not uncommon—the new theater etiquette necessitated silence and decorum and was about spectating and passively consuming the story on stage. In mainstream theater this shift was much more amenable to women. The growth in Scottish Rite ritual was at the forefront of a more pervasive transition to consumption. As a leisure activity its growth occurred at a time, after 1880, when, as Richard Butsch explains, "commercialization began in earnest" in the United States.[35] That said, the social and group identification aspects of Scottish Rite ritual were fortified by the larger context in which it was mostly performed, as part of three- or four-day "reunions" that interspersed ritual initiations with hearty banquets and drinking sessions. Any "feminization" that might have accompanied the shift to spectacle was offset by the explicitly male public sphere depicted on stage and the fact that all the players were male.

The complaints of one Masonic commentator who expressed disquiet over how ritual was marketed contained more than a kernel of truth. He worried that Scottish Rite Masons were effectively using manufactured sensation, using "moving wires . . . walking ghosts, diaphanous forms, unearthly yells, groans, shrieks, flashing lights, storms, earthquakes" and thus "selling degrees" and capitalizing on "one of the greatest money-making businesses of the day."[36] In the early twentieth century Masonic ritual, with its moral and personal underpinnings, morphed dangerously into popular theater and spectatorship rather than active participation in ritual performance. Masonry's emphasis on moral instruction gave way to an emphasis on leisure and consumption. Yet theater and spectacle were a primary but, it is important to note, not sole reason for fraternal success in the early decades of the twentieth century. Theater alone cannot wholly account for the fraternity's abiding attractions over time. Even so by 1920 the Scottish Rite had grown seventeenfold, to half a million members, a spectacular growth that continued after 1945, when it numbered over 1.1 million.[37]

The Red Men and Their Ilk

By 1834 Freemasonry had provided a model for a new sort of primitivist fraternalism, the Red Men, the first home-grown American adult, fully secret society. Ironically, although created specifically to honor Native Americans, it was in fact one of the most exclusive fraternities. Until 1974 it would bar actual Native Americans from entry, keeping its commitment to Indian culture purely in the realm of the imagination. It was exclusively to an inner Indianness that the organization spoke; real Indians were an awkward invasion into the Red Men fantasy.

The fraternity took up the mantle of invented Indianness from earlier organized groups, such as the New York St. Tammany Society, founded in 1789. Tammany used an invented form of public costumed Indianness to further its Nativist and fraternal aims and to signal its aspirations for an egalitarian United States, but eventually it gained more symbolic purchase by emphasizing a female embodiment of Americanness, Columbia, and the historical Columbus. The anti-Masonry movement of the 1820s, immigrant tensions, and then cholera in 1832 put paid to the Red Men, but the organization was revived in 1834 with an emphasis on temperance and the middle class as the Improved Order of Red Men. The IROM saw themselves as custodians of a vanished Indianness, a sort of social version of the impulse to record and preserve evident in salvage anthropology and expressed in subsequent decades in the nation's museums. Despite the dogged persistence of Indian communities in the face of sustained material, physical, and cultural attack in the nineteenth century, the IROM kept up its equally dogged work to ignore actual Indians and instead to preserve Indian "traditions" they themselves had invented. Because the fraternity maintained that Indian peoples either had disappeared or were about to disappear, its sentimental honoring of them at no point required that they do anything to stem the catastrophic loss of Indian land, resources, and population that characterized the period.

Fraternally the Red Men were not alone in their racial exclusion. The Order of United American Mechanics, Modern Woodmen, the Loyal Order of the Moose, and the Patriotic Order of the Sons of America all admitted only whites by charter. When lesser fraternities did accept Native American members, as with the Independent Order of Foresters, who had the witty and charismatic Mohawk doctor Oronhyatekha as their Supreme Ranger from 1881 to 1907, they tended to be exceptional figures. The Foresters saw Oronhyatekha, whom they described as a "noble chief," as a terrific membership-winning asset. Although an Indian exception to the more general whites-only emphasis of fraternities, he was also more than happy to maintain the organization's exclusion of blacks. That said, it is worth noting that even though fraternities applied the color line, racial exclusion was no more their primary purpose than it was that of all the other major institutions in American society of the time who did the same.

"Righteous Satisfaction": Nostalgia and the Rise and Decline of Fraternalism

How should we think about twentieth-century American Freemasonry? Clawson writes that Masonry's significance lies not just in the social networks it created, displayed, and reinforced but also in "the meanings it articulated, the cultural context it provided for social action." She argues that Masonry was about the denial of class, putting in its place gender and race as categories for organizing collective identity. Ritual's purpose was to help reconcile social differences. Yet, as we have seen, class was in fact the bedrock on which Masonry was based; membership in the United States from Masonry's beginnings was by invitation and selection, it presupposed a certain class status, and it required tangible proof of a man's ability to pay and to keep paying for new initiations, regular lodge dinners, paraphernalia, Masonic jewels, annual lodge dues, and more. Freemasonry did help to smooth over a number of socially disruptive conflicts at the turn of the century, when it becomes Clawson's focus, and more generally, but much more was also going on. Given the Indian's privileged status within it and the organization's abiding attraction for non-whites it did more than simply reiterate an "idealized solidarity amongst white men."[38]

For Carnes, Freemasonry spoke essentially to concerns about masculinity. Within lodges "long and 'perilous' initiatory journeys facilitated the young man's transition to, and acceptance of, a remote and problematic conception of manhood in Victorian America." The lodge was primarily a retreat for men to learn the deeper secrets of that mysterious thing: what it means to be a man. When a young Victorian male "left the home for the lodge several evenings a week, keeping his wife in the dark about what transpired there, he imparted to her a painful message about the marital relation. When he performed the roles of Old Testament fathers or Indian chiefs, he re-enacted paternal roles replete with gender significance. And when he ventured into the deepest recesses of fraternal secrets, he encountered ideas about gender expressed nowhere else in Victorian America."[39]

So is Freemasonry primarily concerned with the construction of social communities, or with the construction of manhood? Both were significant, but only something else can account for Freemasonry's powerful and abiding significance in so many men's lives over time: the sustenance Masonry provided and for some continues to provide for the life of the spirit. There is much to suggest that for many Masons part of that spiritual sustenance came from a sense of moral certainty the fraternity provided, a sense that a man was doing the right thing with his life. As the Seneca writer Arthur Parker put it in 1923, "Most normal men seek a fraternity and find in it the satisfaction of every fundamental desire in the male heart—the desire to be, to have, to rank, to know, to feel, to fit. Through the righteous satisfaction of these desires men grow in social and spiritual qualities."[40]

Performing regularly as a Freemason also allowed a man to feed an inner nostalgia for the times talked about by his father and grandfather, before American laborers lost their status as skilled craftsmen. Freemasonry allowed a man to take on the persona of an artisan long after the social position of the master craftsman had been fundamentally eroded. It is an analogous nostalgia to that which has also seduced many historians of the artisan. They have written movingly about how the onset of an exploitive, impersonal market system tore the heart out of a seemingly almost ideal pre-industrial American working life. According to Ronald Schultz, for example, capitalism destroyed society within the working life of a great many. "From the day he signed on as an apprentice, the young artisan witnessed everyday democracy in action," he writes. "Working life in these settings was necessarily intimate and governed by overarching norms of mutuality and cooperation."[41]

The death of such an ideal political community, with its small-shop harmony between masters and journeymen, has become central to how republicanism is explained in early American history and central to the debate about how men thought about themselves at the end of the eighteenth century. If we accept such readings, Freemasonry's emphasis on and ennobling of the artisan can be seen as tying succeeding generations who reenacted the artisan's world within the lodge to the republican virtues associated with previous generations. It also reenacted what was all the more coveted because it was lost: a prior era of harmony in work, when men were much more closely connected to their creative selves. Before labor was divided and work mechanized, a man was required to be both self-sufficient and versatile. As Noah Webster wrote in 1785, "In countries thinly inhabited, or where people live principally by agriculture, as in America, every man is in some measure an artist—he makes a variety of utensils, rough indeed, but such as will answer his purpose—he is a husbandman in summer and mechanic in winter."[42] Nineteenth-century Freemasons attached themselves, if only in their social and fraternal lives, to the classic republicanism of the eighteenth century and expressed within the lodge their unease over the tension between virtue and commerce, between the self and the market. If nineteenth-century males in a heteroglot and rapidly industrializing America could not be sure of harmony within their working lives or of ever gaining the psychological empowerment that accompanies self-sacrifice for the good of a wider community, then they could at least reenact such a world ritually within the darkened reaches of the fraternal lodge. Blue Lodge ritual, the root from which fraternal ritual of all hues flowered in the nineteenth century, was explicit about the respect due to the artisan, about his erudition, skills, and accompanying virtue. Within the lodge at least a worker was paid his due and his skill properly recognized and rewarded.

There were perhaps fifty-five thousand American Masons in 1879 and more than a million by 1900. Fraternalism by this stage was firmly entrenched as a cultural industry, with organizers and their affiliates making thousands of dollars out of repeated initiations and the costs that accompanied a man remaining in "good standing." As Clawson explains, "Regalia manufacturers and merchants, job printers, physicians, and above all fraternal agents and leaders found in the fraternal order a source of material benefit and personal advance." Added to this, many fraternal organizations ran fairly large-scale beneficial societies which by 1898 had more than two and a half million members, nearly half a million more policy holders than private U.S. companies.[43] But even without taking into account the insurance revenue, the income of the various Masonic bodies alone ran to the hundreds of millions. The membership boom that occurred after the First World War may have had something to do with the desire to get ahead at a time when, according to Dumenil, membership may have been more materially beneficial than in the past.[44] Despite the explosion of fraternal invention that happened between 1865 and 1899, Masonry always remained the model for these societies. To a greater or lesser extent they retained the basic Masonic pattern, with degrees of initiation and some form of accessorized drama to accompany them. Yet Thoreau had a point as far back as 1848, when he bemoaned the sort of man non-Masonic fraternities cultivated: "The American has dwindled into an Odd Fellow,—one who may be known by the development of his organ of gregariousness, and a manifest lack of intellect and cheerful self-reliance."[45]

As the twentieth century progressed Freemasonry gradually found itself swamped by competition from service clubs. The fundamental shift was from a greater or lesser emphasis upon ritual (Masons, Knights of Pythias, Red Men, Odd Fellows) toward an explicit emphasis upon conviviality (Rotary, Lions, Kiwanis). Many of the new clubs, such as the Elks (1868), Eagles (1898), and Sons of the American Revolution (1889), were essentially middle-class retreats for white, native-born men. The decline in Freemasonry's popularity, if not in absolute numbers, had actually taken root in the wake of the First World War. Although one source argues that American Masonry reached its peak in the 1930s, with membership at a record 12 percent of the white male adult population, in fact by 1925 fraternalism had already lost some of its luster.[46] Male bonding now took place at work and in newly available forms of leisure, especially sports. Although the

1920s saw an increase in overall numbers, criticism became more prevalent and penetrating. Michael Kimmel in *Manhood in America* quotes one commentator of the time who summed up the restrictive clannishness and inherent childishness at the heart of the hunger for gregariousness expressed by middle-class males. Ritual, by this stage, had lost both its charm and its transformative allure: "Once in so often you march around your lodge room in the wake of the Grand Exalter of the Holy Mackerel and absorb a certain luster from his glittering insignia. . . . You get the same thrill from the secret grip and password that you got from the gang which met after school in the Enchanted Haymow of the Sacred Neighborhood Barn."[47]

Here we can see the beginning of perhaps the deepest criticism possible of fraternalism: that it was self-deceiving rather than, as Masons would prefer, self-realizing. Sinclair Lewis's character George Babbitt epitomized the nativist, suburban foolishness that fraternalism seemed to engender in the 1920s. America was encouraged to laugh at Babbitt's misplaced respect for the man who "belongs to the Boosters or the Rotarians or the Kiwanis, to the Elks or Moose or Red Men or Knights of Columbus or any one of a score of organizations of good, jolly, kidding, laughing, sweating, upstanding, lend-a-handing Royal Good Fellows, who plays hard and works hard, and whose answer to his critics is a square-toed boot that'll teach the grouches and smart alecks to respect the He-man and get out and root for Uncle Samuel, U.S.A."[48]

We are all inheritors of this scorn, so much so that today respect for fraternalism can prompt almost immediate derision, perhaps especially from liberal intellectuals. However, a long look at history suggests such scorn is misplaced. We must remember the good reasons why Freemasonry became a particular focus of attack by Nazi Germany in the period surrounding the Second World War. As Arthur M. Schlesinger astutely pointed out in

1944, joiners of all sorts are generally among the very first casualties of any totalitarian system. Axis dictators with "calculated foresight" repressed or destroyed these "guardians of the people's liberties" and saw them, in Hobbes's phrase, as "worms within the entrails of a natural man, detracting from the absolute allegiance which they believed citizens to owe to the state."[49] Freemasons across Europe during the Second World War became a key focus for assault in this regard, an attack that gained impetus from the most famous hoax document of all time, *The Protocols of the Elders of Zion*. This publication listed the supposed minutes from meetings of a Jewish ruling group that was intent on taking over the world, with Freemasons as part of the fabricated conspiracy. The conflation of Jewish and Masonic prejudice proved to be highly serviceable. Those seizing power particularly resented the way the fraternity had historically separated matters of belief from matters of state.

As part of Hitler's Weltanschauung, Freemasons were accused of being party to a Jewish-Masonic worldwide conspiracy, of being tools of a supposed evil Jewish plot to rule the world. German Masons suffered especially, their lodges deemed "hostile to the state" and their property confiscated. German Freemasonry eventually attempted to stem the attack by adopting Nazi ideology, but even this strategy had little impact. Individual Masons lost their Civil Service jobs, and in occupied countries being a Mason placed individuals under direct threat. Hitler ordered Alfred Rosenberg in 1942 to accelerate the intellectual and physical fight against Masonry, and anti-Masonic propaganda claimed that Jews and Masons had caused the war against the German Reich, part of a vast plan spearheaded by the Freemason American president Franklin Delano Roosevelt. Freemasons joined the list of those deemed unacceptable and therefore forced into the horrors of slave work, the millions of Ukrainians, Poles, Russians,

Latvians, French, Greeks, Italians, Gypsies, and Jehovah's Witnesses who suffered Hitler's policy of "extermination through labor." Nazis made a point of turning the Grand Lodges in Paris, The Hague, and Brussels into museums for the display of anti-Masonic propaganda.

A key element in the Nazi hatred of Masons, Piatigorsky suggests, was the organization's tendency to look inward and to focus backward, to be nostalgic for civilizations of the past. The Nazis "could not help sensing that Freemasonry, apart from being avowedly cosmopolitan and trans-ethnic . . . was irredeemably *historical*."[50] As such it threatened the negative Nazi view of Europe's decadent history.[51] With its commitment to the past, its strong if highly selective forms of inclusion, and its ability to focus men on spiritual and community-oriented development, Freemasonry was thus a precious defense against repression. As we now turn to consider the reasons behind the fraternity's seemingly irrevocable decline in the early twenty-first century, it is appropriate to remember this and to keep in mind that Masonry and fraternalism more generally lost status only five to seven generations ago.

On Television's Deathblow to Fraternalism

Understanding Associationalism and the Declining Role of Fraternalism in American Life

10

As we have seen, a number of influential historians have tended to see Freemasonry primarily as a gendered phenomenon and have explained its decline in the same terms. Viewing the fraternity as a refuge for beleaguered males from the vicissitudes of the parlor, they claim that refuge was no longer needed as the 1920s began and couples increasingly socialized together, at the movies, beside the radio, and in each other's homes playing cards.[1] For Carnes in particular (invoking the anthropologist John M. W. Whiting), late nineteenth-century Masonry provided the male initiation rites required by any society that exposed boys to powerful mothers and then needed to connect them with their fathers as they approached manhood, a context that began to dissolve in the 1920s.

However, Freemasonry's twentieth-century decline deserves a broader context. It is true that fraternalism's institutional foundations began to quake in the 1920s and that the Depression saw a depletion in numbers, especially in groups such as the Improved Order of Red Men and the Knights of Pythias. For its part, Freemasonry lost more than six hundred thousand members between 1930 and 1935 alone. It survived the Depression era somewhat better than other fraternities, although younger men proved less keen on joining. Perhaps there was indeed less of a perceived need for younger men to bond through ritual with their older male peers, less of a need for men both young and old to reckon with the perceived authority of quintessentially male figures, be they Old Testament patriarchs or "ancient" or actual Native Americans. By now middle-class families were more financially secure, and men were able to pay increasing attention to their roles as fathers and grandfathers. Undoubtedly the lodge was losing some of its attraction as a site for intergenerational exchange, but more important, its ritual was also losing respect as a spiritual activity. The idea of spending substantial sums on costumes and pins, jewelry, scarves, sashes, aprons, and swords in addition to paying fees, dues, and dinner costs began to seem less than worthwhile. At the same time the symbolism of Masonic minidramas and the amateur theater they required paled as the melodramas of the Victorian age gave way to more technological and immediate forms of popular culture.

By the 1920s fraternalism and Freemasonry, its mainstay, had become the butt of ribald jokes. Lampooned on all fronts, fraternalism was deemed fit only for the great uncultured mass of the foolish, the folk the newspaper man H. L. Mencken dubbed "the booboisie." It was a joke at the expense of previous fraternally minded generations, and its enduring power can be traced in mainstream media right up to the present day. In 1933 Laurel and Hardy brought out the film *Sons of the Desert*, which took fraternalism to new heights of ridicule. *Amos 'n' Andy*, in its original form from 1951, was specifically designed as a Masonic parody, with the three key characters all members of the Mystic Knights of the Sea. By 1955 television's *The Honeymooners* had its ludicrous Royal and Ancient Order of Raccoons. Then in 1960 there was Fred Flintstone, the cartoon caveman with all the characteristics of suburbia, a stalwart member along with his friend Barney Rubble of the Loyal Order of Water Buffaloes Lodge No. 26; the

Lodge was featured in twenty episodes. Beginning in 1974 the immensely popular *Happy Days* had its Leopard Lodge No. 462, beloved of its "Grand Poobah," the affable, tolerant, unflappable, but slightly silly store owner and paterfamilias Howard Cunningham.

Today the joke continues, with the ubiquitous Homer Simpson a member and one-time supreme leader of the Masonic-sounding Sacred Order of the Stonecutters. In one sense television's dancing on the grave of Freemasonry is a trumpeting of that medium's greatest asset: its own never-ending variety. In performance terms memorized ritual, delivered live week after week, can hardly compete with polished, constantly developing small-screen entertainment. As one author put it succinctly in 1959, "The members of the Lodge are tired of watching third-rate actors, out of character, out of time, muttering the same old stuff."[2] Leading contemporary sociologists have similarly isolated atrophy as the main reason for the fraternity's decline. Freemasonry's solid constitutionalism and its refusal to modify ritual and rules, to engage in "goal succession" and revoke "terminal values," are all held up as the main reasons why it will fail to prosper in the twenty-first century.[3] It would seem that Freemasonry's "timelessness" has somehow begun to look dated.

Television's attacks are stinging, but in fact the most penetrating early criticism of traditional fraternalism came from its main competitors: service clubs. Just as the sociologists would in decades to come, service clubs derided the older lodges as anachronistic, corrosively insular, and out of touch. Their ritual was held to be symptomatic of traditional fraternalism's basic lack of fit with the progressive new world. By comparison, the service clubs that began their ascent in the 1920s and started the slow hemorrhage of numbers from Freemasonry placed little emphasis on ritual and were focused outward rather than inward. In this sense their rise links to the argument put forward by David Riesman about America's shift at this time to "other directedness," or as Christopher Lasch put it decades later, "towards a society that demands submission to the rules of social intercourse but refuses to ground those rules in a code of moral conduct."[4] Service clubs spoke to the active business networking the age required, as opposed to the inner, individual spiritual journey promoted by Freemasonry. Of course in time the service ethos too found itself bound up in the widespread ridicule to which fraternalism in general was exposed. Service clubs became easy targets as places where foolish, childish conformists gathered, desperate to get ahead, places full of a pathetic, misplaced positivism. Places, it was supposed, for the Babbitts of this world.

When Arthur Schlesinger wrote his important essay "Biography of a Nation of Joiners" in 1944 he was convinced that American secret fraternal orders had reached their peak membership in the mid-1920s at over ten million. Actually, as America's foremost fraternity Freemasonry was to enjoy its greatest growth spurt during the Second World War. It was not until about 1960 that it reached its largest overall numbers, when it claimed almost one in twenty American men, 4.2 million members out of perhaps 88 million American males. Thereafter, however, it entered the kind of steady numerical decline Schlesinger foresaw, and it is a decline that continues today. Citing Noel P. Gist's *Secret Societies*, Schlesinger laid a sizable part of the blame for the decline in numbers on "such competing attractions as the cheap motor car, the talking movies, and the radio."[5] But just how responsible modern living and in particular modern communication were for the losses deserves deeper consideration, as does the associated question of to what extent a loss of fraternal membership points to a more widespread loss of American associational life, something long connected with the strength and vitality of American democracy itself. While the issues surrounding gender and fraternalism with which this chapter began are indisputably important and valid, it is perhaps this connection, between fraternal activity and the dynamism or otherwise of American democratic life, that is ultimately more significant.

Is Freemasonry's Decline Symptomatic of America Bowling Alone?

Jeremiads declaiming American decline from a lost Eden of social cohesion or republican virtue have constituted a rich seam in American writing for most of the nation's history. In this sense Riesman's and Lasch's work has much in common with Robert Putnam's *Bowling Alone*; each connects with American concerns over the recent past and the perceived direction of the American future. Interestingly such books about the need to shore up American community life have tended to attract widespread comment, not least from politicians, even those as high up as the White House.[6] Freemasons themselves have joined in expressing this perceived sense of loss in American community life and have tended to see the fraternity's steep decline since the 1960s as symbolic of a more general national malaise, of a pervasive wearing away of the ties that have bound the best of Americans together. A number of older fraternal members have echoed this thinking directly to me, adding that they blame the advent of television as a too readily available alternative to face-to-face fraternal association. Here I suggest that we must be wary of what Miranda Joseph calls "the romance of community," of elegizing social capital that has not necessarily been lost but instead has only changed its form and degree of measurability.[7] In truth Freemasonry's decline, if permanent, is but the decline of one form of community within one segment of American society, and its loss of numbers does not necessarily indicate a more general loss of societal cohesion. That said, the fraternity's loss of membership does point to important larger changes in American associational life, and it is important to see the changes it has experienced in relation to other, broader shifts in how American men, women, and families relate to one another.

This argument might seem unusual in light of Robert Putnam's conclusions in *Bowling Alone*, a highly influential, thoughtful, sometimes misunderstood, and occasionally refreshingly humorous book on how Americans relate to one another socially.[8] Putnam tells a general tale of woe, suggesting that contemporary Americans are dangerously low on social capital, that set of reciprocal connections, networks, and trust among individuals that historically have made America strong. Americans, he bemoans, have stopped associating even at the most informal level, that of "schmoozing" one another, to use the Yiddish term. Worryingly, Putnam notes, "Americans have been dropping out in droves, not merely from political life, but from organized community life more generally." What has taken place is nothing less than an eerie "silent withdrawal from social intercourse." Americans therefore need to reconnect forthwith, since all the classic institutions of American civic life, both religious and secular, have now been "hollowed out." American social capital, Putnam tells us, has followed the same basic pattern (more or less) that I outlined for Freemasonry and fraternal groups over time: "modest growth in the first third of the century; rapid growth coming out of the Depression and World War II; a high plateau from the 1950s into the 1960s; and a sharp, sustained decline during the last third of the century."[9]

Putnam explains these changes by praising his own generation and their good judgment in making specific associational choices. A secondary explanation concerns the growth of technology, television in particular. He does, however, add a dash of hope by suggesting that the young of the 1990s might just be gearing up to pick up the civic-minded mantle of their forebears. Putnam explains that his own generation, those born between 1910 and 1940, now over sixty at the close of the century, have been "good citizens," thoroughly ready to trust, to join up, and to take part in community life. They are the "long civic generation." New forms of communication, especially the telephone, electronic media generally, and television specifically, have tended to foster privatism over time and have discouraged the Americans that followed this generation from meeting with one another. Putnam reserves the bulk of his ire for television, linking it, quite correctly in the developed world at least, to a host of negatives, from financial anxiety to lethargy, weight gain, passivity, loneliness, unhappiness, and most specifically a direct reduction in social, recreational, and community activity. "Television," he explains, "privileges personalities over issues and communities of interest over communities of place. In sum, television viewing may be so strongly linked to civic disengagement because of the psychological impact of the medium itself."[10] He references Sven Birkerts's important point that something changed in the 1950s such that our experience became increasingly mediated and arrested at a stage children normally outgrow, that of "parallel play" in front of an external stimulus. Birkerts explains that this shift caused by technology was one that fundamentally alters our means of comprehending society:

> There is a ledge, a threshold, a point after which everything is different. I would draw the line, imprecisely, somewhere in the 1950s. That was when television worked its way into the fabric of American life, when we grew accustomed to the idea of parallel realities— the one that we lived in, the other that we stepped into whenever we wanted a break from our living. People born after the mid-1950s are the carriers of the new; they make up the force that will push us out of our already-fading rural/small-town/urban understanding of social organization. The momentum of the change has already made those designations all but meaningless.[11]

According to Putnam, there is a normal generational time-lag that explains how this change occurred in the 1950s, but the loss of numbers in associational groups became evident only in the 1960s. Masonry, we recall, lost almost half of its membership between 1959 and 1995.

Given Putnam's conclusions, are Freemasons right to blame television and technology for delivering a deathblow to their organization?[12] Were the generation born in the late 1920s and '30s simply, as the sociologist Charles Tilly put it, "the last suckers" who entered the world just before an unprecedented quantum leap in social experience?[13] If so this is only a part of the answer. As Theda Skocpol and others have explained, civic associational membership has always boomed in the United States following war, and this was certainly the case after the First and Second World Wars.[14] Indeed major conflicts have always forced Americans to respond as a group to the giant changes they unleash. The Second World War and the immediate decades afterward brought unique levels of equality and union engagement. Added to this was significant military spending connected with conflicts in Korea and Vietnam and in the context of the cold war. It is more accurate therefore to view Tilly's "last sucker" generation as a group who responded to exceptional circumstances quite sensibly by banding together, given that, as Quesenberry has pointed out, "outside of . . . unique war-related circumstances—during the Progressive Era, the 1920s, and the last three decades—American economic history has generally been one of ever-growing inequality."[15] According to Putnam, Americans today are dangerously bereft of community and are "*right* to fear that this transformation has very real costs." They therefore urgently need "to reinvent the twenty-first-century equivalent of the Boy Scouts or the settlement house or the playground or Hadassah or the United Mine Workers or the NAACP"—or, he might have added, the Freemasons.[16]

However, if Quesenberry is right, and bearing mind that Put-nam's "long civic generation" grew up during a unique period, when America turned its face away from international trade, such a reorientation is simply not possible without deeper, structural change. Television and other forms of electronic media have with-out question come to dominate aspects of American social life, but they exist as part of a much larger shift in which corporate power has taken on wholly new dimensions in all of our lives. Since the late 1960s, and in particular since the early 1980s, a great wave of globalization, free market thinking, deregulation, and privatiza-tion has played a key role in depoliticizing and disengaging indi-viduals. If television has destroyed social capital and taken men away from the lodge and their peers it has done so in part by rep-resenting the interests of ever-growing global big business. Ironi-cally it was the commercialization of leisure from the 1880s that it-self helped to spark the great boom in fraternal activity that lasted until the 1930s. The larger societal shift, from home-grown enter-tainment to commercial, marketed, professionalized theater, was, we should remember, what helped Scottish Rite Masonry reach its stellar membership heights.

Masonic ritual performance can in this sense be seen as part of a long-term shift away from self-generated, participatory enter-tainment toward the passive consumerism and commercialized leisure so prevalent today. Especially since the 1950s television has powerfully connected the most personal and intimate needs of in-dividuals to the imperative to buy things. Rather than encourag-ing community, ethnic, or class associations, television works to make the family into a consumer unit. As George Lipsitz explains, its stories, interspersed with regular instructions to purchase, fos-ter an infantile narcissism and strive to convince viewers that by consuming, they will achieve a better, truly American life.[17] Even when collective memory does appear in the storied world of television, it is most often used not to reinforce moral messages but to sanction the pursuit of material rewards. In the second half of the twentieth century the communally generated alternative realities conjured by ritual within the Freemasonic lodge struggled to compete with the externally generated alternative realities created in the home by television. Whereas Masonic ritual contains a panoply of timeless heroes (knights, Indian chiefs, artisans) capable of delivering enduring psychological nourishment through their death-defying example, television offers heroes of such constantly varying diversity that, superficially at least, it seems to offer the potential to boost individual self-esteem without limit.[18] Significantly, however, the satisfactions offered by Masonic ritual and its heroes are social and rooted in an awareness of community, whereas the passively consumed and limited pleasures of television revolve around what Habermas has dubbed "civil and familial privatism."[19] With television's rise and fraternal associations' decline we have indeed lost some of what once joined families and communities together. Men have shifted away from one of the primary sources from which they gained psychological succor, away from human associations that invoked giving as opposed to consuming. Instead they spend time with mediated products that place consumer choice far above decisions concerning social and community life.

However, a number of complications arise with all of these changes. One stems from seeing voluntarism as a panacea for all of democracy's perceived ills; clearly it is not. There is also a danger in seeing the highly segregated forms of associational life of the past as the only positive paradigm for association today and in the future. Consider that while the decades since the 1960s have seen a decline in participation in organizations such as Freemasonry, they have also seen an upswing in tolerance, both in terms of racial, sexual, and social legislation and in aspects of culture more generally. This is not to suggest that high levels of social capital, as Putnam defines it, in the 1950s and early 1960s are directly interlinked with institutional racial segregation and with limits on women's power and agency within society, but they may be. Any such link deserves further detailed investigation. We may not go as far as Jason Kaufman, who connects nineteenth-century fraternalism as a self-interested phenomenon to a whole host of liberal evils, from gun loving to racial prejudice, special-interest politics, weak labor unions, and resistance to universal health care, but it seems plausible that fraternalism may not have been an unalloyed good and that it is at least as flawed, complex, and problematic as any other form of relatively large-scale social interaction.[20]

Furthermore it is important to recognize that all association, and this very much applies to Freemasonry, is not a priori political. (Tocqueville, after all, subdivided associational groups into four, each of them operating in a separate sphere from that of the state or government.)[21] Neither of course is all association per se necessarily a good thing in the way Putnam suggests. As Schlesinger reminds us, nearly every great national crisis has brought about the formation of internal American law-defying organizations, and today flourishing forms of antigovernment sentiment operate within oath-bound militia groups.[22] There are yet other issues that connect to the recent emphasis on social capital as an idea. Some have suggested that the fuss that surrounded *Bowling Alone* arose in the first place because Putnam's arguments and his focus on social capital suit a conservative political agenda. In contrast, the answers to society's evils may in fact lie with government rather than with the individual. As Bob Edwards and Michael Foley point out rather wryly, "If social capital is America's elixir for the twenty-first century, conservatives of all stripes can take heart that its source lies in civil society, in private initiative and individual dispositions, not in public action and governmental regulation. A national remedy of civil society and social capital is clearly consistent with a policy agenda of privatization and devolution."[23] Thus our worries about a decline in membership of fraternal organizations as symptomatic of a larger decline in social association more generally can be seen as useful to an agenda that has been blamed for causing some of the problems American associations developed to tackle in the first place: social inequality, loss of kinship, and loss of community. It is worth remembering that for writers of the late 1950s and thereafter, Masonic associations were seen as a means of allowing social mobility, where the regular guy might rub shoulders with the upper classes. While the lodges persisted they brought together a limited span of the American social order until "the upper classes abandoned the lodges almost completely in favor of their exclusive civic-type groups; and typically, the lower classes have not been able to follow them into these."[24]

To the extent that it signals an erosion of voluntarism and a consequent general loss of American social capital, Freemasonry's decline touches a chord in us all. After all, few of us relish the thought of a pervasive loss of national trust and cohesion. Both emotionally and intellectually the idea of the United States as a unique "nation of joiners" is deeply embedded. This is perhaps less true today than it was when Schlesinger described the American ability to resort to collective action as "one of the strongest taproots of the nation's well-being" and as "a great cementing force for national integration."[25] Even so, joining, the ability to band together as individuals to help one another, is centrally tied up with our understanding of American democracy, because within an aristocracy there is less need for it. Within an aristocracy "every wealthy and powerful citizen constitutes the head of a permanent and compulsory association, composed of all those who are dependent upon him, or whom he makes subservient to the execution of his designs."[26] There are those of course (among them Francis Fukuyama) who dispute this link and who also dispute that increased associational participation is in any case necessarily a sign of democratic health. But something has certainly been lost since the late 1950s. This was the point when national, democratically governed, cross-class voluntary groupings began to lose potency and the richest Americans began to choose as never before to associate almost exclusively with themselves. As the privileged elite have detached, civic life has begun to be ever more "niche," inward-looking, limited, and professionalized. Perhaps, as Beito has suggested, this can be linked to the growth of American governmental welfare since the mid-1930s and a concurrent shift of Americans away from binding together for mutual aid toward a new reliance on a paternalistic and largely impersonal welfare state.[27]

Recent developments may yet provide much-trumpeted hope. Without doubt new kinds of associations helped the Obama administration gain control of the White House in 2009. The first "Web president" was able to get Americans to associate in fresh ways and to get out the vote from groups hitherto estranged from the democratic process. His powerful online presence garnered a host of small donations, and significantly these translated into offline action. Thus we may be forgiven for being reassured. Contemporary Americans may not feel the need for the same kind of protected private sphere as previous generations of largely WASP males did in the Masonic lodge, but the urge to associate with kindred spirits to foster personal and societal change is still part of the nation's agenda. Even so a number of modern thinkers are less than sanguine about the Internet's capability for fostering binding community. They compare new virtual networks to "windblown dunes of quicksand" and suggest that in a world increasingly dominated by the imperatives of consumerism all bonds are destined to remain frail, brittle, and acutely temporary. The risk-free socializing of the Internet, though it offers some of the same opportunities for experimenting with identity once offered by the robing rooms of the Masonic lodge, is too often ultimately devoid of the sort of durable commitment that, for better or worse, once made fraternities the backbone of American democracy.[28] In sum, it seems that the loss of the kinds of associational life that characterized previous centuries will affect how democracy is practiced in the United States in the future. Traditions matter, but as significant as their decline is, it is the larger shifts of which their loss is a harbinger that are most important. Examining Freemasonry's decline directs our attention to accelerating social stratification, burgeoning privatism, and the ever-advancing scope of corporate influence. How we manage these issues and what traditions we invoke or invent to do so are among the most pressing challenges of the future.

It is appropriate to give the final word on the oldest and most copied associational model of the past two centuries to a Mason. According to Jim Tresner of the Guthrie Scottish Rite bodies, there are clear signs that young American males are beginning to return to fraternal life. Even though the average American Mason is now likely to be in his late sixties, the trend for the average age for men entering Freemasonry is downward. It very much depends on the area, but it seems that Masonry as "a permanent form of connectedness" is again appealing to the middle-aged.[29] In a reversal of the established pattern, sons are now bringing their fathers into the fold and in so doing reconnecting the 1960s generation to fraternal and community life. As Tresner points out, that same 1960s generation were the ones who had ignored Freemasonry academically and intellectually. Perhaps in a strange way

Freemasonry's very prevalence within so many individual American family histories made it easy for them to ignore. I hope that in a small way this book will help to redress that omission and allow Freemasonry as a phenomenon to be seen in its true light, as a sometimes intercultural locus truly significant to many American men that uniquely reflected their wishes and aspirations as well as providing a special context for their own spiritual progress. For many remarkable Indian men it provided social shelter and the opportunity, not to forget about race, but to be Indian among friends and peers in a context in which certain important Indian values did not seem out of place.

As I have emphasized throughout this book, among the most profound contributions Masonry has made and will continue to make to a host of men's lives is the solace it offers in death. The isolated cemetery up a country lane on Choctaw Road in southeastern Logan County, Oklahoma, is a stark but positive reminder of this. Evansville Cemetery, also called Tohee Cemetery and Bobby Ford Cemetery, lies at the end of a dead-end road with black jack trees surrounding it on the righthand side blackened from a long-ago extinguished fire. About an acre in size, the cemetery is divided in two by a fence, the right side for blacks and the left for whites. It is known as the resting place of mixed-bloods, blacks, Indians, and whites, a fair number of whom were Masons. The righthand cemetery has gravestones with Masonic markings: "32nd degree," "Prince Hall Mason," often a lodge number and sometimes inset marble to give color. While the fence (and who knows, the fire?) kept each ethnicity apart in this world, it seems that Masonry gave all those brothers who rest there common comfort and the security that in the next world the Mason's shared sense of time, myth, brotherhood, and ritual would hold true.[30] That is an interracial legacy of which the fraternity can be proud, a hidden but important history that should not be forgotten.

Notes

A Note on Terms

1. For example, on September 18, 1793, or in the year of Masonry 5793, President and Freemason George Washington dedicated the U.S. Capitol in his ritual attire.

2. R. Williams, *Keywords*, 268–69.

3. Marx, *The Eighteenth Brumaire of Louis Bonaparte* (1855), in *Karl Marx and Frederick Engels*, 97; Habermas, "A Review of Gadamer's *Truth and Method*," 268, 270.

4. Krupat, *All That Remains*, xii.

5. Spilka, *Spirituality*, 1.

6. An indigenous discussion of religion and the sacred is the subject of the initial chapter of Beck, Walters, and Francisco, *The Sacred*, 3–31.

1. Approaching Freemasonry, Part One

1. Gist, "Secret Societies," 81.

2. Bullock, *Revolutionary Brotherhood*, 77, 241–43. Bullock makes this claim more than once (241–43), and given his masterful command of Freemasonry in the revolutionary era it must be respected. It seems, however, to be at least partially contradicted by evidence elsewhere in his text (140), and overall it is difficult to see how such a claim could be fully substantiated.

3. Fliegelman, *Declaring Independence*, 3, 48.

4. Mary Ann Clawson has provided good evidence of groups such as the Knights of Pythias toward the end of the nineteenth century that were cross-class and male fraternity, providing an alternative to class differentiation (*Constructing Brotherhood*, 104–5). But the costs of repeated initiation and of membership, as well as the bulk of the data examined here, suggest that Freemasonry was predominantly a middle-class phenomenon.

5. Fliegelman, *Declaring Independence*, 32.

6. Despite his respect for rhetoric Jefferson was not himself a Freemason. He participated in the laying of a Masonic cornerstone at his University at Charlottesville and on that occasion praised Freemasonry, but his own writing suggests that he was never a member of any Masonic grouping. See Thomas Jefferson to Bishop James Madison, January 31, 1800, in Hirst, *Life and Letters*, xvii.

7. Jefferson quoted in Fliegelman, *Declaring Independence*, 99, and more extensively in Cappon, *The Adams-Jefferson Letters*, 307.

8. Jefferson, *Notes*, 102.

9. Fliegelman, *Declaring Independence*, 194–95.

10. Lauzon quoted in Conn, *History's Shadow*, 84.

11. Wallace, *Jefferson and the Indians*, 20, 21.

12. McKenney, *Memoirs*, 2:88.

13. Conn, *History's Shadow*, 101.

14. Jefferson, *Notes*, 101.

15. B. Anderson, *Imagined Communities*, 133.

16. Adams quoted in Gustafson, *Eloquence*, xiii.

17. Conn, *History's Shadow*, 86.

18. Fliegelman, *Declaring Independence*, 4, 24.

19. Reid quoted in Fliegelman, *Declaring Independence*, 47.

20. Lott, "Love and Theft," 23. See Bhabha, "The Other Question"; R. Williams, *Marxism and Literature*.

21. Roach, *Cities of the Dead*, xii.

22. Roach, "Joseph Roach Talks to Ned Sublette."

23. Roach, *Cities of the Dead*, 5.

24. Roach, *Cities of the Dead*, 4.

25. Holland, *Raising the Dead*, 40.

26. Brooks, *American Lazarus*, 48, 46, 12, 147, 150.

27. In 1848 Douglass bemoaned the fact that Freemasonry's "glittering follies of artificial display" displaced black energies that would have been better spent agitating for equality (quoted in Kantrowitz, "'Intended for the Better Government,'" 1001).

28. Fanon, "On National Cultures," in *The Wretched of the Earth*, 210.

29. S. Hall, "Cultural Identity and Diaspora," 393–94.

30. Rosaldo, *Culture and Truth*, 20.

31. H. White, *Metahistory*, 8.

32. Parkman, *The Conspiracy of Pontiac*, 43–45.

33. Piatigorsky, *Freemasonry*, 39.

34. Vigneras, *The Journal of Christopher Columbus*, 194–200.

35. Much has been written about the cultural arrogance and ethnocentrism inherent in the notion that Columbus "discovered" the American land mass and its diverse set of peoples. The idea that the American land mass is younger relative to elsewhere on Earth has its roots in early Christian orthodoxy. For more, readers may wish to consult Berkhofer, *The White Man's Indian*, 1–55; Charles C. Mann's bestseller, *1491: New Revelations of the Americas before Columbus*; Pratt, *Imperial Eyes*.

36. Williams quoted in Berkhofer, *The White Man's Indian*, 35–37.

37. Berkhofer, *The White Man's Indian*, 38.

38. Jennings, *The Invasion of America*, 52–53.

39. John Eliot in Shepard, *Clear Sun-shine*, 115, quoted in Bellin, *Demon*, 4.

40. Mather quoted in Gill, *Native American Religions*, 10.

41. Thornton quoted in Niezen, *Spirit Wars*, 8–9. For a fuller discussion of the hotly contested issue of Indian population decline and of Indian population calculation mores, readers may wish to consult Porter, "Population Matters in Native America," and the references therein.

42. Niezen, *Spirit Wars*, 9.

43. For more on this theme consult Knaut, *The Pueblo Revolt*, 55; Reff, "'The Predicament of Culture,'" 71.

44. Thwaites, *The Jesuit Relations*, 11, 89. For the past twenty years at least there is evidence of a reversal of the Christianizing approach to missionary work among several evangelical groups and of a shift toward what has been dubbed the "InIndianization" of Christianity. See Stogre, *That the World May Believe*.

45. Harriott, *A Briefe and True Report*, 41.

46. Perhaps because of the unique conceptual space Indians occupied within the American mind, in comparison with poor whites and blacks they received what in dominant non-Indian terms might be deemed preferential treatment when it came to education.

47. Irwin quoted in Bellin, *Demon*, 5; T. Morgan, "Rules for Indian Courts" (1892), in Prucha, *Documents*, 186–87.

48. For more on potlatch, see Jonaitis, *Chiefly Feasts*.

49. Hoxie, *A Final Promise*, xiii.

50. Niezen, *Spirit Wars*, 161.

51. Radin, *The Road*, 265.

52. Regrettably the process of Indian sacred material finding its way to publication continues. See, for example, one of the last works of the anthropologist William Fenton, *The Little Water Medicine Society of the Senecas* (2002), a publication I found he could not be talked out of letting see print. His opinion on the matter is perhaps best summed up by his remarks in a 1995 publication: "A new generation of younger Iroquois, unsure of their own culture but eager to restore it, while beset by a fallacy that one must have native genes to appreciate Iroquois culture, have closed the longhouse doors to outsiders who might assist them" (introduction to *Midwinter Rites*, ix–x). Many Iroquois also criticized Fenton for publishing ceremonial knowledge in *The False Faces of the Iroquois* in 1987. See also material on Fenton's role in resisting early attempts at cultural repatriation waged by Onondaga Indians in the "Great Wampum War of 1970" (restricted access, Fenton, "The New York State Wampum Collec-

tion: The Case for the Integrity of Cultural Treasures," *American Philosophical Society Proceedings* 11, no. 6 [1971]); McCarthy, "Iroquoian and Iroquoianist."

53. Niezen, *Spirit Wars*, 173–74.

54. Copway, *Life*, 1850 ed., 43–44, emphasis in original.

55. See Rexroth, "American Indian Songs."

56. John Collier, "Indian Religious Freedom and Indian Culture," Circular No. 2970, January 3, 1934, Bureau of Indian Affairs, Department of the Interior, Washington DC.

2. Approaching Freemasonry, Part Two

1. Bellin, *Demon*, 9.

2. Bellin, *Demon*, 2.

3. Kohl quoted in Bellin, *Demon*, 10.

4. Phelan, *Unmarked*, 146.

5. Clifford, *The Predicament of Culture*, 23.

6. Bellin, *Demon*, 11; Roach, *Cities of the Dead*, 6, 30.

7. Silko, *Ceremony*, 126.

8. R. White, *The Middle Ground*, xv.

9. Bellin, *Demon*, 121.

10. Bakhtin, *Speech Genres*, 2.

11. Rosaldo, *Culture and Truth*.

12. Conquergood, *Rethinking Ethnography*, 184; Clifford, *Predicament*, 15.

13. Clifford, *Predicament*, 338.

14. Eric Lott provided a trenchant and witty rebuttal of aspects of the "politically unserious" nature of the postethnic turn in American studies. A key problem with its emphasis on America's ethnically mixed cultures, he explained, was the way it ignored "the degree to which racial and ethnic codes have a way of disciplining the mongrels" ("Review," 117).

15. Bank, *Theatre Culture in America*, 463.

16. Diamond, *In Search of the Primitive*, 1.

17. Diamond, *In Search of the Primitive*.

18. Trevor-Roper quoted in Achebe, "The Role of the Writer," 74; recapitulated in Trevor-Roper, "The Past and Present," 6.

19. Conquergood, *Rethinking Ethnography*, 188, 190.

20. Worthen, "Drama, Performativity, and Performance," 1099.

21. Diamond, *In Search of the Primitive*, 39.

22. For a fuller discussion of the Scottish and English roots of Freemasonry, see chapter 3.

23. The transgressive element in performance has been highlighted by John

McKenzie in *Perform or Else*; the legal roots of performance as an idea have been explored by Oliver Gerland in "From Playhouse to P2P Network" (83).

24. Jocks quoted in Irwin, *Native American Spirituality*, 66.

25. Means quoted in Ridington in Irwin, *Native American Spirituality*, 116.

26. Churchill, *Indians Are Us?*, 213.

27. V. Deloria, *The World We Used to Live In*.

28. Roach, *Cities of the Dead*, 4, 5.

29. Bellin, *Medicine Bundle*, 25.

30. P. Deloria, *Playing Indian*, 187.

31. Morgan, *League*, 444.

32. Stern, *Lewis Henry Morgan*.

33. Resek, *Lewis Henry Morgan*, 24, 39; P. Deloria, *Playing Indian*, 78.

34. See Bellin, "Being and Becoming 'Indian,'" in *Medicine Bundle*.

35. Bellin, *Medicine Bundle*, 128.

36. For analyses of colonial mimicry and how assimilation for the colonized is limited in the sense that they can be "white but not quite," see Gates, *The Signifying Monkey*; Bhabha, "Of Mimicry and Man." This has certainly been true in the Native American context, especially in the nineteenth century, when full assimilation for Indians was much touted rhetorically but almost entirely unavailable in practice.

37. Bellin, *Medicine Bundle*, 136, 138.

38. Bellin, *Medicine Bundle*, 145.

39. Bellin, *Medicine Bundle*, 158.

40. The Ghost Dance has been variously interpreted from the beginning as operating along exclusionary or inclusionary principles. For a discussion of cultural incomprehension and the Ghost Dance as well as its lost potential in the years following the 1890s in terms of tribal sovereignty and revitalization, see M. Elliott "Ethnography." Consider also its myriad legacy in "new Ghost Dance literature" and writers such as D'Arcy McNickle, Linda Hogan, Gerald Vizenor, Leslie Marmon Silko, and James Welch.

41. Bellin's own unease over performance in the context of Indian history is evident in his inconclusive conclusion to *Medicine Bundle*. Here he belatedly references previous critics who state that the commodification and consumption of Indian medicine has always been a matter of power (194).

42. Cantwell, *Ethnomimesis*, 226, 181.

43. Scheiber, "Mirrors and Menageries," 369.

44. Rosaldo, *Culture and Truth*, 198, 199, 71.

45. Shohat and Stam, *Unthinking Eurocentrism*, 42.

46. On colonial cannibalism, see Barker, Hulme, and Iversen, *Cannibal-*

ism. On the imagined loquaciousness of the colonial cannibal, see Lestringant, *Cannibals*; Cheyfitz, *The Poetics of Imperialism*, 142–72.

47. Root, *Cannibal Culture*, 18.

48. It could perhaps be said that a number of the "performance" texts produced subsequent to those of Roach and Bellin have not paid the same sort of attention to the complexities of performance in intercultural context or to the complexities of the approach's roots within performance theory itself. However, the approach continues to thrive and its applications within Indian studies to widen. Susan Castillo's *Colonial Encounters in New World Writing, 1500–1786: Performing America* is magisterial in scope and examines a great wealth of encounters between Natives and Spanish, English, and French settler communities, situating performance simply as "the site in which colonial difference is enacted" (16). Even so, it remains the case that it is in early American studies that performance has had its greatest purchase, in books such Jeffrey Richards's *Drama, Theatre, and Identity in the American New Republic*, Sandra M. Gustafson's *Eloquence Is Power: Oratory and Performance in Early America*, and David Waldstreicher's *In the Midst of Perpetual Fetes: The Making of American Nationalism, 1776–1820*.

49. W. Meserve, *An Emerging Entertainment*, 5–6.

50. P. Deloria, *Indians in Unexpected Places*, 231, 232.

51. Another relative, the Reverend Vine V. Deloria, was also a Freemason. See P. Deloria, "Vine V. Deloria Sr., Dakota," 85; R. Denslow, *Masonic Portraits*, 152–57.

52. See O. Anderson, *400 Years*, 106.

53. For more on the Society of American Indians, which listed key Indian figures of the era such as Charles Eastman (Freemason), Carlos Montezuma (Freemason), Thomas Sloan, and Arthur Hewitt among its membership, see Porter, *To Be Indian*, chapter 5 and the references therein.

54. V. Deloria, *Singing for a Spirit*, 69.

55. Ella Deloria quoted in Gardner, *A Vision of Double Woman*, 23.

56. Ella Deloria quoted in Gardner, *A Vision of Double Woman*, 22.

57. Philip J. Deloria quoted in Gardner, *A Vision of Double Woman*, 56.

58. Diamond, *In Search of the Primitive*.

3. A History of Freemasonry

1. Foucault, *The Archaeology of Knowledge*. Drawing on Nietzsche, Foucault urged us to see that the point of a genealogical analysis is to show that a given system of thought is rooted not in rationally inevitable trends but in contingent turns of history.

2. Nye, *Bound to Lead*. Nye has defined soft power as "the ability to get what

you want through attraction rather than coercion." He first put the idea forward in 1990 in *Bound to Lead: The Changing Nature of American Power* and developed it further in 2004 in *Soft Power: the Means to Success in World Politics*.

3. Here I echo Paul J. Rich, who argues, "There is no political life without rituals" (*Chains of Empire*, 296).

4. See, for example, much of the scholarship in the journal of Masonic history, *Ars Quatuor Coronatorum*.

5. Paine, *Origin of Freemasonry*, 224.

6. Knoop and Jones, *Genesis*, 5.

7. Roberts, "Freemasonry," 325.

8. Gist, "Secret Societies," 70–73.

9. Perhaps the earliest record of a Masonic body is connected with the initiation of Elias Ashmole in 1646 in England (Yates, *The Art of Memory*, 294), although Knoop and Jones in *Genesis* indicate that Freemasonry may have existed in England as early as 1500.

10. Stevenson makes the point that in Scotland virtually all the pre-1710 lodges were and often long remained closely tied to the mason trade (*The Origins of Freemasonry*, 10), in contrast with England's early lodges, which were often made up entirely of nonoperatives. Thus following Stevenson's argument, "speculative" concerns originated in an operative, Scottish context around 1600. For a discussion of operative, accepted, and speculative Masonry, see Lisa Kahler, "Scottish Definitions and Transitions," 3–18, in de Hoyos and Morris, *Freemasonry in Context*.

11. Stevenson, *The Origins of Freemasonry*, 6, 11. For more on the origins of the word, see also Ward, "The Crisp English Word Freemason"; Matthew Scanlon in Weisberger, McLeod, and Morris, *Freemasonry on Both Sides of the Atlantic*, 155.

12. Thomas quoted in Stevenson, *The Origins*, 78.

13. For more on the distinction between "real" and "fictitious" memory places, see Yates, *The Art of Memory*, 317.

14. Stevenson, *The Origins*, 96.

15. Stevenson, *The Origins*, 115.

16. Stevenson, *The Origins*, 120, 124.

17. Momaday, *The Man Made of Words*, 104.

18. See Stevenson on the journey from Hiram in the Bible to Hiram Abiff in Masonic rhetoric (*The Origins of Freemasonry*, 144).

19. Stevenson, *The Origins of Freemasonry*, 144.

20. Stevenson, *The Origins of Freemasonry*, 233.

21. Newton of course was himself seemingly anachronistic. He was a herald of the modern but was also steeped in occult concerns, several of which

were shared by Freemasons, in particular a fascination with the meanings behind the dimensions of Solomon's temple. See M. White, *Isaac Newton*; A. Hall, *Isaac Newton*.

22. See Tawney, *Religion and the Rise of Capitalism*; Hill, *The Century of Revolution*; Crosby, *The Measure of Reality*.

23. Jacob, "The Origins of Freemasonry," 326.

24. Jacob, *The Radical Enlightenment* (1981), 79.

25. For trenchant criticism of *The Radical Enlightenment*, see reviews by Carla H. Hay and in particular G. C. Gibbs. *Enthusiasm*, perhaps ironically, was also a term used to critique Masons in the eighteenth century. Because of its commitment to values and beliefs of the past and because it was supposed to reveal experience of the divine, it was deemed to represent an explicit threat to established authority.

26. Jacob, *The Radical Enlightenment* (1981), 21, 43.

27. See reviews by Hay, Gibbs, Heyd, La Vopa.

28. Jacob, *The Radical Enlightenment* (1981), 113.

29. Quoted in Jacob, *The Radical Enlightenment* (1981), 96.

30. As subsequent discussion will show, Masonry's support for free thinking led to its being condemned by the Catholic Church. The Vatican issued the first Papal Bull against it in 1737, and even during the progressive reign of John XXIII in the 1960s the fraternity remained "not forgiven."

31. Benedict, review, 728.

32. Toland is also said to have been born in Donegal, but here I agree with Daniel (*John Toland*, 5).

33. Jacob, *The Radical Enlightenment* (1981), 123.

34. For a discussion of the vexed question of what *Celtic* means, readers may wish to begin with Wells, "Who, Where and What Were the Celts?"

35. As with so much nostalgia for a lost past, this re-visioning of Druidic societies was rose-tinted; figures as early as Rousseau were to point out that non-Christian faiths did not necessarily encourage international harmony and brotherhood or prevent xenophobia (*Emile*, 39–40).

36. Jacob, *The Radical Enlightenment* (1981), 123.

37. Jacob, *The Radical Enlightenment* (1981), 191, 192. Toland was the first author to use the term *pantheism* but was resistant to the idea that the philosophy could be reduced to a set of doctrines understood in terms of an *ism*.

38. Paine quoted in Foner, *The Complete Writings*, 833, 835.

39. Toland shared his period's respect for eloquence and for mnemonics as a means of communicating swiftly and efficiently. He wrote, he said, for the "man running" (see Daniel, *John Toland*, 131, 137).

40. Francis Yates has written a fascinating discussion of Bruno's relation-

ship with Masonry in *The Art of Memory*, putting forward the theory that Freemasonry's speculative origins can be directly connected to the "architecture of the art of memory" (295).

41. Daniel, *John Toland*, 209, 214, 218.

42. Beiser, *The Sovereignty of Reason*, 230, 243.

43. Koch, *Republican Religion*, 291, 292.

44. Habermas, *The Structural Transformation of the Public Sphere*.

45. On aspects of female Masonry, see Burke and Jacob, "French Freemasonry," and in particular Jacob's revealing chapters "Women in the Lodges" in *The Origins of Freemasonry* (92–129) and "Freemasonry, Women and the Paradox of the Enlightenment" in *Living the Enlightenment* (12–142). It is thought that the first lodge to admit women was in The Hague in 1752, followed by French lodges in the 1770s and 1780s.

46. Elliott and Daniels, "The 'School,'" 228.

47. Fraser, "Rethinking the Public Sphere," 64, 60.

48. Bourdieu, *Distinction*.

49. For Furet, the French Revolution was a revolution in how power communicated, a change in semiotic politics.

50. Burke and Jacob, "French Freemasonry," 513.

51. Jacob, *Living the Enlightenment*, 10–22.

52. Jacob, *The Origins of Freemasonry*, 15, 22, 24, 47.

53. Jacob, *Living the Enlightenment*, 22.

54. J. Anderson, *Constitutions*, 68.

55. Jacob, *The Origins of Freemasonry*, 243.

56. Thrupp quoted in Black, *Guilds and Civil Society*, 9; Black, *Guilds and Civil Society*, 31.

57. Hobsbawm, *Primitive Rebels*, 162.

58. J. Smyth, *The Men of No Property*, 45–46, 86–88.

59. Hobsbawm, *Primitive Rebels*, 163.

60. Kant, *Critique of Pure Reason*, 9.

61. Black, *Guilds and Civil Society*, 43.

62. Roberts, "Freemasonry," 323.

63. Quoted in Jacob, *Living*, 147.

64. Jacob, *Living*, 149.

65. Stevenson, *The First Freemasons*, 13.

66. A. Anderson, "Cosmopolitanism," 265–89.

67. Rev. Dr. Twining, "A Vast Chain Extending round the Whole Globe," oration, *Freemason's Chronicle*, June 24, 1841, reprinted in *Freemason's Quarterly Review*, September 1841, 357.

68. Hyam, *Britain's Imperial Century*, 300.

69. Harland-Jacobs, "Hands across the Sea," 241.

70. Coil, *Coil's Masonic Encyclopedia*, 81; F. Smyth, "The Master-Mason-at-Arms," 227.

71. "Annual Address," 157.

72. "Children of the Empire: Empire Lodge Welcomes Canadian Masons," *The Freemason*, January 2, 1915, 347.

73. Dumenil describes Masonry as "expressive" in comparison with other organizations, such as trade unions and political parties, which are "instrumental" and mediate between the individual and society (*Freemasonry and American Culture*, xii).

74. J. Anderson, "The Charges," 254.

75. J. Brownrigg, "Consecration of the Empire Lodge, No. 2108," *The Freemason*, November 28, 1885, 579.

76. See Rich, *Chains of Empire*, on ritual (28) and on the affectation of having ancient origins shared both by Masonry and British public schools (66).

77. Hamill, *The Craft*, 80–81.

78. Piatigorsky (*Freemasonry*, 164) disputes Dumenil's characterization of Masonry as "white, male, primarily native, Protestant" (*Freemasonry and American Culture*, xi), but it is in fact accurate. Protestant American Masons ignored the dissonance involved in their practicing ritual given how their faith viewed it, and there is little evidence that Federalist anti-Masonry had the impact on nativism he suggests.

79. Harland-Jacobs, "All in the Family," 453.

80. Howe, *The Freemason's Manual*, 78.

81. "Brother Grant's Address," 415–19.

4. Freemasonry as Ornamentalism

1. Rich, *Elixir of Empire*, 73.

2. Harland-Jacobs, *Builders of Empire*, 17.

3. Hyam, *Britain's Imperial Century*, 310.

4. Kupperman, *Settling with the Indians*, 2.

5. Cannadine, *Ornamentalism*, 9.

6. I recognize that there are conceptual difficulties with the use of the term *class* to describe communities prior to 1800, but this book uses the term in its broadest sense. In this I follow E. P. Thompson, who argued that classes are, simply, the effect of struggles. One of the best discussions of the thorny topic of who and what constitutes class is Antoine Joseph's "Modes of Class Formation."

7. As with many books that make a truly new contribution in the face of existing intellectual orthodoxies, reviewers found in *Ornamentalism*'s reading of the past a direct threat to the present. Preposterously an American-based

reviewer even suggested "to dismiss or even subordinate race to class is to risk turning a blind eye to its ongoing impact in Britain, from London to Oldham and beyond" (Burton, review, 499).

8. Cannadine, *Ornamentalism*, 85, 90.

9. Rich, *Chains of Empire*, 18, 73.

10. Cannadine, *Ornamentalism*, 95.

11. Hill quoted in Skocpol, *Diminished Democracy*, 105.

12. Cannadine, *Ornamentalism*, 125.

13. B. Anderson, *Imagined Communities*.

14. Dermott, *Ahiman Rezon*.

15. Fay, *Revolution and Freemasonry*, 249.

16. Brooks, "Early American Public Sphere," 74.

17. On African Americans in New Jersey and elsewhere being accepted into mainstream Masonry, see Voorhis, *Our Colored Brethren*.

18. L. Williams, *Black Freemasonry*, 98. See also Schmidt and Babchuk, "The Unbrotherly Brotherhood."

19. Skocpol and Oser, "Organization Despite Adversity," 402; Myrdal, *An American Dilemma*, 952.

20. As well as those mentioned previously, twentieth-century black Freemasons include Duke Ellington and Count Basie.

21. Goldberg, *Enemies Within*, 69.

22. Quoted in Piatigorsky, *Freemasonry*, 171.

23. According to A. C. Parker, William Parker kept the parcel of books hidden in his Tonawanda reservation home. It was finally opened to reveal *Jachin and Boaz, an Authentic Key to Freemasonry*, "written by a gentleman and published at Poughkeepsie, 1811." There was also a complete handwritten Monitor of the Ancient and Accepted Scottish Rite bound in silk with a description in French of the thirty-three degrees dated New Orleans, 1812. The books were given to the Supreme Council, Northern Masonic Jurisdiction, in Boston. See Parker, "Ely S. Parker," 231.

24. W. Denslow, "Freemasonry and the American Indian," 131.

25. R. Morris, *William Morgan*, 197.

26. Vaughn, *The Antimasonic Party*, 5.

27. Lipson, *Freemasonry*, 170, 174.

28. Cross, *The Burned-over District*, 116.

29. Kutolowski, "Antimasonry Reexamined," 285.

30. Bullock, *Revolutionary Brotherhood*, 283–85.

31. Clawson, *Constructing Brotherhood*, 15.

32. Bullock, *Revolutionary Brotherhood*, 318–19.

33. Quoted in Jacob, *Living the Enlightenment*, 23.

34. Leo XIII, *Humanum Genus*, 6, 7.

35. Jacob, *The Radical Enlightenment* (1981), 280. Jacob's book contains the full text of James Anderson's *Constitutions*.

36. J. Anderson, *Constitutions*, 249, 253.

37. One of the few pieces of extended research to bring Mormonism and Masonry together is the thoughtful but deeply flawed *Equal Rites: The Book of Mormon, Masonry, Gender, and American Culture* by Clyde R. Forsberg.

38. Brodie, *No Man Knows My History*, 65.

39. Brodie, *No Man Knows My History*, 281–82, 393–94. Mormon rituals were fundamentally revised in 1990. Furthermore non-Indian studies using DNA have long discounted Mormon claims for Hebrew ancestry for Native Americans. In 2006 a new edition of the Book of Mormon sanctioned by the Church diluted such claims, stating only that the Lamanites were "among the ancestors of the American Indians." Defenders of the Mormon faith have responded to criticism by noting that in a living church such revisions are to be expected.

40. Forsberg, *Equal Rites*, xxii.

41. Davies, "Mormonism," in Lewis and Hammer, *The Invention of Sacred Tradition*, 66.

42. Quoted in Farmer, "Displaced from Zion," 1.

43. Farmer, "Displaced from Zion," 3.

44. Pearce, *The Savages of America*, 55.

45. See Murphy, "From Racist Stereotype to Ethnic Identity."

46. See Farmer, *On Zion's Mount*.

47. Brooke, *The Refiner's Fire*.

48. S. Morris, "Boom to Bust."

49. Stinchcombe, "Social Structure and Organizations," 142–93.

50. Skocpol, *Diminished Democracy*, 47.

51. Stevens, *The Cyclopedia of Fraternities*, 113–14.

52. De Hoyos and Morris, *Freemasonry in Context*, xii.

53. Geertz, "Deep Play," 9.

54. Nelson, *National Manhood*, x.

55. Clawson, *Constructing Brotherhood*, 131–32.

56. L. Williams, *Black Freemasonry*, 67.

57. Harland-Jacobs, *Builders of Empire*, 98.

58. For more on indigenous nineteenth-century Hawaiian Freemasonry, see Karpiel, "Mystic Ties of Brotherhood."

5. The Attractions of Freemasonry, Part One

1. Malinowski's definition, "Religion refers to the fundamental issues of human existence while magic always turns round specific, concrete and detailed

problems," has long ago been reassessed (*A Scientific Theory of Culture*, 200). But it remains the case that in discussing nonorthodox belief systems in English we are still left with these heavily laden, often Eurocentric terms.

2. Thompson, *The Making of the English Working Class*.

3. Thomas, *Religion*, ix, 45.

4. Butler, *Awash in a Sea of Faith*, 9.

5. Thomas, *Religion*, 165.

6. Thomas, *Religion*, 267, 643.

7. Thomas, *Religion*, 61.

8. Although I do not agree that the medieval period was a "Golden Age of Faith" (in the sense of the Christian faith), I do view it as an intensely religious period in the sense that there was widespread belief in powerful supernatural entities with moral purpose. For more on this question, see Bruce, "The Pervasive World-View."

9. Butler, *Awash in a Sea of Faith*, 66, 83. A difficulty with Butler's otherwise excellent work is his tendency to perceive finite and sharp time-specific contrasts in the spiritual history of the United States, perhaps as a result of reliance on Church sources. Also, apart from one brief discussion (155–56), he ignores indigenous faith in his analysis. He writes movingly of an African spiritual holocaust in the New World resulting from slavery but ignores the unprecedented spiritual warfare practiced over time against Native American communities.

10. D. Hall, *Worlds of Wonder*.

11. Of course in another sense the United States remains Indian. As D. H. Lawrence pointed out in *Studies in Classic American Literature*, the very soul of America is Indian. Furthermore "intellectual discovery" of just how much was culturally borrowed from Indian sources remains in its infancy. See, for example, the hotly contested evidence for Indian forms of governance adopted by early America in Grinde and Johansen, *Exemplar of Liberty*.

12. Malinowski, "Magic, Science and Religion," in Needham, *Science, Religion and Reality*.

13. Weber, *From Max Weber*, 265.

14. Weber, *From Max Weber*, 155.

15. Hill, *Society and Puritanism*, 486.

16. The word *magic* can be traced back to the Magi or "wise men" in the Bible who came from the East, but the term solidified in meaning only during the early nineteenth century.

17. See Eisenstadt, "Multiple Modernities"; Gaonkar, *Alternative Modernities*.

18. Taylor, *A Secular Age*, 25–26.

19. Hume, *History of Great Britain*, quoted in Pocock, *Barbarism and Religion*, 203; Taylor, *A Secular Age*, 239.

20. Taylor, *A Secular Age*, 293.

21. Weber, "Religious Rejections of the World and Their Directions," in *From Max Weber*, 331.

22. Taylor in Gaonkar, *Alternative Modernities*, 193.

23. Schmidt, *Hearing Things*, 192.

24. Goldberg, *Enemies Within*.

25. Newcomb, *Pagans in the Promised Land*.

26. Bauman, *Intimations*, vii. See also Gane, *Max Weber*.

27. Jacob, *The Origins of Freemasonry*, 99.

28. Although Clawson and others have asserted that Masonry is "multiclass," as Beito has pointed out, the case for this remains unproven (Clawson, *Constructing Brotherhood*, 24–25; Beito, *From Mutual Aid*, 9).

29. Douglas, *Purity and Danger*.

30. V. Deloria, *The World We Used to Live In*, 53.

31. Schechner, *The Future of Ritual*, 260.

32. Johnson, *Beginnings of Freemasonry in America*, 383.

33. A. Ortiz, *New Perspectives on the Pueblos*, 139.

34. Bell, *Ritual Theory*, 54.

35. Turner, *From Ritual to Theater*, 82.

36. Rappaport, *Ritual and Religion*, 107, 71.

37. Hobsbawm, "Fraternity," 472.

38. Piatigorsky, *Freemasonry*, 299, 302.

39. Turner, *The Anthropology of Performance*, 150.

40. Booth quoted in Newton, "Edwin Booth as a Mason," 100.

41. A. Clark, *The Masonic Chronicle*, 91.

42. Turner, *Forest of Symbols*, 30.

43. Lukes, "Political Ritual," 301–2.

44. Bourdieu, *Outline of a Theory of Practice*, 207; Douglas, *Natural Symbols*, 41–58.

45. Bell, *Ritual Theory*, 221–22.

46. Rappaport, *Ritual and Religion*, 278–79.

47. Ness, "Going Back to Bateson," 16. See Bateson, "Bali."

48. This differs from Bourdieu's idea of *habitus*, which is unconscious. See *Outline of a Theory of Practice*.

49. Turner defined ritual as "the performance of a complex sequence of symbolic acts" (*The Anthropology of Performance*, 75).

50. Pike, "Gnosticism," and *Morals and Dogma*, 246.

51. Carnes, *Secret Ritual*, 73–79.

52. Pike, "Knights of the Sun," in Blanchard, *Scotch Rite Masonry*, 213.

53. Erdoes and Lame Deer, *Lame Deer*, 109.

54. Mackey, Clegg, and Haywood, *Encyclopedia*, 619.

55. Whalen, *Christianity and American Freemasonry*, 114.

56. For a more recent annunciation of the "serious sin" involved in Masonic affiliation, see "Declaration of the Sacred Congregation for the Doctrine of the Faith, 1983," issued by Joseph Cardinal Ratzinger (now pope) and Jerome Hamer, in Whalen, *Christianity and American Freemasonry*, 195–96.

57. See Fingarette, *Confucius*.

58. Geertz, "Deep Play," 90.

59. Durkheim, *The Elementary Forms of Religious Life*, 52.

60. Kipling, "In the Interests of the Brethren." For a broader discussion of definitions of both religion and spirituality, see Fontana, *Psychology, Religion and Spirituality*, chapter 2.

61. Jacob, *Living the Enlightenment*, 66. That Masons should use such a subservient gendered term about their own organization suggests irony.

62. Dumenil, *Freemasonry and American Culture*, 66.

63. Bullock, *Revolutionary Brotherhood*, 169.

64. Pike quoted in Carnes, *Secret Ritual*, 75.

65. Pike, *Morals and Dogma*, 625.

66. MacDonald, *The Catholic Church*, 100; Mackay, *Masonry Defined*, 71.

67. Pike, *Morals and Dogma*, 589–99.

68. Preston, *Illustrations of Masonry*, 75–76.

69. Dumenil, *Freemasonry and American Culture*, xiv.

70. Turner in Schechner and Appel, *By Means of Performance*, 13.

71. Blau in Schechner and Appel, *By Means of Performance*, 270.

72. Goldenweiser, "Loose Ends"; Fenton, *The Iroquois Eagle Dance*, 207, 208. Goldenweiser describes culture patterns that reach a definitive form and then develop only through "progressive complication, a variety within uniformity, virtuosity within monotony" (81).

73. J. Anderson, *Constitutions*, 10, 6.

74. Mallery, *Introduction to the Study of Sign Language among the North American Indians*.

75. MacNulty, "A Philosophical Background for Masonic Symbolism," in de Hoyos and Morris, *Freemasonry in Context*.

76. MacNulty, *The Way of the Craftsman*, 37.

77. MacNulty, *Freemasonry*, 7.

78. For more on Jung, see Dunne, *Carl Jung*.

79. Turner, *The Ritual Process*, 125–29.

80. MacNulty, *Freemasonry*, 28.

81. MacNulty, *Freemasonry*, 32.

82. Clawson, *Constructing Brotherhood*, 83.

83. See A. Ben-Amos, *Funerals, Politics, and Memory*, 146.

84. Ariès, *Western Attitudes towards Death*, 27–52.

85. Freud, *Totem and Taboo*.

86. MacCannell, *The Regime of the Brother*. MacCannell's idea of a fraternal regime is not new in feminist scholarship; see Pateman, *The Sexual Contract*.

87. Freud, *Totem and Taboo*, 146.

88. One of the best discussions of the changing context for death remains Feifel, *The Meaning of Death*.

89. *Murrow Masonic Monitor*, 85, 102, Box Oklahoma: R42, Rittenhouse Collection.

90. Jacob, *Living the Enlightenment*, 67. There is confusion over the role of drinking in Freemasonry stemming from Carnes's assertion that after the 1830s middle-class American Masons banned alcohol and replaced drinking songs with fraternal hymns (*Secret Ritual*, 33). Carnes's source for this assertion is the Reverend A. B. Grosh's *Odd Fellow's Improved Manual*. A curtailment of Odd Fellows' drinking may have occurred in this period, but in general there is no broad-based evidence of drinking being banned or conviviality suppressed in Freemasonry or other linked fraternities. On the contrary, there is much evidence of alcohol being integral to American Masonry over time. For an appreciative discussion of the varieties of drinks and the large quantities consumed at Masonic events in the colonial period, see "From Labor to Refreshment" in Cole, *Masonic Gleanings*, 167–70.

91. The Independent Order of Odd Fellows was the Masonic-type group most readily associated prior to 1820 with drinking; their early emphasis was explicitly on "conviviality" or group drinking.

92. A. Parker to A. DeCora, October 23, 1911, Papers of the Society of American Indians, ten microfilm reels, held at University of Rochester, New York.

93. For more on sacred language in the Masonic tradition, see Arturo de Hoyos, "The Mystery of the Royal Arch Word," in de Hoyos and Morris, *Freemasonry in Context*.

94. Momaday, *The Man Made of Words*, 104.

95. Rasmussen, *The Netsilik Eskimo*, 278.

96. For a discussion of Masonic orality and secrecy, see Mackey, *Masonry Defined*, chapter 6.

97. See S. Brent Morris's study "The Post Boy Sham Exposure of 1723" in de Hoyos and Morris, *Freemasonry in Context*.

98. For more, see Leyland, *Thomas Smith Webb*.

99. Parker, "Secret Medicine Societies of the Seneca."

100. Fenton, *The Iroquois Eagle Dance*, 18, 19, 24, 134, 123.

101. Fenton, *The Iroquois Eagle Dance*, 164, 171.

102. Speck, *Midwinter Rites*, 121.

103. Fenton, *The Iroquois Eagle Dance*, 173.

104. Fenton, *The Iroquois Eagle Dance*.

105. Parker quoted in Fenton, *The Iroquois Eagle Dance*, 80.

106. Morgan, *League of the Ho-De'-No-Sau-Nee*, 60.

107. Langford, *Englishness Identified*, 255, 239, 259, 260.

108. Trilling, *The Liberal Imagination*, 209.

109. Beito, *From Mutual Aid to the Welfare State*, 14, 10, 3, 27.

110. Channing, "Remarks on Associations," in *Works*, 149; Schlesinger, "Biography of a Nation of Joiners," 24. Channing's "Remarks on Associations" first appeared in *Christian Examiner* 7 (1829): 105–40.

111. Money, "The Masonic Moment," 370.

112. P. Clark, *British Clubs*, 336.

113. Elliott and Daniels, "The 'School.'"

114. Muraskin, *Middle-Class Blacks*, 27.

115. For more on the meaning of parade performance, see Fernandez, *Persuasions and Performances*.

116. Roach, "Mardi Gras Indians and Others," 478.

6. The Attractions of Freemasonry, Part Two

1. There is also a lesser tradition of Masonic writers deflating the idea. George A. Newbury and Louis L. Williams, for example, in *A History of the Supreme Council 33°*, write concerning Indian Masonic origins that such "nursery tales must henceforth be confined to the nursery" (29). Ossian Lang, who wrote *History of Freemasonry in the State of New York*, was even more explicit: "The yarns about Masonry among the aborigines, among the Jews at Newport, Rhode Island, in 1656, and the like, are spun of mungo and thin air" (6).

2. Spainhour quoted in Yarrow, *Introduction to the Study of Mortuary Customs*, 28–29.

3. Davis and Tresner, *A Shared Spirit*, 18.

4. Schoolcraft, *Historical and Statistical Information*, 5:474; Vecsey, *Traditional Ojibwa Religion*, 174.

5. Vecsey, *Traditional Ojibwa Religion*, 174.

6. Schoolcraft, *Historical and Statistical Information*, 5:434.

7. Ridge, "North American Indians."

8. There is much evidence of female "medicine" or spiritual agency in a great number of Native American traditions. See, for example, Greg Sarris's work with Mabel McKay in *Keeping Slug Woman Alive: A Holistic Approach to American Indian Texts*.

9. Wright, *Indian Masonry*, 3, 108–9.

10. Wright, *Indian Masonry*, 6, 16, 26.

11. Wright, *Indian Masonry*, 73.

12. Wright, *Indian Masonry*, 109.

13. Blanchard, *Scotch Rite Masonry Illustrated*, 1:42.

14. Wright, *Indian Masonry*, 10.

15. I believe William R. Denslow to be the son of the longtime Grand Secretary of the Grand Lodge of Missouri, the Royal Arch Mason Ray Vaughn Denslow (b. 1885).

16. See Kantrowitz, "'Intended for the Better Government of Man,'" 1014.

17. Perhaps a majority of historians agree with Philip L. Barbour in *The Three Worlds of Captain John Smith* that rather than save Smith's life, Pocahontas was simply playing her part in a ritual adoption (441).

18. Mackey, Clegg, and Haywood, *Encyclopedia of Freemasonry*, 481–83.

19. W. Denslow, "Freemasonry and the American Indian," 182.

20. Copway, *The Life*, 1847 ed., 39.

21. See J. Meserve, "Chief Pleasant Porter," 333.

22. W. Denslow, "Freemasonry and the American Indian," 54.

23. W. Denslow, "Freemasonry and the American Indian," 173.

24. W. Denslow, "Freemasonry and the American Indian," 69, 73.

25. W. Denslow, "Freemasonry and the American Indian," 16, 37.

26. For further discussion and bibliography on both Parkers, see Porter, *To Be Indian*.

27. A 1855 daguerreotype of Ely S. Parker wearing the Red Jacket medal is in the Western Reserve Historical Society, Cleveland, Ohio. According to Parker records, after Red Jacket's death the medal passed to Ely's grandfather, Sose-ha-wa, or James Johnson, a nephew of Red Jacket's who was also a grandson of Handsome Lake.

28. A. Parker quoted in W. Denslow, "Freemasonry and the American Indian," 19.

29. A. Parker quoted in W. Denslow, "Freemasonry and the American Indian," 167.

30. E. Parker quoted in Armstrong, *Warrior in Two Camps*, 70.

31. Konkle, *Writing Indian Nations*, 261. Perhaps less convincingly, Konkle asks us to forgive Parker's and Red Jacket's endorsement of racial difference in this and other speeches, arguing that such racialism must be viewed against the wider contemporary context of a racial politics bent on splitting Native communities apart (260).

32. Dirlik, *Postmodernity's Histories*, 183–84.

33. C. Moore, *The Freemason's Monthly Magazine*, 135.

34. See W. Denslow, "Freemasonry and the American Indian," 151.

35. That is, he persistently connected genetic or innate factors within populations or groups that are not in fact linked. See Porter, *To Be Indian*, 215.

36. Parker, "New York Indians and the Craft," 41.

37. Parker, "Why All This Secrecy?," 361.

38. Hoxie, *A Final Promise*, 241.

39. Masonic sources suggest that Parker was not the first Indian thirty-third-degree Mason, the honor going to Chief Crazy Bull, great-grandson of Sitting Bull of Suffolk Lodge No. 60 in Port Jefferson, New York (Cole, *Masonic Gleanings*, n.p.).

40. Mackey, Clegg, and Haywood, *Encyclopedia of Freemasonry*, 703.

41. A. Parker to George L. Tucker, September 22, 1923, Arthur Caswell Parker Papers, Rush Rhees Library, University of Rochester, New York.

42. Parker, *American Indian Freemasonry*, 13, 22, 16.

43. Parker, "Neh Ho-non-tci-noh-geh" and "Secret Medicine Societies of the Seneca."

44. Fenton, *The Little Water Medicine Society of the Senecas*, 86. On Fenton, please see chapter 1, n. 52.

45. Fenton, *The Little Water Medicine Society of the Senecas*, 22, xiii, 48–49, xiii, 68.

46. Fenton, *The Little Water Medicine Society of the Senecas*, 4.

47. M. Duncan, *Duncan's Masonic Ritual and Monitor*, 122, 120, 121.

48. Parker, "New York Indians and the Craft," 234.

49. Clawson, *Constructing Brotherhood*, 82.

50. Arthur C. Parker, "The Age-old Appeal of Universal Freemasonry," on the occasion of the sesquicentennial of Franklin Lodge, No. 4, F. & A.M. of St. Albans, Vermont, October 15, 1947, Arthur Caswell Parker Papers, University of Rochester, New York.

51. Graymont, *Fighting Tuscarora*, 40, 42, 77, 105, 135.

52. "First Inaugural Address," 271.

53. Kammen, *Mystic Chords of Memory*, 101.

54. Foucault, "Film and Popular Memory"; B. Anderson, *Imagined Communities*.

55. "Knights of the Sun," in Blanchard, *Scottish Rite Masonry*, 213.

56. R. Lewis, *The American Adam*, 5.

57. Catlin quoted in Bellin, *Medicine Bundle*, 48.

58. "Brother Square Toes" is collected in Kipling, *Rewards and Fairies*.

59. Kipling's Masonic poems also include "Banquet Night" and stories connected to the Lodge of Faith and Works, No. 5837, English Constitution, such as "In the Interests of the Brethren" and "The Janeites." One of the best books on his life is Andrew Lycett's *Rudyard Kipling*.

60. Fussell, "Irony, Freemasonry," 228.

61. Fussell, "Irony, Freemasonry," 224.

62. Pratt, *Imperial Eyes*, 7. Juliet Flower MacCannell has fleshed out a similar idea—The Good of the Whole—drawing on Rousseau; see "The Post-Colonial Unconscious, or the White Man's Thing."

63. Pratt, *Imperial Eyes*, 84.

64. Rogin, *Fathers and Children*, 24, 30, 5, 6.

65. Tocqueville quoted in Janara, "Brothers and Others," 782.

66. Janara, "Brothers and Others," 782, 795.

67. Harland-Jacobs, *Builders of Empire*, 238.

7. The Revolutionary Era

1. Smith, "Beyond Tocqueville," 550.

2. Butler, *Awash in a Sea of Faith*, 196.

3. Koch, *Republican Religion*, 253–84; Barkun, *A Culture of Conspiracy*, 15–39.

4. Hatch, *The Democratization of American Christianity*.

5. Quoted in Minges, "All My Slaves," 13. See also Cotterill, *The Southeastern Indians*.

6. Bullock, *Revolutionary Brotherhood*, 113.

7. See Johansen, *Debating Democracy*; Grinde and Johansen, *Exemplar of Liberty*.

8. P. Deloria, *Playing Indian*, 8.

9. Bakhtin, *Rabelais and His World*.

10. Snow, review, 192.

11. Kelsay, *Joseph Brant 1743–1807*.

12. Sidney Hayden in C. Moore, *Leaflets of Masonic Biography*, 147.

13. Joseph Brant's Masonic certificate is held at the Royal Ontario Museum, University of Toronto.

14. Robertson, *The History of Freemasonry in Canada*, 1:688; Kelsay, *Joseph Brant*, 172.

15. Stone, *Life of Joseph Brant*, 251.

16. For more on Brant's pension, see Captain Brant to Sir Evan Nepean, n.d., in Stone, *Life of Joseph Brant*, 257.

17. Kelsay, *Joseph Brant*, 536. Brant is also listed by the Grand Lodge of British Columbia and Yukon A.F. & A.M. as founder in 1798 of Brantford Lodge No. 31. See freemasonry.bcy.ca/biography/brant-j/brant-j.html (accessed November 11, 2009).

18. Quoted in Stone, *Life of Joseph Brant*, 338.

19. For an account of Brant's protecting infants in war, see Stone, *Life of Joseph Brant*, 126.

20. McLeod quoted in Davis and Tresner, *A Shared Spirit*, 52.

21. Davis and Tresner, *A Shared Spirit*.

22. Fellows, *An Exposition*, v.

23. Bresee, *Along Masonic Trails*, 59–60.

24. Johnson never lost his respect for elemental powers or for indigenous means of healing and is known to have sought relief at a magical healing stream shown to him by Iroquois sachems in 1767 (Flexner, *Mohawk Baronet*, 314).

25. O'Toole, *White Savage*, 59.

26. O'Toole, *White Savage*, 62.

27. Hendrick quoted in Flexner, *Mohawk Baronet*, xviii.

28. Sullivan et al., *The Papers of Sir William Johnson*, 2:487.

29. O'Toole, *White Savage*, 164.

30. Flexner, *Mohawk Baronet*, 54.

31. V. Deloria, *The World We Used to Live In*, 115.

32. O'Toole, *White Savage*, 312.

33. For more on Johnson and Highland Scots, see Calloway, "Sir William Johnson."

34. Hamilton, *Papers of Sir William Johnson*, 12:1075.

35. Fenton, *The Great Law*, 571.

8. The "Settlement" of the West

1. Limerick, *The Legacy of Conquest*, 26.

2. See d'Errico, "John Marshall," 28.

3. Davis and Tresner, *A Shared Spirit*, 28.

4. W. Denslow, "Freemasonry and the American Indian," 183.

5. The Creek lodge's charter was eventually revoked by the Grand Lodge in 1867.

6. Latham, *The Story of Oklahoma Masonry*, 8.

7. Haywood, *The Well-Springs of American Freemasonry*, 120–56.

8. Parker quoted in W. Denslow, "Freemasonry and the American Indian," 85.

9. Andrew Jackson's seventh annual message to Congress, December 7, 1835, available at http://millercenter.org.

10. Latham, *The Story of Oklahoma Masonry*, 2; Minges, "The Keetoowah Society," 125; Woodward, *The Cherokees*, 204–12.

11. R. Duncan, *Reluctant General*, 135.

12. See Franks, "The Implementation of the Confederate Treaties," 21.

13. Perdue, *Slavery*, 57.

14. Patrick Minges is a Blue Lodge Mason (personal correspondence, January 7, 2009). W. R. Denslow, in contrast, states only that it is probable that

Pike conferred the thirty-second degree on Boudinot in 1886 ("Freemasonry and the American Indian," 189).

15. Minges, *Slavery in the Cherokee Nation*, 103.

16. Moulton, *John Ross*, 7.

17. W. Denslow, "Freemasonry and the American Indian," 75.

18. Minges, *Slavery in the Cherokee Nation*, 135.

19. See Franks, "The Implementation," 30.

20. Pike to Secretary of War J. P. Benjamin, November 27, 1861, in R. Duncan, *Reluctant General*, 186.

21. See Franks, "The Implementation"; Kremm and Neal, "Crisis of Command."

22. Pike quoted in Kremm and Neal, "Crisis of Command," 33.

23. Albert Pike, Walnut Springs, to Peter Pitchlyn, January 21, 1864, Box 4, Peter Pitchlyn Collection, Western History Collections, University of Oklahoma.

24. Carnes, *Secret Ritual*, 145.

25. Pike, *Morals and Dogma*, 861.

26. Pike quoted in R. Duncan, *Reluctant General*, 144.

27. Wright, *Indian Masonry*, 105.

28. McLoughlin and Conserv, *The Cherokees and Christianity*, 279.

29. Butler, *Awash in a Sea of Faith*, 235.

30. Quoted in Piatigorsky, *Freemasonry*, 176–79.

31. Latham, *The Story*, 10.

32. For more on Rogers's Masonry, see Wertheim et al., *The Papers of Will Rogers*, 280.

33. Rogers quoted in Carter, *Never Met a Man I Didn't Like*, 272.

34. Roosevelt quoted in Milsten, *Will Rogers*, 8.

9. The Nineteenth and Twentieth Centuries

1. S. Ortiz, "The Historical Matrix," 65.

2. Piatigorsky, *Freemasonry*, 200.

3. Berkhofer, *The White Man's Indian*; Fabian, *Time and the Other*.

4. For more on Masonic time, see "Daily Lives as Measured in Masonic Time," chapter 2 in Jacob, *The Origins of Freemasonry*.

5. H. Jackson, *Century of Dishonor*.

6. Rotundo, *American Manhood*, 3–7, 222.

7. Rotundo, *American Manhood*, 63.

8. Thoreau quoted in Rotundo, *American Manhood*, 105.

9. Carnes, *Secret Ritual*, 1.

10. Rotundo, *American Manhood*, 146. There is little evidence to support

Rotundo's claim that Masonic rituals "focused in great measure on men's feelings about women" (201).

11. Rotundo, *American Manhood*, 228.

12. Published by the Oklahoma Lodge of Research in October 1967, excerpted in Davis and Tresner, *A Shared Spirit*.

13. Davis and Tresner, *A Shared Spirit*, 41, 42.

14. Carnes, *Secret Ritual*, 123–25.

15. Harwood, "Secret Societies," 622–23.

16. Schlesinger, *Paths to the Present*, 48–50; Handlin and Handlin, *The Dimensions of Liberty*, 111.

17. Arnold quoted in R. Williams, *Culture and Society*, 118–19.

18. Levine, *Highbrow Lowbrow*, 233, 146.

19. Carnes, *Secret Ritual*, 28.

20. Lynes, *The Lively Audience*.

21. On women's support of Freemasonry in this period, see W. Moore, "Funding the Temples."

22. There are twenty-nine Scottish Rite regular degrees, which follow the three degrees conferred in Craft lodges: Entered Apprentice, Fellowcraft, and Master Mason.

23. Pike, *Moral and Dogma*, 625.

24. Brockman cited in de Hoyos and Morris, *Freemasonry in Context*, 62.

25. Brockman, *Theatre of the Fraternity*, 21.

26. Moore quoted in Brockman, *Theatre of the Fraternity*, 38.

27. Brockman, *Theatre of the Fraternity*, 119.

28. Quoted in Brockman, *Theatre of the Fraternity*, 62.

29. Brockman, *Theatre of the Fraternity*, 45.

30. Adams quoted in Davis and Tresner, *A Shared Spirit*, 1.

31. Quoted in Brockman, *Theatre of the Fraternity*, 66.

32. Clawson quoted in Brockman, *Theatre of the Fraternity*, 53.

33. Stevens, *Cyclopedia of Fraternities*, xvi; Swiencicki, "Consuming Brotherhood," 779, 796.

34. See Lynn Dumenil's analysis of Live Oak Lodge in California in 1880–1920 (*Freemasonry and American Culture*, 15–23).

35. Butsch, *For Fun and Profit*, 14.

36. Quoted by Clawson, in Brockman, *Theatre of the Fraternity*, 66.

37. Brockman, *Theatre of the Fraternity*, 68.

38. Clawson, *Constructing Brotherhood*, 11, 14, 18.

39. Carnes, *Secret Ritual*, 256, 3, ix.

40. Parker, "Why All This Secrecy?," 361.

41. Schultz, *The Republic of Labor*, 7. To get a different emphasis, one that

focuses on economics rather than ideology, see Commons, *Labor and Administration*, 219–66.

42. Webster quoted in Laurie, *Artisans into Workers*, 15.

43. Clawson, *Constructing Brotherhood*, 213; Carnes, *Secret Ritual*, 10.

44. Dumenil, *Freemasonry and American Culture*, 220.

45. Thoreau, *Cape Cod and Miscellanies*, in *Complete Works*, 364–65.

46. Piatigorsky, *Freemasonry*, 190.

47. Kimmel, *Manhood in America*, 130.

48. S. Lewis, *Babbitt*, 161.

49. Schlesinger, "Biography of a Nation of Joiners," 25.

50. Piatigorsky, *Freemasonry*, 348.

51. A useful Masonic guide to Masonic persecution during the Second World War can be found in chapters 6 and 7 of R. Denslow, *Masonic Portraits*.

10. On Television's Deathblow to Fraternalism

1. See Clawson, *Constructing Brotherhood*; Carnes, *Secret Ritual*.

2. Van Cott, *Freemasonry*, 155.

3. Schmidt and Babchuk, "Formal Voluntary Organizations," 46.

4. Riesman, *The Lonely Crowd*; Lasch, *The Culture of Narcissism*, 41.

5. Schlesinger, "Biography of a Nation of Joiners," 20.

6. Elisabeth Bumiller, "Bush Embraces His Roots and Some Connecticut Money, Too," *New York Times*, April 10, 2002.

7. M. Joseph, *Against the Romance of Community*.

8. Putnam's title is catchy but misleading; as he admits, bowling has in fact bucked the trend and held basically steady in the face of a more general lessening of informal ties (*Bowling Alone*, 113).

9. Putnam, *Bowling Alone*, 64, 115, 72, 80. John L. Belton has pointed out that although it is true that American Masonic numbers peaked at around four million in 1960, if we measure Masonic involvement against base male population figures rather than against absolute numbers, Masonic popularity was actually lower after the Second World War than after the First (cited in de Hoyos and Morris, *Freemasonry in Context*, 315).

10. Putnam, *Bowling Alone*, 132, 237, 239, 242.

11. Birkerts quoted in Putnam, *Bowling Alone*, 246.

12. Previously historians have seen technology not as mitigating against an American passion for joining together organizationally but as serving to stimulate it. However, it was not television and electronic media that authors such as William Channing and Arthur Schlesinger had in mind when they made this point, but innovations such as the post office, the railroad, and the steam-

boat, which served to telescope distance for Americans. See William E. Channing quoted in Schlesinger, "Biography of a Nation of Joiners," 9.

13. Tilly quoted in Putnam, *Bowling Alone*, 255.

14. Skocpol et al., "War and the Development of American Civil Society."

15. Quesenberry, "Bowling Together during War," 1034.

16. Putnam, *Bowling Alone*, 401.

17. Lipsitz, *Time Passages*, 39–76.

18. For more on heroes and immortality, see Rank, *Art and Artist*, 407; Becker, *The Denial of Death*, 131, 129.

19. Habermas, *Legitimation Crisis*, 71–75.

20. Kaufman, *For the Common Good?*

21. Hannah Arendt also carefully defined *association* and strictly separated social association analytically from political association (*On Revolution*, 182). Those interested in a careful analysis of nineteenth-century associationalism and the difficulty of assessing its impact may wish to consult Jason Kaufman, "Three Views of Associationalism."

22. Schlesinger, "Biography of a Nation of Joiners," 23–24. Putnam says that he prefers "bridging" social capital, where connections are made across diverse social groups, as opposed to "bonding" social capital that reifies homogeneous social groups.

23. Edwards and Foley, "Much Ado about Social Capital," 230.

24. Packard, *The Status Seekers*, 192–93. As Clawson accepts in *Constructing Brotherhood* (95–106), Freemasonry as an elite fraternity offered less opportunity than other groups for cross-class bonding. However, it has historically provided a structure whereby those on one social plane could meaningfully interact with those on another, and its decline lessens this opportunity.

25. Schlesinger, "Biography of a Nation of Joiners," 25.

26. Tocqueville quoted in Schlesinger, "Biography of a Nation of Joiners," 2.

27. Beito, *From Mutual Aid*, 228.

28. Bauman, *Consuming Life*, 107, 115.

29. Jim Tresner, interview with author.

30. See the survey of Evansville Cemetery (Tohee or Bobby Ford) carried out by Nelda Brown Alkadhimi on behalf of Logan County Genealogical Society, Inc., Guthrie, Oklahoma. Available at Logan County Genealogical Society, Inc., Library, Oklahoma Territorial Museum, Guthrie.

Bibliography

Achebe, C. "The Role of the Writer in a New Nation." In *African Writers on African Writing*, edited by G. D. Killam. London: Heinemann, 1978.

Anderson, Amanda. "Cosmopolitanism, Universalism, and the Divided Legacies of Modernity." In *Cosmopolitics: Thinking and Feeling beyond the Nation*, edited by Peng Cheah and Bruce Robbins. Minneapolis: University of Minnesota Press, 1998.

Anderson, Benedict. *Imagined Communities: Reflections on the Origin and Spread of Nationalism*. New York: Verso, 1991. (Orig. pub. 1983.)

Anderson, J. "The Charges of a Free-Mason Extracted from the Ancient Records of Lodges Beyond the Sea, and Those in England, Scotland, and Ireland, for the Use of the Lodges in London: To Be Read at the Making of New Brethren, or When the Master Shall Order It." 1723. In *The Radical Enlightenment: Pantheists, Freemasons, and Republicans*, by Margaret C. Jacob. London: Allen and Unwin, 2006.

———. *The Constitutions of the Free-Masons. Containing the History, Charges, Regulations, & c. of that most Ancient and Right Worshipful Fraternity. For the Use of the Lodges*. London: William Hunter, 1723.

Anderson, Owanah. *400 Years: Anglican/Episcopal Missions among American Indians*. Cincinnati OH: Forward Movement, 1997.

"Annual Address of the Grand Master, 30 November." In *Proceedings of the Grand Lodge of Scotland*. Edinburgh: Grand Lodge of Scotland, 1888.

Arendt, Hannah. *On Revolution*. London: Penguin, 1990. (Orig. pub. 1963.)

Ariès, Philippe. *Western Attitudes towards Death: From Middle Ages to the Present*. Translated by P. Ranum. Baltimore: Johns Hopkins University Press, 1974.

Armstrong, William H. *Warrior in Two Camps: Ely S. Parker*. Syracuse NY: Syracuse University Press, 1978.

Baird, David W. *Peter Pitchlyn: Chief of the Choctaws*. Norman: University of Oklahoma Press, 1986.

Bakhtin, Mikhail. *Rabelais and His World*. Cambridge MA: MIT Press, 1968.

———. *Speech Genres*. Edited by Carol Emerson and Michael Holquist. Austin: University of Texas Press, 1986.

Bank, Rosemarie K. "Staging the 'Native': Making History in American Theatre Culture, 1828–1838." *Theatre Journal* 45 (1993): 93–102.

———. *Theatre Culture in America, 1825–1860*. New York: Cambridge University Press, 1997.

Bann, Stephen. *Romanticism and the Rise of History*. New York: Twayne, 1995.

Barbour, Philip L. *The Three Worlds of Captain John Smith*. Boston: Houghton Mifflin, 1964.

Barker, Francis, Peter Hulme, and Margaret Iversen. *Cannibalism and the Colonial World*. Cambridge: Cambridge University Press, 1998.

Barkun, Michael. *A Culture of Conspiracy: Apocalyptic Visions in Contemporary America*. Berkeley: University of California Press, 2003.

Bataille, Gretchen. *Native American Representations: First Encounters, Distorted Images, and Literary Appropriations*. Lincoln: University of Nebraska Press, 2001.

Bateson, Gregory. "Bali: The Value System of a Steady State." In *Social Structure: Studies Presented to A. R. Radcliffe-Brown*, edited by M. Fortes. Wolton-under-Edge, Gloucestershire: Clarendon Press, 1949.

Bauman, Zygmunt. *Consuming Life*. Cambridge: Polity Press, 2007.

———. *Intimations of Post-Modernity*. London: Routledge, Chapman and Hall, 1992.

Beck, Peggy V., Anna Lee Walters, and Nia Francisco. *The Sacred: Ways of Knowledge, Sources of Life*. Tsaile AZ: Navajo Community College Press, 1992.

Becker, Ernest. *The Denial of Death*. New York: Free Press, 1973.

Beiser, Frederick C. *The Sovereignty of Reason: The Defense of Rationality in the Early English Enlightenment*. Princeton NJ: Princeton University Press, 1996.

Beito, David. *From Mutual Aid to the Welfare State: Fraternal Societies and Social Services, 1890–1967*. Chapel Hill: University of North Carolina Press, 2000.

Bell, Catherine. *Ritual Theory, Ritual Practice*. Oxford: Oxford University Press, 1992.

Bellin, Joshua David. *The Demon of the Continent: Indians and the Shaping of American Literature*. Philadelphia: University of Pennsylvania Press, 2001.

———. *Medicine Bundle: Indian Scared Performance and American Literature, 1824–1932*. Philadelphia: University of Pennsylvania Press, 2008.

Ben-Amos, Avner. *Funerals, Politics, and Memory in Modern France, 1789–1996*. New York: Oxford University Press, 2000.

Ben-Amos, Dan, and Kenneth S. Goldstein, eds. *Folklore: Performance and Communication*. The Hague: Mouton, 1975.

Benedict, Ruth. Review of *Secret Societies* by Noel P. Gist. *American Sociological Review* 7, no. 5 (1942): 728–30.

Berkhofer, Robert F., Jr. *The White Man's Indian: Images of the American Indian from Columbus to the Present*. New York: Vintage Books, 1979.

Bhabha, Homi K. "Of Mimicry and Man: The Ambivalence of Colonial Discourse." In *The Location of Culture*. London: Routledge, 1994.

———. "The Other Question: The Stereotype and Colonial Discourse." *Screen* 24, no. 6 (1983): 18–36.

Bird, Robert Montgomery. *Nick of the Woods, or The Jibbenainosay: A Tale of Kentucky*. Philadelphia: Carey, Lea and Blanchard, 1837.

Black, Antony. *Guilds and Civil Society in European Political Thought from the Twelfth Century to the Present*. London: Methuen, 1984.

Blanchard, Jonathan. *Scotch Rite Masonry Illustrated: The Complete Ritual of the Ancient and Accepted Scottish Rite*. Vols. 1 and 2. Chicago: Ezra A. Cook, 1887.

———. *Scottish Rite Masonry Illustrated*. Chicago: Ezra A. Cook, 1882.

Bourdieu, Pierre. *Distinction: A Social Critique of the Judgement of Taste*. Translated by R. Nice. London: Routledge. 1984. (Orig. pub. 1979.)

———. *Outline of a Theory of Practice*. Translated by Richard Nice. Cambridge MA: Harvard University Press, 1977.

Bresee, Wilmer Edgar. *Along Masonic Trails*. Cooperstown NY: The Freeman's Journal, 1961. Held in The Masonic Library and Museum of Pennsylvania, Philadelphia.

Brockman, C. Lance. *Theatre of the Fraternity: Staging the Ritual Space of the Scottish Rite of Freemasonry, 1896–1929*. Minneapolis: Frederick R. Weisman Art Museum, University Press of Mississippi, 1996.

Brodie, Fawn M. *No Man Knows My History: The Life of Joseph Smith, the Mormon Prophet*. 2nd ed. rev. New York: Knopf, 1986.

Brooke, John L. *The Refiner's Fire: The Making of Mormon Cosmology, 1644–1844*. Cambridge: Cambridge University Press, 1994.

Brooks, Joanna. *American Lazarus: Religion and the Rise of African-American and Native American Literatures*. New York: Oxford University Press, 2003.

———. "The Early American Public Sphere and the Emergence of a Black Print Counterpublic." *William and Mary Quarterly* 62, no. 1 (2005): 67–92.

"Brother Grant's Address to Londonderry Freemasons." June 24, 1850. *Freemasons' Quarterly Review* (September 1850): 415–19.

Brown, Walter Lee. *A Life of Albert Pike*. Fayetteville: University of Arkansas Press, 1997.

Bruce, Steve. "The Pervasive World-View: Religion in Pre-Modern Britain." *British Journal of Sociology* 48, no. 4 (1997): 667–80.

Bullock, Steven C. *Revolutionary Brotherhood: Freemasonry and the Transformation of the American Social Order, 1730–1840*. Chapel Hill: University of North Carolina Press, 1996.

Burke, Janet M., and Margaret C. Jacob. "French Freemasonry, Woman and Feminist Scholarship." *Journal of Modern History* 68, no. 3 (1996): 513–39.

Burton, Antoinette. Review of *Ornamentalism* by David Cannadine. *American Historical Review* 107, no. 2 (2002): 497–98.

Butler, Jon. *Awash in a Sea of Faith: Christianizing the American People.* Cambridge MA: Harvard University Press, 1990.

Butsch, Richard. *For Fun and Profit: The Transformation of Leisure into Consumption.* Philadelphia: Temple University Press, 1990.

Calloway, Colin G. "Sir William Johnson, Highland Scots, and American Indians." *New York History* 89, no. 2 (2008): 163–77.

Cannadine, David. *Ornamentalism: How the British Saw Their Empire.* London: Allen Lane, 2001.

Cantwell, Robert. *Ethnomimesis: Folklife and the Representation of Culture.* Chapel Hill: University of North Carolina Press, 1992.

Cappon, Lester J., ed. *The Adams-Jefferson Letters.* Chapel Hill: University of North Carolina Press, 1959.

Carnes, Mark C. *Secret Ritual and Manhood in Victorian America.* New Haven CT: Yale University Press, 1989.

Carter, Joseph H. *Never Met a Man I Didn't Like: The Life and Writings of Will Rogers.* New York: Avon, 1991.

Castillo, Susan. *Colonial Encounters in New World Writing, 1500–1786: Performing America.* London: Routledge, 2005.

Channing, W. E. *Works.* Boston, 1875.

Cheyfitz, Eric. *The Poetics of Imperialism: Translation and Colonization from* The Tempest *to Tarzan.* Philadelphia: University of Pennsylvania Press, 1991.

Churchill, Ward. *Indians Are Us? Culture and Genocide in Native North America.* Monroe ME: Common Courage Press, 1994.

Clark, Arthur W. *The Masonic Chronicle* 5, no. 8 (1886): 91.

Clark, P. *British Clubs and Societies 1580–1800: The Origins of an Associational World.* Oxford: Oxford University Press, 2000.

Clawson, Mary Ann. *Constructing Brotherhood: Class, Gender and Fraternalism.* Princeton NJ: Princeton University Press, 1989.

Clifford, James. *The Predicament of Culture: Twentieth-Century Ethnography, Literature, and Art.* Cambridge MA: Harvard University Press, 1988.

Cohen, Kenneth. "A Mutually Comprehensible World? Native Americans, Europeans, and Play in Eighteenth Century America." *American Indian Quarterly* 26 (2002): 67–93.

Coil, H. *Coil's Masonic Encyclopedia.* New York: Macoy Publishing and Masonic Supply Co., 1961.

Cole, Robert Glenn. *Masonic Gleanings.* Chicago: Kable, 1954.

Commons, John R. "American Shoemakers, 1648–1895." In *Labor and Administration.* New York: Macmillan, 1913.

Conn, Steven. *History's Shadow: Native Americans and Historical Consciousness in the Nineteenth Century.* Chicago: University of Chicago Press, 2004.

Conquergood, Dwight. "Rethinking Ethnography: Towards a Critical Cultural Politics." *Communication Monographs* 58 (June 1981): 179–94.

Cooper, James Fenimore. *The Last of the Mohicans.* New York: Penguin, 1986.

———. *The Prairie.* New York: New American Library, 1964.

Copway, George. *The Life, Letters and Speeches of Kah-ge-ga-gah-bowh.* New York: S. W. Benedict, 1850. (Orig. pub. as *The Life, History, and Travels of Kah-ge-ga-gah-bowh* [Albany: Weed and Parsons, 1847].)

Cotterill, R. S. *The South-eastern Indians: The Story of the Civilized Tribes before Removal.* Norman: University of Oklahoma Press, 1963. (Orig. pub. 1954.)

Crosby, Alfred W. *The Measure of Reality: Quantification and Western Society, 1250–1600.* Cambridge: Cambridge University Press, 1997.

Cross, Whitney R. *The Burned-over District: The Social and Intellectual History of Enthusiastic Religion in Western New York, 1800–1850.* Ithaca NY: Cornell University Press, 1950.

Daniel, Stephen H. *John Toland: His Methods, Manners and Mind.* Kingston, Canada: McGill-Queen's University Press, 1984.

Davies, Douglas J. "Mormonism." In *The Invention of Sacred Tradition*, edited by James R. Lewis and Olav Hammer. Cambridge: Cambridge University Press, 2007.

Davis, Robert G., and Jim Tresner. *A Shared Spirit: Freemasonry and the Native American Tradition.* Guthrie OK: Masonic Service Association of North America and the Most Worshipful Grand Lodge of Oklahoma, 2001.

de Hoyos, Arturo, and S. Brent Morris, eds. *Freemasonry in Context: History, Ritual, Controversy.* Oxford: Lexington Books, Scottish Rite Research Society, 2004.

Deloria, Philip J. *Indians in Unexpected Places.* Lawrence: University Press of Kansas, 2004.

———. *Playing Indian.* New Haven CT: Yale University Press, 1998.

———. "Vine V. Deloria Sr., Dakota." In *The New Warriors: Native American Leaders Since 1900*, edited by R. David Edmunds. Lincoln: University of Nebraska Press, 2001.

Deloria, Vine, Jr. *Singing for a Spirit: A Portrait of the Dakota Sioux.* Santa Fe NM: Clear Light, 1991.

———. *The World We Used to Live In.* Golden CO: Fulcrum, 2006.

Denslow, Ray V. *Masonic Portraits.* Jefferson MO: Board of Publication for the Missouri Lodge of Research, 1972.

Denslow, William R. "Freemasonry and the American Indian." *Transactions of the Missouri Lodge of Research* 13 (1956).

Densmore, Frances. *Chippewa Music*. Bureau of American Ethnology Bulletin 45. Washington DC, 1910.

Dermott, Lawrence. *Ahiman Rezon: or a Help to a Brother; showing the Excellency of Secrecy, and the first cause or motive of the Institution of Masonry; the Principles of the Craft; and the Benefits from a strict Observance thereof, etc., etc.; also the Old and New Regulations, etc. To which is added the greatest collection of Masons' Songs, etc. By Bro. Laurence Dermott, Secretary*. London: James Bedford, 1756.

d'Errico, Peter. "John Marshall: Indian Lover?" *Journal of the West* 39, no. 3 (2000): 19–30.

Diamond, Stanley. *In Search of the Primitive: A Critique of Civilization*. New Brunswick NJ: Transaction, 1974.

Dirlik, Arif. *Postmodernity's Histories: The Past as Legacy and Project*. Lanham MD: Rowman and Littlefield, 1999.

Douglas, Mary. *Natural Symbols*. New York: Random House, 1973.

———. *Purity and Danger: An Analysis of Concepts of Pollution and Taboo*. London: Routledge, 1991.

Dumenil, Lynn. *Freemasonry and American Culture, 1880–1930*. Princeton NJ: Princeton University Press, 1984.

Duncan, Malcolm C. *Duncan's Masonic Ritual and Monitor*. 3rd ed. New York: Crown, 1986. (Orig. pub. 1886.)

Duncan, Robert Lipscomb. *Reluctant General: The Life and Times of Albert Pike*. New York: E. P. Dutton, 1961.

Dunne, Claire. *Carl Jung: Wounded Healer of the Soul*. London: Continuum International, 2002.

Durkheim, Émile. *The Elementary Forms of Religious Life*. 1912. Translated by J. Swain. New York: Collier, 1961.

Edwards, Bob, and Michael W. Foley. "Much Ado about Social Capital." *Contemporary Sociology* 30, no. 3 (2001): 227–30.

Eisenstadt, Shmuel, ed. "Multiple Modernities." Special issue of *Daedalus* (Winter 2000).

Eliot, T. S. "Tradition and the Individual Talent." 1919. In *Selected Essays*. London: Faber and Faber, 1986.

Elliott, Michael A. "Ethnography, Reform and the Problem of the Real: James Mooney's *Ghost Dance Religion*." *American Indian Quarterly* 22, no. 2 (1998): 201–33.

Elliott, Paul, and Stephen Daniels. "The 'School of True, Useful and Universal Science'? Freemasonry, Natural Philosophy and Scientific Culture in Eighteenth-century England." *British Journal of the History of Science* 39, no. 2 (2006): 207–29.

Erdoes, Richard, and John Lame Deer. *Lame Deer: Seeker of Visions*. New York: Simon and Schuster, 1972.

Fabian, Johannes. *Time and the Other: How Anthropology Makes Its Object*. New York: Columbia University Press, 1983.

Fanon, Frantz. *The Wretched of the Earth*. New York: Grove, 1963.

Farmer, Jared. "Displaced from Zion: Mormons and Indians in the 19th Century." *Historically Speaking* 10, no. 1 (2009): 40–42.

———. *On Zion's Mount: Mormons, Indians, and the American Landscape*. Cambridge MA: Harvard University Press, 2008.

Fay, Bernard. *Revolution and Freemasonry, 1660–1800*. Boston: Little, Brown, 1935.

Feifel, Herman. *The Meaning of Death*. New York: McGraw-Hill, 1959.

Fellows, John. *An Exposition of the Mysteries, Or, Religious Dogmas and Customs of the Ancient Egyptians, Pythagoreans, and Druids: An Inquiry into the Origin, History, and Purport of Freemasonry*. New York: Gould, Hanks, 1835.

Fenton, William N. *The False Faces of the Iroquois*. Norman: University of Oklahoma Press, 1987.

———. *The Great Law and the Longhouse: A Political History of the Iroquois Confederacy*. Norman: University of Oklahoma Press, 1998.

———. Introduction to *Midwinter Rites of the Cayuga Long House*, by Frank Speck. Lincoln: University of Nebraska Press, 1995.

———. *The Iroquois Eagle Dance: An Offshoot of the Calumet Dance*. Smithsonian Institution Bureau of American Ethnology Bulletin 156. Washington DC, 1991. (Orig. pub. 1953.)

———. *The Little Water Medicine Society of the Senecas*. Norman: University of Oklahoma Press, 2002.

Fernandez, James W. *Persuasions and Performances: The Play of Tropes in Culture*. Bloomington: Indiana University Press, 1986.

Fingarette, Herbert. *Confucius: The Secular as Sacred*. New York: Harper and Row, 1972.

"First Inaugural Address: Final Text." March 4, 1861. In *The Collected Works of Abraham Lincoln*, edited by Roy P. Basler, et al. Vol. 4. New Brunswick NJ: Rutgers University Press, 1953.

Flexner, James Thomas. *Mohawk Baronet: A Biography of Sir William Johnson*. Syracuse NY: Syracuse University Press, 1959.

Fliegelman, Jay. *Declaring Independence: Jefferson, Natural Language, and the Culture of Performance*. Stanford: Stanford University Press, 1993.

Foner, Philip S. *The Complete Writings of Thomas Paine*. New York: Citadel, 1969.

Fontana, David. *Psychology, Religion and Spirituality*. Oxford: Blackwell, 2003.

Forbes, Jack D. *Africans and Native Americans: The Language of Race*. Urbana: University of Illinois Press, 1993.

Forsberg, Clyde R., Jr. *Equal Rites: The Book of Mormon, Masonry, Gender, and American Culture.* New York: Columbia University Press, 2004.

Foucault, Michel. *The Archaeology of Knowledge.* Translated by A. M. Sheridan Smith. New York: Pantheon Books, 1972. (Orig. pub. 1969.)

———. "Film and Popular Memory." In *Foucault Live (Interviews, 1966–84)*, edited by Sylvere Lotringer. Translated by John Johnston. New York: Semiotext(e), 1989.

Franks, Kenny A. "The Implementation of the Confederate Treaties with the Five Civilized Tribes." *Chronicles of Oklahoma* 51 (Spring 1973): 21–33.

Fraser, Nancy. "Rethinking the Public Sphere: A Contribution to the Critique of Actually Existing Democracy." *Social Text*, nos. 25/26 (1990): 56–80.

Freud, Sigmund. *Totem and Taboo.* London: Routledge and Kegan Paul, 1960. (Orig. pub. 1912–13.)

Frye, Northrop. *Anatomy of Criticism.* Princeton NJ: Princeton University Press, 1957.

Furet, François. *Interpreting the French Revolution.* Translated by Elborg Forster. Cambridge: Cambridge University Press, 1981. (Orig. pub. 1978.)

Fussell, Paul, Jr. "Irony, Freemasonry, and Humane Ethics in Kipling's 'The Man Who Would Be King.'" *ELH* 25, no. 3 (1958): 216–33.

Gane, Nicholas. *Max Weber and Postmodern Theory: Rationalization versus Re-enchantment.* New York: Palgrave, 2002.

Gaonkar, Dilip Parameshwar. *Alternative Modernities.* Durham NC: Duke University Press, 2001.

Gardner, Susan. *A Vision of Double Woman: Ella Cara Deloria and the Profession of Kinship.* Lincoln: University of Nebraska Press, forthcoming.

Gates, Henry Louis, Jr. *The Signifying Monkey: A Theory of Afro-American Literary Criticism.* New York: Oxford University Press, 1988.

Geertz, Clifford. "Deep Play: Notes on the Balinese Cockfight." In *The Interpretation of Cultures.* New York: Basic Books, 1973.

Gerland, Oliver. "From Playhouse to P2P Network: The History and Theory of Performance under Copyright Law in the United States." *Theatre Journal* 59, no. 1 (2007): 75–95.

Gibbs, G. C. Review of *The Radical Enlightenment* by Margaret C. Jacob. *British Journal for the History of Science* 17, no. 1 (1984): 67–81.

Gill, Sam D. *Native American Religions: An Introduction.* Belmont CA: Wadsworth, 1982.

Gilroy, Paul. *The Black Atlantic: Modernity and Double Consciousness.* Cambridge MA: Harvard University Press, 1993.

Gist, Noel P. "Secret Societies: A Cultural Study of Fraternalism in the United States." *University of Missouri Studies* 15, no. 4 (October 1940).

Goldberg, Robert Alan. *Enemies Within: The Culture of Conspiracy in Modern America*. New Haven CT: Yale University Press, 2001.

Goldenweiser, Alexander. "Loose Ends of a Theory on the Pattern and Involution in Primitive Society." In *Essays in Anthropology Presented to A. L. Kroebes*, edited by R. Lowie. Berkeley: University of California Press, 1936.

Graymont, Barbara. *Fighting Tuscarora: The Autobiography of Chief Clinton Rickard*. Syracuse NY: Syracuse University Press, 1973.

Grinde, Donald G., and Bruce E. Johansen. *Exemplar of Liberty: Native America and the Evolution of Democracy*. Los Angeles: University of California Press, 1991.

Gustafson, Sandra M. *Eloquence Is Power: Oratory and Performance in Early America*. Chapel Hill: University of North Carolina Press, 2001.

Habermas, Jürgen. *Legitimation Crisis*. Boston: Beacon Press, 1975.

———. "A Review of Gadamer's *Truth and Method*." In *Hermeneutics and Modern Philosophy*, edited by Brice R. Wachterhauser. Translated by F. Dallmayr and T. McCarthy. Albany: State University of New York Press, 1986.

———. *The Structural Transformation of the Public Sphere: An Inquiry into a Category of Bourgeois Society*. 1962 translation by Thomas Burger with Frederick Lawrence. Cambridge MA: MIT Press, 1989.

Hall, A. Rupert. *Isaac Newton: Adventurer in Thought*. Cambridge: Cambridge University Press, 1996.

Hall, David D. *Worlds of Wonder, Days of Judgement: Popular Religious Belief in Early New England*. New York: Knopf, 1989.

Hall, Stuart. "Cultural Identity and Diaspora." In *Colonial Discourse and Postcolonial Theory: A Reader*, edited by Patrick Williams and Laura Chrisman. New York: Columbia University Press, 1994.

Hamill, John. *The Craft: A History of English Freemasonry*. London: Aquarian Press, 1986.

Hamilton, Milton, comp. *The Papers of Sir William Johnson*. Vol. 12. Albany: State University of New York Press, 1957.

Handlin, Oscar, and Mary Handlin. *The Dimensions of Liberty*. Cambridge MA: Belknap Press of Harvard University Press, 1984.

Harland-Jacobs, Jessica L. "All in the Family: Freemasonry and the British Empire in the Mid-Nineteenth Century." *Journal of British Studies* 42, no. 4 (2003): 448–82.

———. *Builders of Empire: Freemasonry and British Imperialism, 1717–1927*. Chapel Hill: University of North Carolina Press, 2007.

———. "'Hands across the Sea': The Masonic Network, British Imperialism, and the North Atlantic World." *Geographical Review* 89, no. 2 (1999): 237–53.

Harriot, Thomas. *A Briefe and True Report of the New Found Land of Virginia*. 1590. New York: Dover, 1972.

Harwood, W. S. "Secret Societies in the United States." *North American Review* 164, no. 485 (1897): 622–23.

Hatch, Nathan. *The Democratization of American Christianity*. New Haven CT: Yale University Press, 1991.

Hawthorne, Nathaniel. *The Scarlet Letter*. Boston: Tricknor, Reed and Fields, 1850.

Hay, Carla H. Review of *The Radical Enlightenment* by Margaret C. Jacob. *Albion: A Quarterly Journal Concerned with British Studies* 15, no. 3 (1983): 244–45.

Haywood, Harry Leroy. *The Well-Springs of American Freemasonry*. Washington DC: Masonic Service Association, 1953.

Herman, Daniel J. "Romance on the Middle Ground." *Journal of the Early Republic* 19 (1999): 279–91.

Heyd, Michael. Review of *The Radical Enlightenment* by Margaret C. Jacob. *Journal of Modern History* 55, no. 2 (1983): 308–9.

Hill, Christopher. *The Century of Revolution 1603–1714*. Edinburgh: Thomas Nelson and Sons, 1961.

———. *Society and Puritanism in Pre-Revolutionary England*. New York: Schocken, 1964.

Hirst, Francis W. *Life and Letters of Thomas Jefferson*. New York: Macmillan, 1926.

Hobsbawm, Eric J. "Fraternity." *New Society* 16, no. 4 (1975): 470–73.

———. *Primitive Rebels: Studies in Archaic Forms of Social Movement in the 19th and 20th Centuries*. New York: Norton, 1959.

Hoffman, Walter J. "The Mide'wiwin or 'Grand Medicine Society' of the Ojibwa." Seventh annual report of the Bureau of Ethnology to the secretary of the Smithsonian Institution, 1885–86. Washington DC, 1891.

Holland, Sharon Patricia. *Raising the Dead: Readings of Death and (Black) Subjectivity*. Durham NC: Duke University Press, 2000.

Howe, J. *The Freemason's Manual: Or, Illustrations of Masonry*. London: John Hogg, 1862.

Hoxie, Frederick E. *A Final Promise: The Campaign to Assimilate the Indians, 1880–1920*. Cambridge: Cambridge University Press, 1984.

Hunt, Lynn. *Politics, Culture, and Class in the French Revolution*. Berkeley: University of California Press, 1984.

Hyam, R. *Britain's Imperial Century, 1815–1914: A Study of Empire and Expansion*. 2nd ed. Lanham MD: Barnes and Noble Books, 1993.

Hymes, Dell. "Breakthrough into Performance." In *Mystic Chords of Memory: The Transformation of Tradition in American Culture*, by Michael Kammen. New York: Vintage, 1991.

Irwin, Lee. *Native American Spirituality: A Critical Reader*. Lincoln: University of Nebraska Press, 2000.

Jackson, Helen Hunt. *Century of Dishonor: A Sketch of the United States Government's Dealings with Some of the Indian Tribes*. New York: Harper, 1881.

Jackson, Shannon. *Professing Performance: Theatre in the Academy from Philology to Performativity*. Cambridge: Cambridge University Press, 2004.

Jacob, Margaret C. *Living the Enlightenment: Freemasonry and Politics in Eighteenth-Century Europe*. Oxford: Oxford University Press, 1991.

———. *The Origins of Freemasonry: Facts and Fictions*. Philadelphia: University of Pennsylvania Press, 2006.

———. "The Origins of Freemasonry: The First Freemasons." *Eighteenth-Century Studies* 23, no. 3 (1990): 322–29.

———. *The Radical Enlightenment: Pantheists, Freemasons and Republicans*. Winchester MA: Allen and Unwin, 1981.

———. *The Radical Enlightenment: Pantheists, Freemasons and Republicans*. Lafayette LA: Cornerstone, 2006.

Janara, Laura. "Brothers and Others: Tocqueville and Beaumont, U.S. Genealogy, Democracy, and Racism." *Political Theory* 32, no. 6 (2004): 773–800.

Jefferson, Thomas. *Notes on the State of Virginia*. Edited by William Peden. Chapel Hill: University of North Carolina Press, 1955.

Jennings, Francis. *The Invasion of America: Indians, Colonialism, and the Cant of Conquest*. New York: Norton, 1975.

Johansen, Bruce. *Debating Democracy: Native American Legacy of Freedom*. Santa Fe NM: Clear Light, 1998.

Johnson, Melvin M. *Beginnings of Freemasonry in America*. London: Kessinger, 1999. (Orig. pub. 1924.)

Jonaitis, Aldona, ed. *Chiefly Feasts: The Enduring Kwakiutl Potlatch*. Seattle: University of Washington Press, 1991.

Jones, Dorothy V. *License for Empire: Colonialism by Treaty in Early America*. Chicago: University of Chicago Press, 1982.

Jones, Tobias. *The Dark Heart of Italy: Travels through Time and Space across Italy*. London: Faber and Faber, 2003.

Joseph, Antoine. "Modes of Class Formation." *British Journal of Sociology* 43, no. 3 (1992): 345–67.

Joseph, Miranda. *Against the Romance of Community*. Minneapolis: University of Minnesota Press, 2002.

Kammen, Michael. *Mystic Chords of Memory: The Transformation of Tradition in American Culture*. New York: Knopf, 1991.

Kant, Immanuel. *Critique of Pure Reason*. Translated by Norman Kemp Smith. New York: St. Martin's Press, 1968.

Kantrowitz, Stephen. "'Intended for the Better Government of Man': The Political History of African American Freemasonry in the Era of Emancipation." *Journal of American History* 96, no. 4 (2010): 1001–26.

Karpiel, Frank J. "Mystic Ties of Brotherhood: Freemasonry, Ritual, and Hawaiian Royalty in the Nineteenth Century." *Pacific Historical Review* 69, no. 3 (2000): 357–97.

Kaufman, Jason. *For the Common Good? American Civic Life and the Golden Age of Fraternity.* New York: Oxford University Press, 2002.

———. "Three Views of Associationalism in 19th-Century America: An Empirical Examination." *American Journal of Sociology* 104, no. 5 (1999): 1296–345.

Kelsay, Isabel Thompson. *Joseph Brant 1743–1807: Man of Two Worlds.* Syracuse NY: Syracuse University Press, 1984.

Kimmel, Michael S. *Manhood in America: A Cultural History.* New York: Oxford University Press, 2006.

Kipling, Rudyard. "In the Interests of the Brethren." *The Builder,* March 1922.

———. *The Man Who Would Be King and Other Stories.* Edited by Louis L. Cornell. Oxford: Oxford University Press, 1999.

———. *Rewards and Fairies.* London: Indypublish, 2002. (Orig. pub. 1910.)

Knaut, Andrew. *The Pueblo Revolt of 1680: Conquest and Resistance in Seventeenth-Century New Mexico.* Norman: University of Oklahoma Press, 1995.

Knoop, Douglas D., and G. P. Jones. *The Genesis of Freemasonry: An Account of the Rise and Development of Freemasonry in Its Operative, Accepted, and Early Speculative Phases.* Manchester, England: University of Manchester Press, 1947.

Koch, Adolf G. *Republican Religion: The American Revolution and the Cult of Reason.* New York: Henry Holt, 1933.

Konkle, Maureen. *Writing Indian Nations: Native Intellectuals and the Politics of Historiography 1827–1863.* Chapel Hill: University of North Carolina Press, 2004.

Kremm, Thomas W., and Diane Neal. "Crisis of Command: The Hindman/Pike Controversy over the Defense of the Trans-Mississippi District." *Chronicles of Oklahoma* 70 (Spring 1992): 26–45.

Krupat, Arnold. *All That Remains: Varieties of Indigenous Expression.* Lincoln: University of Nebraska Press, 2009.

Kupperman, Karen Ordahl. *Settling with the Indians: The Meeting of English and Indian Cultures in America, 1580–1640.* Totowa NJ: Rowman and Littlefield, 1980.

Kutolowski, Kathleen Smith. "Antimasonry Reexamined: Social Bases of the Grass-Roots Party." *Journal of American History* 71, no. 2 (1984): 269–93.

Lang, Ossian. *History of Freemasonry in the State of New York*. New York: Grand Lodge of New York, F. & A.M., 1922.

Langford, Paul. *Englishness Identified: Manners and Character 1650–1850*. Oxford: Oxford University Press, 2000.

Lasch, Christopher. *The Culture of Narcissism: American Life in an Age of Diminishing Expectations*. New York: Norton, 1979.

———. *The Lonely Crowd: A Study of the American Character*. New Haven CT: Yale University Press, 1991. (Orig. pub. 1979.)

Latham, J. Fred. *The Story of Oklahoma Masonry*. Oklahoma City: Grand Lodge of Oklahoma, 1957.

Laurie, Bruce. *Artisans into Workers: Labor in Nineteenth-century America*. Urbana: University of Illinois Press, 1997.

La Vopa, Anthony J. Review of *Living the Enlightenment* by M. Jacob. *Journal of Modern History* 66, no. 2 (1994): 351–54.

Lawrence, D. H. *Studies in Classic American Literature*. London: Penguin Classics, 1990. (Orig. pub. 1923.)

Leo XIII. *Humanum Genus: Encyclical Letter of His Holiness Pope Leo XIII, April 20, 1884*. Rockford IL: Tan Books, 1978.

Lestringant, Frank. *Cannibals: The Discovery and Representation of the Cannibal from Columbus to Jules Verne*. Translated by Rosemary Morris. Cambridge: Polity Press, 1997.

Levine, Lawrence W. *Highbrow Lowbrow: The Emergence of Cultural Hierarchy in America*. Cambridge MA: Harvard University Press, 1988.

Lewis, James R., and Olav Hammer, eds. *The Invention of Sacred Tradition*. Cambridge: Cambridge University Press, 2007.

Lewis, R. W. B. *The American Adam: Innocence, Tragedy, and Tradition in the Nineteenth Century*. Chicago: University of Chicago Press, 1955.

Lewis, Sinclair. *Babbitt*. New York: Harcourt, Brace and World, 1950. (Orig. pub. 1922.)

Leyland, Herbert T. *Thomas Smith Webb: Freemason, Musician, Entrepreneur*. Dayton OH: Otterbein Press, 1965.

Limerick, Patricia. *The Legacy of Conquest: The Unbroken Past of the American West*. New York: Norton, 1987.

Lipsitz, George. *Time Passages: Collective Memory and American Popular Culture*. Minneapolis: University of Minnesota Press, 1990.

Lipson, Dorothy Ann. *Freemasonry in Federal Connecticut*. Princeton NJ: Princeton University Press, 1977.

Lott, Eric. *Love and Theft: Blackface Minstrelsy and the American Working Class*. New York: Oxford University Press, 1993.

————. "Love and Theft: The Racial Unconscious of Blackface Minstrelsy." *Representations*, no. 39 (Summer 1992): 23–50.

————. "Review: The New Cosmopolitanism." *Transition*, no. 72 (1996): 108–35.

Lucas, Stephen E. "Justifying America: The Declaration of Independence as a Rhetorical Document." In *American Rhetoric: Context and Criticism*, edited by Thomas W. Benson. Carbondale: Southern Illinois University Press, 1989.

Lukes, Steven. "Political Ritual and Social Integration." *Sociology: Journal of the British Sociological Association*, no. 2 (1975): 289–308.

Lycett, Andrew. *Rudyard Kipling*. London: Weidenfeld and Nicolson, 1999.

Lynes, Russell. *The Lively Audience: A Social History of the Visual and Performing Arts in America 1890–1950*. New York: Harper and Row, 1985.

MacCannell, Juliet Flower. "The Post-colonial Unconscious, or the White Man's Thing." *Journal for the Psychoanalysis of Culture and Society* 1 (Spring 1996): 27–41.

————. *The Regime of the Brother: After the Patriarchy*. New York: Routledge, 1991.

MacDonald, Fergus. *The Catholic Church and the Secret Societies in the United States*. Edited by Thomas J. McMahon. United States Catholic Historical Society Monograph Series 22. New York: United States Catholic Historical Society, 1946.

Mackey, Albert Gallatin. *Masonry Defined: A Liberal Masonic Education*. Compiled from the writing of Dr. Albert G. Mackey by E. R. Johnston. Rev. ed. Shreveport LA: National Masonic Press, 1930.

Mackey, Albert Gallatin, Robert Ingham Clegg, and H. L. Haywood. *Encyclopedia of Freemasonry & Its Kindred Sciences Compromising the Whole Range of Arts, Sciences and Literature as Connected with the Institution*. Rev. ed. London: Kessinger, 1946. (Orig. pub. 1905.)

MacNulty, W. Kirk. *Freemasonry: A Journey through Ritual and Symbol*. London: Thames and Hudson, 1991.

————. *The Way of the Craftsman: A Search for the Spiritual Essence of Craft Freemasonry*. London: Routledge, 1988.

Malinowski, Bronislaw. "The Role of Magic and Religion." 1931. In *Reader in Comparative Religion: An Anthropological Approach*, edited by William A. Lessa and Evon Z. Vogt. 4th ed. New York: Harper and Row, 1979.

————. *A Scientific Theory of Culture and Other Essays*. Chapel Hill: University of North Carolina Press, 1944.

Mallery, Garrick. *Introduction to the Study of Sign Language among the North American Indians as Illustrating the Gesture Speech of Mankind*. 1880. In

Aboriginal Sign Language of the Americas and Australia, edited by D. Jean Umiker-Sebeok and Thomas A. Sebeok. New York: Plenum Press, 1978.

Mann, Charles C. *1491: New Revelations of the Americas before Columbus*. New York: Knopf, 2005.

Marx, Karl. *Karl Marx and Frederick Engels: Selected Works*. New York: International Publishers, 1984.

McCarthy, Theresa L. "Iroquoian and Iroquoianist: Anthropologists and the Haudenosaunee at Grand River." *Histories of Anthropology Annual* 4 (2008): 135–71.

McClenachan, Charles T. *The Book of Ancient and Accepted Scottish Rite of Freemasonry*. New York: Masonic Publishing, 1867.

McKenny, Thomas. *Memoirs, Official and Personal*. 2 vols. in 1. New York: Paine and Burgess, 1846.

McKenzie, John. *Perform or Else: From Discipline to Performance*. London: Routledge, 2004.

McLoughlin, William Gerald, and William H. Conserv. *The Cherokees and Christianity, 1794–1870: Essays on Acculturation and Cultural Persistence*. Athens: University of Georgia Press, 1994.

McLuhan, Marshall. *The Mechanical Bride: Folklore of Industrial Man*. New York: Vanguard, 1951.

Melville, Herman. *The Confidence-Man: His Masquerade*. New York: Dix and Edwards, 1857.

Meserve, John Bartlett. "Chief Pleasant Porter." *Chronicles of Oklahoma* 9, no. 3 (1931): 318–34.

Meserve, Walter J. *An Emerging Entertainment: The Drama of the American People to 1828*. Bloomington: Indiana University Press, 1977.

Milsten, David Randolph. *Will Rogers: The Cherokee Kid*. Tulsa OK: Coman, 1987.

Minges, Patrick Neal. "'All My Slaves, Whether Negroes, Indians, Mustees, or Mulattoes': Towards a Thick Description of 'Slave Religion.'" 1999. Available at http://are.as.wvu.edu/minges.htm.

———. "The Keetoowah Society and the Avocation of Religious Nationalism in the Cherokee Nation 1855–1867." PhD dissertation, Union Seminary, New York, 1999. UMI No: 9930856.

———. *Slavery in the Cherokee Nation: The Keetowah Society and the Defining of a People 1855–1867*. New York: Routledge, 2003.

Momaday, N. Scott. *The Man Made of Words: Essays, Stories, Passages*. New York: St. Martin's Griffin, 1997.

Money, J. "The Masonic Moment; Or, Ritual, Replica, and Credit: John Wilkes, the Macaroni Parson, and the Making of the Middle-class Mind." *Journal of British Studies* 32 (1993): 359–95.

Moore, Charles Whitlock. *The Freemason's Monthly Magazine*, March 1863. Original in New York Public Library.

Moore, Cornelius. *Leaflets of Masonic Biography, or Sketches of Eminent Free-masons*. Cincinnati: Mason's Review Office, 1863.

Moore, William D. "Funding the Temples of Masculinity: Women's Roles in Masonic Fairs in New York State, 1870–1930." *Nineteenth Century* 14, no. 1 (1994): 19–25.

Morgan, Lewis Henry. *League of the Ho-De'-No-Sau-Nee, Iroquois*. Secaucus NJ: Citadel, 1962. (Orig. pub. 1851.)

Morris, Robert. *William Morgan: Or, Political Anti-Masonry, Its Rise, Growth and Decadence*. New York: Robert MaCoy, 1883.

Morris, S. Brent. "Boom to Bust in the Twentieth Century: Freemasonry and American Fraternities." 1988 Anson Jones Lecture, Texas Lodge of Research, March 19, 1989.

Moulton, Gary E. *John Ross: Cherokee Chief*. Athens: University of Georgia Press, 1978.

Muraskin, William. *Middle-Class Blacks in a White Society: Prince Hall Free-masonry in America*. Berkeley: University of California Press, 1975.

Murphy, Thomas W. "From Racist Stereotype to Ethnic Identity: Instrumental Uses of Mormon Racial Doctrine." *Ethnohistory* 46, no. 3 (1999): 451–80.

Myrdal, Gunnar. *An American Dilemma*. Vol. 2, *The Negro Social Structure*. New York: McGraw-Hill, 1964. (Orig. pub. 1944.)

Nash, Gary. "The Hidden History of Mestizo America." *Journal of American History* 82, no. 3 (1995): 941–64.

Needham, Joseph, ed. *Science, Religion and Reality*. London: Macmillan, 1925.

Nelson, Dana D. *National Manhood: Capitalist Citizenship and the Imagined Fraternity of White Men*. Durham NC: Duke University Press, 1998.

Ness, Sally A. "Going Back to Bateson: Toward a Semiotics of (Post-)Ritual Performance." In *Ritual and Event*, edited by Mark Franco. London: Routledge, 2007.

Newbury, George A., and Louis L. Williams. *A History of the Supreme Council 33°*. Lexington MA: The Supreme Council, AASR, 1987.

Newcomb, Steven T. *Pagans in the Promised Land: Decoding the Doctrine of Christian Discovery*. Golden CO: Fulcrum, 2008.

Newton, Joseph Fort, "Edwin Booth as a Mason." *The Builder*, May 1915.

Niezen, Ronald. *Spirit Wars: Native North American Religions in the Age of Nation Building*. Berkeley: University of California Press, 2000.

Nye, Joseph. *Bound to Lead: The Changing Nature of American Power*. New York: Basic Books, 1990.

———. "The Misleading Metaphor of Decline." *Atlantic Monthly*, March 1990.

———. *Soft Power: The Means to Success in World Politics*. New York: Public Affairs, 2004.

Ortiz, Alfonso, ed. *New Perspectives on the Pueblos*. Albuquerque: University of New Mexico Press, 1972.

Ortiz, Simon J. "The Historical Matrix towards a National Indian Literature: Cultural Authenticity in Nationalism." In *Critical Perspectives on Native American Fiction*, edited by Richard F. Fleck. Washington DC: Three Continents, 1993.

O'Toole, Fintan. *White Savage: William Johnson and the Invention of America*. New York: Farrar, Straus and Giroux, 2005.

Owens, Louis. "As If an Indian Were Really an Indian: Native American Voices and Postcolonial Theory." In *Native American Representations: First Encounters, Distorted Images, and Literary Appropriations*, edited by Gretchen Bataille. Lincoln: University of Nebraska Press, 2001.

Packard, Vance. *The Status Seekers*. New York: David MacKay, 1959.

Paine, Thomas. *Origin of Freemasonry*. In *The Works of Thomas Paine*. New York: E. Haskell, 1854.

Parker, Arthur C. *American Indian Freemasonry*. Buffalo NY: Buffalo Consistatory AASR NMJUSA, 1919.

———. "Ely S. Parker: Man and Mason." *Transactions of the American Lodge of Research—Free and Accepted Masons* 8, no. 2 (1961): 229–47.

———. "Neh Ho-non-tci-noh-geh, the Guardians of the Little Waters, a Seneca Medicine Society." In *Myths and Legends of the New York State Iroquois*, by Harriet Maxwell Converse. Edited by Arthur C. Parker. New York State Museum Bulletin 125. Albany, 1908.

———. "New York Indians and the Craft." *Masonic Outlook*, October 1928.

———. "Secret Medicine Societies of the Seneca." *American Anthropologist*, n.s. 11, no. 2 (1909): 161–85.

———. "Why All This Secrecy?" *The Builder*, December 1923.

Parkman, Francis. *The Conspiracy of Pontiac and the Indian War after the Conquest of Canada*. 9th ed. Boston: Little, Brown, 1891.

Pateman, Carole. *The Sexual Contract*. Cambridge: Polity Press, 1988.

Pearce, Roy Harvey. *The Savages of America: A Study of the Indian and the Idea of Civilization*. Rev. ed. Baltimore: Johns Hopkins University Press, 1965.

Perdue, Theda. *Slavery and the Evolution of Cherokee Society, 1540–1866*. Knoxville: University of Tennessee Press, 1979.

Phelan, Peggy. *Unmarked: The Politics of Performance*. New York: Routledge, 1993.

Piatigorsky, Alexander. *Freemasonry: The Study of a Phenomenon*. London: Harvill Press, 1999.

Pike, Albert. "Gnosticism, the Kabbala, and the Mysteries as Connected with and Illustrating Masonry." *American Quarterly Review of Freemasonry*, nos. 1–5 (July 1858).

———. *Morals and Dogma*. Published by the Supreme Council of the Thirty-Third Degree for the Southern Jurisdiction of the United States Charleston, 1871. Reprint, Whitefish MT: Kessinger, 2004.

Pocock, John Greville Agard. *Barbarism and Religion*. Vol. 2, *Narratives of Civil Government*. Cambridge: Cambridge University Press, 1999.

Porter, Joy. "Population Matters in Native America." In *America's Americans: Population Issues in U.S. Society and Politics*, edited by Philip Davies and Iwan Morgan. London: Institute for the Study of the Americas, 2007.

———. *To Be Indian: The Life of Iroquois-Seneca Arthur Caswell Parker*. Norman: University of Oklahoma Press, 2001.

Pratt, Mary Louise. *Imperial Eyes: Travel Writing and Transculturation*. London: Routledge, 1992.

Preston, William. *Illustrations of Masonry*. London: William Preston, 1772.

The Protocols of the Meetings of the Learned Elders of Zion with Preface and Explanatory Notes. Dearborn MI: Dearborn Independent, 1934. (Orig. pub. 1920–22.)

Prucha, Francis Paul, ed. *Documents of United States Indian Policy*. 2nd ed., expanded. Lincoln: University of Nebraska Press, 1990.

Putnam, Robert. *Bowling Alone*. New York: Simon and Schuster, 2000.

Quesenberry, Preston. "Bowling Together during War." *Yale Law Journal* 111, no. 4 (2002): 1031–38.

Radin, Paul. *The Road of Life and Death*. New York: Pantheon Books, 1945.

Rank, Otto. *Art and Artist: Creative Urge and Personality*. New York: Knopf, 1932.

Rappaport, Roy A. *Ritual and Religion in the Making of Humanity*. Cambridge: Cambridge University Press, 1999.

Rasmussen, K. *The Netsilik Eskimo: Social Life and Spiritual Culture. Report of Fifth Thule Expedition 1921–4*. Copenhagen: Gyldendalske Boghandel, 1931.

Reff, Daniel T. "'The Predicament of Culture' and Spanish Missionary Accounts of the Tepehuan and Pueblo Revolts." *Ethnohistory* 42, no. 1 (1995): 63–90.

Resek, Carl. *Lewis Henry Morgan: American Scholar*. Chicago: University of Chicago Press, 1960.

Rexroth, Kenneth. "American Indian Songs." In *Assays*. New York: New Directions, 1961.

Rich, Paul. J. *Chains of Empire: English Public Schools, Masonic Cabalism, Historical Causality, and Imperial Clubdom*. London: Regency, 1991.

———. *Elixir of Empire: The English Public Schools, Ritualism, Freemasonry, and Imperialism*. London: Regency, 1989.

Richards, Jeffrey. *Drama, Theatre, and Identity in the American New Republic.* Cambridge: Cambridge University Press, 2005.

Ridge, John Rollin. "North American Indians." *Hesperian* 8 (May 1962): 99–109.

Riesman, David, Nathan Glazer, and Reuel Denney. *The Culture of Narcissism: American Life in the Age of Diminishing Expectations.* New York: Norton, 1991. (Orig. pub. 1979.)

Riesman, David, with Reuel Denny and Nathan Glazer. *The Lonely Crowd.* New Haven CT: Yale University Press, 1950.

Roach, Joseph. *Cities of the Dead: Circum-Atlantic Performance.* New York: Columbia University Press, 1996.

——. "Joseph Roach Talks to Ned Sublette." 2005. Available at www.afropop.org/multi/interview/ID/68/Joseph+Roach+talks+to+Ned+Sublette.

——. "Mardi Gras Indians and Others: Genealogies of American Performance." *Theatre Journal* 44 (1992): 461–83.

Roberts, John M. "Freemasonry: Possibilities of a Neglected Topic." *English Historical Review* 84, no. 331 (1969): 323–35.

Robertson, John Ross. *The History of Freemasonry in Canada.* Vol. 1. Toronto: Hunter, Rose, 1899.

Rogin, Michael Paul. *Fathers and Children: Andrew Jackson and the Subjugation of the American Indian.* New York: Vintage Books, 1976.

Root, Deborah. *Cannibal Culture: Art, Appropriation and the Commodification of Difference.* Boulder CO: Westview Press, 1996.

Rosaldo, Renato. *Culture and Truth: The Remaking of Social Analysis.* Boston: Beacon, 1989.

Rotundo, Anthony E. *American Manhood: Transformations in Masculinity from the Revolution to the Modern Era.* New York: Basic Books, 1993.

Rousseau, Jean-Jacques. *Emile; or, On Education.* Translated by Allan Bloom. New York: Basic Books, 1979.

Rusbridger, Alan. "Matter for Paranoia." *Times Literary Supplement,* April 1989.

Russell, Bertrand. *Unpopular Essays.* London: Bertrand Russell Peace Foundation, 2009.

Said, Edward. *Orientalism.* New York: Vintage Books, 1978.

Sarris, Greg. *Keeping Slug Woman Alive: A Holistic Approach to American Indian Texts.* Berkeley: University of California Press, 1993.

Schechner, Richard. *The Future of Ritual: Writings on Culture and Performance.* New York: Routledge, 1995.

Schechner, Richard, and Willa Appel, eds. *By Means of Performance: Intercultural Studies of Theatre and Ritual.* Cambridge: Cambridge University Press, 1990.

Scheiber, Andrew J. "Mirrors and Menageries: Criticism, Ethnography, and

Multiculturalism in Contemporary Literary Praxis." *American Literary History* 8, no. 2 (1996): 364–87.

Schlesinger, Arthur M. "Biography of a Nation of Joiners." *American Historical Review* 50, no. 1 (1944): 1–25.

———. *Paths to the Present*. New York: Macmillan, 1949.

Schmidt, Alvin J., and Nicholas Babchuk. "Formal Voluntary Organizations and Change over Time: A Study of American Fraternal Association." *Nonprofit and Voluntary Sector Quarterly* 1, no. 1 (1972): 46–55.

———. "The Unbrotherly Brotherhood: Discrimination in Fraternal Orders." *Phylon* 34, no. 3 (1973): 275–82.

Schmidt, L. E. *Hearing Things: Religion, Illusion and the American Enlightenment*. Cambridge MA: Harvard University Press, 2000.

Schoolcraft, Henry Rowe. *Historical and Statistical Information Respecting the History, Condition and Prospects of the Indian Tribes of the United States*. Vol. 5. Philadelphia: Lippincott, Grambo, 1856.

Schultz, Ronald. *The Republic of Labor: Philadelphia Artisans and the Politics of Class, 1720–1830*. Ithaca NY: Cornell University Press, 1990.

Sennet, Richard. *The Craftsman*. London: Penguin, 2008.

Shepard, Thomas. *The Clear Sun-shine of the Gospel Breaking Forth upon the Indians in New-England*. In *The Eliot Tracks, with Letters from John Eliot to Thomas Throwgood and Richard Baxter*, edited by Michael P. Clark. Westport CT: Praeger, 2003.

Shohat, Ella, and Robert Stam. *Unthinking Eurocentrism: Multiculturalism and the Media*. New York: Routledge, 1994.

Silko, Leslie Marmon. *Ceremony*. New York: Penguin, 1986.

Simmel, Georg, and Camilla H. Wedgewood. "The Sociology of Secrecy and of Secret Societies." *American Journal of Sociology* 11 (January 1906): 441–98.

Skocpol, Theda. *Diminished Democracy: From Membership to Management in American Civic Life*. Norman: University of Oklahoma Press, 2003.

Skocpol, Theda, and Jennifer Lynn Oser. "Organization Despite Adversity: The Origins and Development of African American Fraternal Associations." *Social Science History* 28, no. 3 (2004): 367–437.

Skocpol, Theda, Jennifer Lynn Oser, Ziad Munson, Marshall Gantz, and Andrew Karch. "War and the Development of American Civil Society." Paper prepared for the annual meeting of the American Sociological Association, Chicago, August 1999.

Smith, Rogers M. "Beyond Tocqueville, Myrdal, and Hartz: The Multiple Traditions in America." *American Political Science Review* 87, no. 3 (1993): 549–66.

Smyth, F. "The Master-Mason-at-Arms: A Short Study of Freemasonry in the Armed Forces." *Ars Quatuor Coronatorum* 104 (1991): 222–36.

Smyth, Jim. *The Men of No Property: Irish Radicals and Popular Politics in the Late Eighteenth Century.* New York: Macmillan, 1998.

Snow, Dean R. Review of *The Great Law and the Longhouse. American Anthropologist* 101, no. 1 (2008): 192–93.

Speck, Frank, with Alexander General (Deskáheh). *Midwinter Rites of the Cayuga Long House.* Lincoln: University of Nebraska Press, 1949.

Spilka, Bernard. *Spirituality: Problems and Directions in Operationalizing a Fuzzy Concept.* Paper presented at the annual conference of the American Psychological Association, Toronto, August 23, 1993.

Stern, Bernhard J. *Lewis Henry Morgan: Social Evolutionist.* New York: Russell and Russell, 1931.

Stevens, Albert C. *The Cyclopedia of Fraternities.* Detroit: Gale Research, 1966. (Orig. pub. 1907.)

Stevenson, David. *The First Freemasons: Scotland's Early Lodges and Their Members.* Aberdeen: Aberdeen University Press, 1988.

———. *The Origins of Freemasonry: Scotland's Century 1590–1710.* Cambridge: Cambridge University Press, 1988.

Stinchcombe, Arthur L. "Social Structure and Organizations." In *Handbook of Organizations,* edited by James G. March. Chicago: Rand McNally, 1965.

Stogre, Michael. *That the World May Believe: The Development of Papal Social Thought on Aboriginal Rights.* Sherbrooke, Quebec: Editions Paulines, 1992.

Stone, William L. *Life of Joseph Brant—Thayendanegea Including the Indian Wars of the American Revolution.* New York: George Dearborn, 1828.

Sullivan, James, Alexander C. Flick, Milton W. Hamilton, and Albert Corey, eds. *The Papers of Sir William Johnson.* 13 vols. Albany: University of the State of New York, 1921–65.

Swiencicki, Mark A. "Consuming Brotherhood: Men's Culture, Style and Recreation as Consumer Culture, 1880–1930." *Journal of Social History* 31, no. 4 (1998): 773–808.

Tawney, Richard Henry. *Religion and the Rise of Capitalism.* Introduction by Adam B. Seligman. New Brunswick NJ: Transaction, 1998. (Orig. pub. 1926.)

Taylor, Charles. *A Secular Age.* Cambridge MA: Belknap Press of Harvard University Press, 2007.

Thomas, Keith. *Religion and the Decline of Magic.* New York: Charles Scribner's Sons, 1971.

Thompson, Edward P. *The Making of the English Working Class.* Harmondsworth, England: Penguin, 1968.

Thoreau, Henry D. *Complete Works.* Boston: Little, Brown, 1929.

Thwaites, R. G., ed., *The Jesuit Relations and Allied Documents*. Cleveland OH: Pagent, 1959.

Tocqueville, Alexis de. *Democracy in America*. Vol. 2. 1840. Translated by Henry Reeve. New York: Schocken, 1961.

Trevor-Roper, Hugh. "The Past and Present: History and Sociology." *Past and Present* 42 (1969): 3–17.

Trilling, Lionel. *The Liberal Imagination*. London: Methuen, 1961. (Orig. pub. 1950.)

Turner, Victor. *The Anthropology of Performance*. New York: PAJ, 1992.

———. *Forest of Symbols: Aspects of Ndembu Ritual*. Ithaca NY: Cornell University Press, 1967.

———. *From Ritual to Theater: The Human Seriousness of Play*. New York: PAJ, 1982.

———. *The Ritual Process: Structure and Anti-Structure*. Ithaca NY: Cornell University Press, 1969.

Van Cott, Charles. *Freemasonry: A Sleeping Giant*. Minneapolis: T. S. Denison, 1959.

Vaughn, William Preston. *The Antimasonic Party in the United States 1826–1843*. Lexington: University Press of Kentucky, 1983.

Vecsey, Christopher. *Traditional Ojibwa Religion and Its Historical Changes*. Philadelphia: American Philosophical Society, 1983.

Verba, Sidney, Kay Lehman Schlozman, and Henry Brady. *Voice and Equality: Civic Voluntarism in American Politics*. Cambridge MA: Harvard University Press, 1995.

Vigneras, L. A. *The Journal of Christopher Columbus*. Revision of translation by Cecil Jane. London: Hakluyt Society, 1960.

Vogel, Dan. *Indian Origins and the Book of Mormon*. Salt Lake City: Signature Books, 1986.

Voorhis, Harold V. B. *Our Colored Brethren: The Story of Alpha Lodge of New Jersey*. New York: Henry Emmerson, 1960.

Waldstreicher, David. *In the Midst of Perpetual Fetes: The Making of American Nationalism, 1776–1820*. Chapel Hill: University of North Carolina Press, 1997.

Wallace, Anthony F. C. *Jefferson and the Indians: The Tragic Fate of the First Americans*. Cambridge MA: Harvard University Press, 1999.

Ward, E. "The Crisp English Word Freemason." *Ars Quatuor Coronatorum* 68 (1956): 58–66.

Warner, Michael. *The Letters of the Republic: Publication and the Public Sphere in Eighteenth Century America*. Cambridge MA: Harvard University Press, 1990.

Webb, Thomas Smith. *The Freemason's Monitor; or, Illustrations of Masonry: In Two Parts.* Albany NY: Spencer and Webb, 1797.

Weber, Max. *From Max Weber: Essays in Sociology.* Translated and edited by H. H. Gerth and C. Wright Mills. New York: Oxford University Press, 1946.

Weisberger, William, Wallace McLeod, and S. Brent Morris. *Freemasonry on Both Sides of the Atlantic: Essays Concerning the Craft in the British Isles, Europe, the United States, and Mexico.* New York: Columbia University Press, 2002.

Wells, Peter S. "Who, Where and What Were the Celts?" Review article. *American Journal of Archaeology* 102, no. 4 (1998): 814–16.

Wertheim, Arthur Frank, Barbara Bair, Steven K. Gragert, and M. Jane Johanssen, eds. *The Papers of Will Rogers.* Vol. 2, *April 1904–September 1908.* Norman: University of Oklahoma Press, 2000.

Whalen, William J. *Christianity and American Freemasonry.* San Francisco: Ignatius Press, 1987. (Orig. pub. 1958.)

White, Hayden. *Metahistory.* Baltimore: Johns Hopkins University Press, 1973.

White, Michael. *Isaac Newton: The Last Sorcerer.* London: Fourth Estate, 1998.

White, Richard. *The Middle Ground: Indians, Empires, and Republics in the Great Lakes Region, 1650–1815.* Cambridge: Cambridge University Press, 1991.

Williams, Loretta J. *Black Freemasonry and Middle-Class Realities.* Columbia: University of Missouri Press, 1980.

Williams, Raymond. *Culture and Society: 1780–1950.* New York: Columbia University Press, 1983.

———. *Keywords: A Vocabulary of Culture and Society.* Oxford: Oxford University Press, 1976.

———. *Marxism and Literature.* New York: Oxford University Press, 1977.

Wills, Garry. *Inventing America: Jefferson's Declaration of Independence.* New York: Doubleday, 1978.

Woodward, Grace Steele. *The Cherokees.* Norman: University of Oklahoma Press, 1963.

Worthen, W. B. "Drama, Performativity, and Performance." PMLA 113, no. 5 (1998): 1093–107.

Wright, Robert C. *Indian Masonry.* Rev. ed. Whitefish MT: R. A. Kessinger, 1993. (Orig. pub. 1907.)

Yarrow, Harry Crécy. *Introduction to the Study of Mortuary Customs among the North American Indians.* Washington DC: Government Printing Office, 1880.

Yates, Francis A. *The Art of Memory.* London: Pimlico, 1984. (Orig. pub. 1966.)

Index

tion of social world, 81; rescue of, by Indian Masons, 198. *See also* aristocracy

Ellington, Duke, 281n20

Enlightenment period, 59, 60–61, 132

ethnographers. *See* anthropologists and ethnographers

Euclid, 55–56

family relationships. *See* kinship

Fenton, William, 273n52

Five Civilized Tribes (Five Nations), 161, 217, 229

Foreman, J., 160

Forten, James, 14

Franklin, Benjamin, 84

fraternalism: as atonement, 137; as consumption, 245, 246, 251–52, 264–65; decline of, in twentieth century, 256–70; in Depression era, 102; and entrepreneurs, 234; and heroic identities, 236; and inclusion of indigenous Others, 77–78, 186; and internal harmony, 221–22; and national boundaries, 73; as self-deceiving, 253; shared, 196

fraternal organizations: and belonging, 168–69; after Civil War, 229; as consumption, 245; educational role of, 148; and gendered change, 221–22; growth of, in nineteenth century, 101–2, 234–37; for Indians, 47; as sanctuary, 110–11; as social safety net, 147; as training, 102. *See also* associational memberships; masculine associational culture

Freemasonry: and affirmation of su-

preme being, 93, 152; and affluence, 139; and alcohol, 286n90; as alternative to Protestantism, 125; benefits of, to Indians, 26, 49, 164, 208; and business support, 146; and Civil War, 224–25; cosmopolitanism of, 72–78; and costs of membership, 139, 249, 257; and cultural exchange, 53; decline of, in twentieth century, 248–53; and the Divine, 128, 132, 133, 134, 135; Druidic influence on, 63–65, 238; and equality, 61–62, 70, 84–85, 86; and the establishment, 61–62; and food and drink, 77; as forum for educating non-Indians, 177, 228; fraternal ethos in, 68, 75–76, 116–17, 129, 138–39, 204, 208, 212; as joke, 257–58; medieval roots of, 109; and merit, 67, 69, 80, 116; as middle-class organization, 3, 253; moral authority of, 86, 128–29, 139; as mystery religion, 126; and Nazi persecution, 254–55; as non-denominational, 63, 93; and oaths, 152; in Oklahoma, 209–11, 243–44; origins of, in Scotland and England, 52; and parades, 149; and performance paradigm, 35–36; and personal advancement, 80; and place, 141; pleasure and camaraderie of, 48, 77, 139, 232; political nature of, 61–62; pre-Christian core of, 60, 125–26, 136–37, 200–201; relaxation as appeal of, 77; as religion, 126–27; respectability as benefit of, 147–48; during revolutionary period, 189–206; and the right to rule, 184–85; and social mobility, 267; and

pan-Indian Messianic movements, 23

pantheism, 60–63, 125, 127

Parker, Arthur C., 15, 50, 140, 161–63, 167–72, 212–13, 250

Parker, Ely S., 14, 50, 162, 163–67

Parker, Gabe E., 159

Parker, Nicholson H., 162

Parker, William, 90, 281n23

Peace Medal (1792), 162, 166–67

performance, scholarship on, 2–16

performance paradigm: Boston Tea Party as, 192–94; and decline of ritual, 129–30; deficiencies in, 28–29, 33, 39–40; as English conception, 34–35; as evidence of Indian humanity, 8; and history, 228; and Indian studies, 18–19; and interconnection between Indians and non-Indians, 57; and Masonic practice, 1–2, 120–21, 125; and ownership, 37; and relationships between cultures, 30–31; unrepeatability of, 29; and William Johnson, 201

Pike, Albert, 87–88, 124, 127, 209, 214–20, 238–39

Pitchlyn, Peter P., 15, 160, 210, 217, 218, 220

Planting Society, 47

Pocahontas syndrome, 156–57

political relationships, 53, 70, 93, 122–23, 186

Porter, Pleasant, 159

potlatch, 23

power relationships, 32–33, 37, 68, 122–23

Preston, William, 129

Prevost, Augustine, 196

"primitive" Others, 187, 230–33, 247

private sphere. *See* public and private spheres

Protestantism, 57–58, 106, 108, 112–13, 125, 191

The Protocols of the Elders of Zion, 88, 254

public and private spheres, 68, 72, 92, 110, 268

Pueblo Indians, 21, 117

Pushmataha (Choctaw), 160, 210

race and racialism, 10, 80–81, 83, 100, 103–4, 248

racial oppression, 87, 185, 266

racism, 165, 168

reciprocity, 37, 185, 200, 204

Red Jacket (Seneca), 6, 90, 158, 162, 166–67, 191

Red Men, 247–48

Reformation. *See* Protestantism

republicanism, 61–65, 68–69, 71, 86, 148, 191, 250–51, 259–61, 267–70

Revere, Paul, 192

Rickard, Clinton, 15, 177

Ridge, John Rollin, 15, 152, 217, 223

rituals: and connections with the dead, 12–13; and flexibility, 122, 126; as form of power, 122–23; functions of, 117–19; funeral, 205–6, 225; Indian, 23, 130–31, 143; initiation, 57, 154, 232–33, 256; as intersection of processes, 16; Masonic, 1, 10, 36, 43, 53, 109, 114–31, 285n72; in Mormonism, 95–96, 101; nature of, 30; participants and observers in, 117, 119, 121, 241, 246, 264–65; psychological aspects of, 121–22; and reducing anxiety, 118; as reminder of homeland, 76; special effects in, 242–43

Tuskeniah (Creek), 192

unity between matter and spirit, 56,
61, 101

vanishing Indian, myth of, 165–66,
168, 230, 247–48
Vann, David, 217
Vann, John S., 160
Vann, Joseph, 217
violence, 116, 121–22, 157
voluntarism, 235–36, 265, 267, 268

Walker, David, 14
Walker, William, 15
Washington, Booker T., 14
Washington, George, 85, 89
Watie, Buck. *See* Boudinot, Elias

Watie, Stand, 15, 217, 220, 223
Williams, Eleazer, 191
women, Iroquois, 144, 201, 202
women, white: and anti-Masonry,
92; exclusion of, from Freemasonry, 67, 221, 279n45; and private sphere, 184–85, 231–32; and
public sphere, 233; and social capital, 266; as supporters of Masonic activities, 102, 238; and theater, 245–46
Wright, Robert C., 153–56
Wyandot Indians, 211

Yahola, Opothle, 210, 218
York Rite, 102, 235, 238

Zuni fraternities, 155

Other Works by Joy Porter

To Be Indian: The Life of Iroquois-Seneca Arthur Caswell Parker.
Foreword by William N. Fenton. Norman:
University of Oklahoma Press, 2001.

The Cambridge Companion to Native American Literature.
Edited by Joy Porter and Professor Kenneth Roemer.
Cambridge: Cambridge University Press, 2005.

Place and Native American Indian History and Culture.
Edited by Joy Porter. Foreword by Alan Trachtenberg.
Oxford: Peter Lang, 2007.

Competing Voices from Native America.
By Joy Porter and Dewi Ball. Oxford and Santa Barbara CA:
Greenwood Press, 2009.

Eco-Justice, Land and Spirit in Native America.
Westport CT: Praeger, forthcoming.

*The American Indian Poet of the First World War: Modernism and
the Indian Identity of Frank "Toronto" Prewett 1892–1962.*
Toronto: University of Toronto Press, forthcoming.